Twayne's English Authors Series

EDITOR OF THIS VOLUME

Herbert Sussman

Northeastern University

J. H. Shorthouse

TEAS 275

J. H. Shorthouse

J. H. SHORTHOUSE

By F. J. WAGNER

University of Regina

TWAYNE PUBLISHERS

A DIVISION OF G. K. HALL & CO., BOSTON

Copyright © 1979 by G. K. Hall & Co.

Published in 1979 by Twayne Publishers,
A Division of G. K. Hall & Co.
All Rights Reserved

Printed on permanent/durable acid-free paper and bound
in the United States of America

First Printing

Frontispiece photo of J. H. Shorthouse
courtesy of Macmillan and Co.
London

Library of Congress Cataloging in Publication Data

Wagner, Frederick J
J. H. Shorthouse.

(Twayne's English authors series; TEAS 275)
Bibliography: p. 180-83
Includes index.
1. Shorthouse, Joseph Henry, 1834-1903—Criticism and inter-
pretation.
PR5451.Z5W3   823'.8   79-13635
ISBN 0-8057-6729-0

Contents

About the Author

F.J. Wagner was born on a Saskatchewan farm. He received his education in Canada and the United States—B.A. from Capital University and an M.A. from the University of Minnesota. He has taught at St. Paul-Luther College in St. Paul, Minnesota and at Luther College, Regina, Saskatchewan, Canada for over thirty years. From 1965 until his retirement in 1976 he taught at the University of Regina, where he still does some part-time teaching. His courses include surveys in English literature, Chaucer, and Practical Criticism.

Most of the research on Shorthouse was done during a sabbatical year at the University of London and another sabbatical semester reading in the British Library. As a preliminary to this book, Professor Wagner has published an annotated bibliography of Shorthouse (*Bulletin of Bibliography and Magazine* Notes, 1971).

Preface

A widening and deepening interest in the minor writers of the nineteenth century, particularly in the wilderness of the "religious" novel, has in the last forty years lured an increasing number of prospectors into a relatively unmapped area on the chance that there they might discover rifts loaded with ore. A succession of studies, more than enough to indicate dimensions and variety of the terrain, has provided, along with some interesting and valuable nuggets, helpful topographical maps as further incitement to exploration: Joseph Ellis Baker, *The Novel and the Oxford Movement* (1932); Amy Cruse, *The Victorians and their Reading* (1935); Leo J. Henkin, *Darwinism in the English Novel 1860–1910* (1940) and *Problems and Digressions in the Victorian Novel* (1944); Andrew L. Drummond, *The Churches in English Fiction* (1950); Margaret Maison, *Search Your Soul, Eustace: A Survey of the Religious Novel in the Victorian Age* (1961); Raymond Chapman, *Faith and Revolt: Studies in the Literary Influence of the Oxford Movement* (1970); Richard Altick, *Victorian People and Ideas* (1975); Valentine Cunningham, *Everywhere Spoken Against: Dissent in the Victorian Novel* (1976); Robert Lee Wolff, *Gains and Losses: Novels of Faith and Doubt in Victorian England* (1977). These have been supported at intervals by new, full-length studies of neglected authors, such as Catherine MacLean's *Mark Rutherford: A Biography of William Hale White* (1955), Robert Lee Wolff's *The Golden Key: A Study of the Fiction of George MacDonald* (1961), and William S. Peterson's *Victorian Heretic: Mrs. Humphry Ward's "Robert Elsmere"* (1976). Still unhonored in this manner, J. H. Shorthouse is one of those minor novelists who deserve more recognition than they have had if the complexities of the religious conflicts and tensions in nineteenth-century England are to be properly understood. He is distinctively illustrative of one of the varied compromises made by those Victorians who could not accept uncritically the orthodoxies of Catholicism, Anglicanism, or Dissent, but who were also unconvinced by proposed substitutes for an apparently dying religion, "culture," "morality," "duty," "aestheticism."

Shorthouse's *John Inglesant* (1880) was one of the bestsellers in the 1880s and 1890s, and was reprinted for the nth time as recently as 1976. Yet Meijer Polak's *The Historical, Philosophical, and Religious Aspects of "John Inglesant"* (Purmerend 1933; Oxford 1934), never in wide circulation and long out of print, has, with all its peculiar limitations, so far been the only full-length study of Shorthouse in English. Three other studies, doctoral dissertations, all in German, have been made: Elfriede Rieger's fairly comprehensive *Joseph Henry Shorthouse und sein "John Inglesant": Ein Beitrag zur Geschichte des englischen Romans im 19. Jahrhundert* (Göttingen 1927); Hanna Frauchiger's more restricted *Das "innere Licht" in "John Inglesant" von Joseph Henry Shorthouse* (Zürich 1928); Herbert Held's *"John Inglesant" und der Römische Katholizismus in England* (Graz 1940). These, as well as Polak's, lean in varying measure and manner on William Kaye Fleming's "Some Truths about 'John Inglesant' " (*Quarterly Review*, July 1925) which shook admirers of *John Inglesant* with chapter-and-verse evidence of wide ranging "plagiarism" in the novel. Though Fleming's article undoubtedly stimulated fresh interest in Shorthouse, it seriously impaired his reputation as an influential, if controversial, writer. Shorthouse became in some minds more interesting as a species of literary pickpocket than as a novelist who was one of the leading spokesmen for cultivated Anglicanism.

Contemporary reviews of Shorthouse's novels neither elevated nor demolished him, but a gradual accumulation of inadvertently repeated errors of fact, most of them innocuous enough, fogged both the facts of his life and his achievement. Shorthouse's waning popularity was halted temporarily, following his death (1903), by a spate of commemorative articles. These reviewed the *corpus* of his writing and resulted in more solid critical pronouncement than that expressed by the earlier reviews. Two years later the gently uncritical, commemorative *Life, Letters, and Literary Remains of J. H. Shorthouse*, by his wife, provided firsthand and limited information about Shorthouse's uneventful life. The publication stimulated another journalistic flurry which was followed by a twenty-year silence broken only intermittently until Fleming's well-intentioned article in 1925 on the unacknowledged borrowings in *John Inglesant* made Shorthouse's name known to a new generation. Since then Shorthouse has occasionally enjoyed the comfort of having a chapter to himself—generally a good chapter—in a book; but normally he has been bedded down in a paragraph (or in a long sentence) to share a skimpy blanket with a variety of other minor writers categorized as historical novelists, romancers, mystics, or propagandists.

A Quaker turned Anglican, Shorthouse wrote five novels, some short stories, and a number of essays which reveal an Anglicanism distinctively his own, a sacramentalism as much aesthetic and cultural as religious. Even if he was perhaps not intentionally or consciously a frontline pikeman in the religious pamphleteering of the nineteenth century his novels and essays cannot be ignored in any critical examination of that great bulk and variety of "religious" novels by which the nineteenth-century reader was entertained, instructed, or influenced. Of the many novels pushing particular religious causes—Romanist, anti-Romanist, evangelical—*John Inglesant* as a creative achievement is foremost among those supporting Anglicanism against the Church of Rome and the Dissenters.

It has been the purpose in the present study, first, to bring together within the covers of one book the ascertainable, pertinent facts of Shorthouse's life and writing career scraped out of many cracks and crannies; then, in a limited space to follow Shorthouse's passage from Quakerism to a distinctive Anglicanism as it is perceptible in his life and writing. The introductory chapter, then, will be concerned with Shorthouse's life, background, and personality. The following chapter takes a cursory glance at his journeyman pieces written for the Friends' Essay Society. The third and longest inspects *John Inglesant*, his greatest achievement. The next two chapters review his remaining novels and the essays which reveal his "churchmanship." The final chapter considers Shorthouse as one voice in the constantly changing discord of Victorian religious belief. Because of limited space the temptation to enlarge on the extent of Shorthouse's debts to Plato and Spinoza has been resisted. No attempt has been made to search out his niche in the category of historical fiction or romance. And it has not been found necessary to garrot him for his "plagiarism" or to psychoanalyze him.

Over the years debts have accumulated. Professor Douglas Bush, long ago, without any premonition of consequences, introduced an aspiring beginner to *John Inglesant*, and this and other greater debts to a great teacher are hereby belatedly but gratefully acknowledged by one of his wayward disciples. Morchard Bishop's interest and encouragement at a time when no book on Shorthouse was more than mildly contemplated make him unintentionally an accessory before the fact, but he is in no way responsible for any shortcomings of this study. From his horde of information, John Hunter kindly answered some queries about Birmingham Friends in the nineteenth century. During the writing Professor Robert Lee Wolff's gracious, generous response to emergency calls from a stranger was most gratifying.

Acknowledgment is made here also of the courtesy and assistance of many librarians wherever they were, particularly those of The British Library, The National Library of Scotland, The Birmingham Reference Library, The Friends' Library, London, and those who shared their treasure through interlibrary loan. Most of all, thanks are due to Mr. S. Harland, Chief Librarian of my own young university library, who in a good cause could wink at strains on departmental allocations; to Miss Margaret Hammond and Mr. Walter Raff whose knowledge of ways and means solved many a bibliographical conundrum; and to the denizens of the interlibrary loans department, with honorable mention to Carol Olive and Paula Bidlo, whose resourcefulness and diligence assured a steady flow of scarce materials over their counter.

My colleague and friend, Dr. L. G. Crossman, extracted some precious time to read the manuscript and with customary modesty to make some valuable suggestions. My wife has been denied the joys of compiling the index, but her practised eye and sensitive ear have reduced infelicities of style in the manuscript to what I hope will be a forgivable number. Pat Detz and Gisela Fiege somehow found time cheerfully to type the manuscript. A grant from the President's Fund, University of Regina, helped to defray unavoidable costs of xerograph materials and typing.

Acknowledgments

I wish to acknowledge with thanks the hospitality and courtesy of Shorthouse's publishers, Macmillan and Company, who kindly permitted me long ago to examine the Shorthouse letters in their London file—now in the *Macmillan Archive*, British Library—and gave me permission to quote generously from Shorthouse's works.

I wish also to thank Garland Publishing, Inc. for permission to quote from *Gains and Losses: Novels of Faith and Doubt in Victorian England*, by Robert Lee Wolff.

Chronology

1834	Joseph Henry Shorthouse born, 9 September, in Great Charles Street, Birmingham, to Quaker parents Joseph Shorthouse, manufacturer of chemicals, and his wife Mary Ann Hawker, daughter of John Hawker, glass manufacturer.
1835	Moved to 30 Calthorpe Street, Edgbaston, a Birmingham suburb.
1838	At Miss Harris's school in Frederick Street; begins to stammer; removed from school and educated by tutors and parents.
1842	Severe attack of typhus fever; slow recovery at Moseley with his grandmother Rebecca Shorthouse; wide reading.
1844	Day pupil at William Lean's Quaker private school, George Street; after a short time again removed from school by parents and tutored at home.
1850	Pupil at Grove House, Tottenham, January to June; on return home tutored in French, Italian, and drawing; enters the family business; with his cousins member of Friends' Essay Society.
1857	Marries Sarah Scott, elder daughter of John Scott, a Birmingham accountant, 19 August; takes up residence on Francis Street.
1858	Fall from a pony at Church Stretton in June; resulting concussion may have affected his health for the rest of his life.
1861	With his wife, baptized 14 August by the Rev. Francis Morse, Anglican, St. John's Ladywood.
1862	Severe attack of epilepsy in January; another attack in September; moves to 6 Beaufort Road, Edgbaston.
1864	Begins a nine-year term as People's Warden, St. John's, Ladywood.
1867	Begins writing of *John Inglesant*.
1876	*John Inglesant* completed in September; rejected by

publishers, manuscript put aside for four years; purchase of "Lansdowne," 60 Wellington Road, Edgbaston, where he was to reside for the rest of his life.

1880   *John Inglesant*, one hundred copies, published 1 July at Shorthouse's expense by Cornish Brothers, Birmingham; attracts little public attention.

1881   *John Inglesant*, two volumes, published by Macmillan on urging of Mrs. Humphry Ward; immediate success. "On the Platonism of Wordsworth," read to the Wordsworth Society, Grasmere, 19 July.

1882   "The Agnostic at Church" published in the *Nineteenth Century* (April 1882). "Introductory Essay to Facsimile Reprint" of George Herbert's *The Temple* issued in June by Fisher Unwin. "An Apologue," a short sketch, published in the *Nineteenth Century* (July 1882). "The Marquis Jeanne Hyacinthe de St. Palaye," a short story, published in *Macmillan's Magazine* (July 1882). "The Baroness Helena von Saarfeld," a short story, published in *Macmillan's Magazine* (August 1882).

1883   "The Humorous in Literature" published in *Macmillan's Magazine* (March 1883). Preface to *Golden Thoughts from the Spiritual Guide of Miguel Molinos, the Quietist* published by David Bryce and Son, Glasgow. "Ellie: A Story of a Boy and Girl," a very short story, five hundred copies, published for private circulation only, by W. R. King, Birmingham. *The Little Schoolmaster Mark, Part I*, published by Macmillan in October; appeared also in November issue of the *English Illustrated Magazine*.

1884   "Frederick Denison Maurice," a review of a biography of Maurice by his son, published in the *Nineteenth Century* (May 1884). *The Little Schoolmaster Mark, Part II* published by Macmillan in December.

1885   *The Little Schoolmaster Mark*, Parts I and II in one volume published by Macmillan in March.

1886   *Sir Percival, a Story of the Past and of the Present* published by Macmillan in September.

1887   "A Teacher of the Violin," a short story, published in *Macmillan's Magazine* (November 1887).

1888   *A Teacher of the Violin and Other Tales*, a collection of his previously published short stories, published by Macmillan in March. Preface to Francis Morse's *Peace the Voice of the Church to her Sick* published by the Christian Knowledge Society. "Of Restraining Self-Denial in Art," an essay, published in the *Century Guild Hobby Horse*. *The Countess Eve, A Novel* published by Macmillan at the end of October.

1891   His last novel, *Blanche, Lady Falaise, A Tale* published by Macmillan in September.

1895   "A Sunday Afternoon," a sketch, published in the *English Illustrated Magazine* (June 1895).

1899   Preface to Arthur Galton's *The Message and Position of the Church of England* published by Kegan Paul.

1900   Invalided with muscular rheumatism in October.

1901   Retires from business in March.

1903   Death at "Lansdowne," Wellington Road, Edgbaston, 4 March.

CHAPTER 1

Prologue

JOSEPH Henry Shorthouse, the author of *John Inglesant*, as distinguished from his contemporary Joseph Henry Shorthouse, M.D. [d. 1883], the founding editor of *The Sporting Times*, was born in 1834, two years after the First Reform Bill and three years before Victoria came to the English throne. In the same year, Charles Lamb and Samuel Taylor Coleridge died, and William Morris and George du Maurier were born. Dickens, Thackeray, Tennyson, and Browning were then in their early twenties, the Brontës and George Eliot in their teens.

Shorthouse died in 1903. In that year George Gissing also died, and Evelyn Waugh and George Orwell were born. Thomas Hardy, and Henry James were by then in their sixties; Shaw, Conrad, and A. E. Housman were already in their forties; Kipling, Yeats, Galsworthy, and H. G. Wells were slightly younger, D. H. Lawrence and T. S. Eliot in their teens. James Joyce and Virginia Woolf had just turned twenty-one. Given a year or two at either end of his life, Shorthouse's exact contemporaries among the nineteenth-century novelists and writers whose productive period coincided with his own were George MacDonald, Margaret Oliphant, "Mark Rutherford," Walter Besant, Edwin Arnold, Lewis Carroll, "Ouida," F. W. Robinson, G. A. Henty, Leslie Stephen, Samuel Butler, and Walter Pater—a rather mixed bag.

During the sixty-eight-year interval between Shorthouse's birth and death an English queen reigned a long reign and inadvertently bequeathed her name to the period. Shorthouse's life, then, spanned what some choose to distinguish as "Early-Victorian," "Mid-Victorian," and "Late-Victorian" periods of literary, political, social, and religious change. In the same time span a procession of prime ministers—Melbourne, Peel, Russell, Derby, Aberdeen, Palmerston, Disraeli, Gladstone, Salisbury, Rosebery, Balfour— crossed the political stage with an almost monotonous alternation of

Whig and Tory, leaving in their wake, sometimes reluctantly, a flutter of Reform Bills, Factory Acts, and Education Bills. Continental friends and foes were shaken by revolutions of varying magnitude. The highly-touted Victorian peace was interrupted with a Crimean War, an Opium War, a Zulu War, a Boer War abroad, and enlivened at home with recurrent riots in the city squares—bread riots, machine-breaking riots, an expression of the symptomatic, convulsive growing pains of a changing economic and social order. At intervals for ten years the Polar seas were scanned for traces of the lost Franklin Expedition. The laying of the transoceanic cable (1857-66) drew the continents more closely together. The industrial smoke from multiplying smokestacks increasingly dimmed the sky of William Blake's "green and pleasant land." The railway carriage, which around mid-century gradually superseded the stagecoach, ran on an ever-enlarging iron network which by 1900 covered the island, and not only facilitated commerce and communication but gave increasing mobility to the "masses," a mobility which—depending on how one viewed it—could be considered either joyful or alarming.

In the same period, one of ceaseless, vigorous speculation and inquiry, the meaning and purpose of religion were seriously examined. The authority of the Bible as the inerrant word of God, the source of history, even of truth, was challenged by David Friedrich Strauss's *Das Leben Jesu, Kritisch Bearbeitet* (1835; translated into English by George Eliot, 1841). Biblical authority was further eroded by an increasing, critical examination of the Bible as a historical document, the "Higher Criticism." Bishop Colenso's *The Pentateuch Critically Examined* (1862) made great cracks in the foundations of religious belief already shaking from "the testimony of the rocks"—chiefly from Sir Charles Lyell's *The Principles of Geology* (1830–33). This "testimony" was supplemented by the exhumation of the Neanderthal Man (1856), the publication of Charles Darwin's *The Origin of Species* (1859) and Lyell's *The Antiquity of Man* (1863). Philosopher-scientists Herbert Spencer and Thomas Huxley, in spite of Prime Minister Gladstone's resistance, continued the rout of religious orthodoxy. Karl Marx completed the first volume of *Das Kapital* (1867) in the refuge of the British Museum Reading Room. The achievements of James Simpson in anaesthesia, Joseph Lister in surgery, Robert Koch and Louis Pasteur in bacteriology made life less uncertain and pain more endurable. Summarized in a well-worn commonplace, the century was a period of steady, improving, sometimes rapidly accelerating, change—agricultural, industrial, political, social, religious, intellectual. Of the tensions which accompanied this period of change those precipitated by the "battle of the churches" were of the most widespread concern to the "Earnest Victorians." And actively concerned in this battle was the Quaker-Anglican, manufacturer-novelist Joseph Henry Shorthouse.

Margaret (Southall) Evans, Shorthouse's cousin, records what her Quaker mother Sarah (Shorthouse) Southall, looking back from her one-hundredth birthday (12 September 1901) could remember of this century of change:

In the century during which she has lived, the greatest changes have taken place in the shortest time. For long after her birth Englishmen and Englishwomen owned slaves. . . . It was deemed right that a man should be hanged if he stole property worth 5/-. The prisons were crowded. . . . Little boys of eight and nine were sent up chimneys to sweep them, and many died in the flues of suffocation. . . . Man-traps, spring-guns, and gins were set in gardens and woods to catch poachers. The Mail coaches all had guards who carried firearms to protect the mails against highwaymen. . . . Criminals were executed in public . . . and their bodies left on the gibbet for years; no laws protected dumb animals from cruelty. . . . Bulls were baited; . . . gentlemen patronized cock-fighting, and the clergy badger-baiting on Sunday evenings after church. . . . Little boys addressed their fathers as 'Sir,' . . . little girls were taught to sit upright and turn out their toes. . . . It cost 1/- to send a letter from Birmingham to London. . . . Ladies wore muslin made in India and linen made in France and Ireland. Goods were taken about the country in stage wagons or on packhorses. People travelled by stage coaches well padded inside, as they were often upset. There were a few steam coaches before 1840, that travelled between London and Birmingham and had a funnel at the back . . . and there were velocipedes made of wood. . . . Most people stayed at home. . . . In the principal streets [of Birmingham] many of the houses were thatched. . . . There were no policemen, only parish constables and night watchmen who called the hour. The town was lit by oil-lamps. . . . Until [she] was over forty years old water was sold in Birmingham streets from carts, as milk is. . . . There was a cherry orchard in the middle of the town where Cherry Street now is, and corn was reaped just to the west of St. Philip's Churchyard. . . Birmingham always had a bad name for coining and coiners. . . Bad money used to be much more common than it is now. . . There was no British Empire when [she] was born. Large parts of India were in the hands of the East India Company. . . . Part of Canada belonged to England. . . . Nelson died on board the "Victory" when [she] was four years old. . . . Australia was discovered by the Dutch and was called "New Holland." The English government formed a penal settlement to which to transport its criminals. . . . The world has moved quickly since [she] was born. It has moved chiefly in one direction—it has found the value of a human life.[1]

Of the world of political change, social adjustment, and industrial expansion, there is little expression in the literary work of Shorthouse. Although he lived all his comfortable life in a rapidly growing industrial city, a manufacturer of chemicals useful to an expanding peacetime industry, and certainly needful in wartime, in his essays and novels there are audible no clinkings of the economic chains which were being forged or broken; there is no expression of either joy or distress about working conditions in the mines and factories, nor any recognition of what Elizabeth Barrett called "The Cry of the Children." There is hardly a hint that the Independent Labor Party had been formed (1893). His writings hark back to other places, to other times than his own or are suspended by the imagination into an other-world romance. The human figures which move through them are unobservant of, or unconcerned about, such urgent but temporary matters as sweatshops, factory smoke, or a growing merchant marine, tariffs, the price of bread, conditions of labor, or agricultural wages, or votes. There are no Oliver Twists, no Alton Lockes, or Squeerses, or Gradgrinds among them, nor, for that matter, any Sam Wellers.

This does not necessarily mean that Shorthouse as a Midlands citizen was unconcerned with domestic social problems. But there is an obvious contrast between the novelist and the manufacturer, that is, between the romances which emanated from his suburban study in "Lansdowne," Edgbaston, and the business post which emanated from the family chemical works in New Market Street, Birmingham.

I

Joseph Henry Shorthouse was born in Great Charles Street, Birmingham, 9 September 1834, the oldest of three sons of well-to-do, liberally conservative (or conservatively liberal) Quaker parents. Apart from the annual fortnight at the seaside, and, after the publication of his first novel, brief visits to Oxford, the cathedral towns, or London, he was confined unobtrusively to Birmingham, and he died 4 March 1903 in Edgbaston, a Birmingham suburb where he had spent almost all his life. Except for the occasional family holiday at Llandudno, in Wales, and, at sixteen, an excursion with his cousins into Scotland as far as Braemar, he was never out of England. But his novels are set in other places and times than his own. *John Inglesant*, his most important novel, is a story of the seventeenth century, set partially in England, but mostly in Italy. *The Little Schoolmaster Mark* is set in eighteenth-century Germany, *The Countess Eve* in eighteenth-century Burgundy. Though *Sir Percival* at the beginning has a vaguely nineteenth-century English setting, the closing letter shifts the scene to Africa, and his last novel *Blanche, Lady Falaise*, with an almost totally English setting, has its Austrian insert.

The facts of his outwardly uneventful life can be easily and briefly summarized. When he was one, his family moved from the industrial encroachments of Birmingham to 30 Calthorpe Street, Edgbaston, then already the prestigious suburban residence of prosperous Birmingham merchants and manufacturers. At the age of four, a sensitive child, he attended for a short time, as a day-pupil, a "Preparatory Establishment for Young Gentlemen" conducted by Miss Elizabeth Harris at 6 Frederick Street, Edgbaston, not far from his home. But he was withdrawn when he developed a stammer, and was thereafter instructed at home by his parents and tutors. Prostrated by a severe attack of typhus fever when he was eight, he spent a long period of convalescence at the home of his grandmother Rebecca Shorthouse, on the one-hundred-and-twenty-acre country estate which his grandfather William Shorthouse had purchased at Moseley in 1801. At ten, he attended a Quaker school on George Street conducted by William Lean, an enlightened disciplinarian, but again developed a painful stammer, and was removed from school for treatment, with little success, by a London physician, John Bishop. With his brother John he was enrolled from 14 January to 13 June 1850, at Grove House, Tottenham, a school for the sons of well-to-do Quakers.[2] But the stammer persisted, and on his return home he was tutored in French, Italian, and drawing (but not in music, as he regretted later). With neither reluctance nor enthusiasm, at sixteen he entered the family business, the manufacture of chemicals, particularly lacquer and vitriol. When he was twenty-three, he married Sarah Scott, two years his senior, also of the Society of Friends, the daughter of Elizabeth and John Scott, a Birmingham accountant of a Cumberland family. On a holiday at Church Stretton shortly after his marriage, a fall from a pony resulted in a concussion which apparently affected his health for the rest of his life. After a long period of indecision and strain, in December 1860 he resigned his membership in the Society of Friends, though for some undisclosed reason his wife did not resign until the following November. They were baptized together in the Church of England, 14 August 1861, and he remained until his death a sincere and congregationally active adherent of the Church of England, serving as People's Warden for nine years between 1864 and 1874.

In 1880 he published at his own expense his first novel, *John Inglesant*, on which he had worked steadily during his evenings and spare time since 1867. The novel was almost unnoticed by the public until Mrs. Humphry Ward urged it on Alexander Macmillan who published it in 1881, when Shorthouse found himself unexpectedly famous. *John Inglesant* was followed by what has been called "weaker tricklings from the same spring": [3] *The Little Schoolmaster Mark* (1883–1885), *Sir Percival* (1886), *A Teacher of the Violin and Other Tales* (1888), *The Countess Eve* (1888), *Blanche, Lady Falaise* (1891).

As one of the first members of the Wordsworth Society he contributed an essay "On the Platonism of Wordsworth" (1881), now decently interred in the *Transactions* of the Society—though Folcroft Press ventured a limited reprint in 1969. To the *Nineteenth Century* (April 1882) he contributed "The Agnostic at Church," an essay provoked by Louis Greg's essay of the same title (January), and in the same year a very short story "An Apologue" (July 1882), later included in *A Teacher of the Violin*. On the solicitation of Maurice's son, he contributed to the *Nineteenth Century* (May 1884) a review of the *Life of Frederick Denison Maurice*, which was elevated to an introduction in later editions of the book. In *Macmillan's Magazine* he published two short stories, "The Marquis Jeanne Hyacinthe De St. Palaye" (July 1882) and "The Baroness Helena von Saarfeld" (August 1882), both later reprinted in *A Teacher of the Violin*, and a longer article "The Humorous in Literature" (March 1883) which had grown out of an earlier essay he had written for the Friends' Essay Society. He wrote an essay "Of Restraining Self-Denial in Art" for the *Century Guild Hobby Horse* (1888), and in the *English Illustrated Magazine* published an undistinguished poem entitled "My Wife's Valentine" (May 1884), and "A Sunday Afternoon" (June 1895), a fictionalized sketch based on a holiday visit to Llanfairfechan near Llandudno the previous September.

He contributed an introductory High Church essay to Fisher Unwin's re-issue of George Herbert's *The Temple* (1882), and short prefaces to *Golden Thoughts from the Spiritual Guide of Miguel Molinos* (1883), his friend Francis Morse's *Peace the Voice of the Church to her Sick* (1888), and his distant cousin Arthur Galton's *The Message and Position of the Church of England* (1899). Apparently, he began a romance of the Italian Renaissance but never finished it. Not until invalided by muscular rheumatism a year or so before his death did he retire from business. Not too much, then, and not too little did Shorthouse write for one who was not making his living with his pen.

II

In what may be called Shorthouse criticism there is a tireless, and unnecessarily tiresome, concern with the provincial manufacturer of chemicals turned author of romance and the Birmingham Quaker turned Edgbaston High Churchman. To reviewers of his work the phenomenon of the Quaker-Anglican-manufacturer-novelist seems to have been as irresistibly worrisome as a loose tooth. A man in a Midlands city occupied during the day with the manufacture and sale of things (or of things to be used in the manufacture of other things) writes fine-spun romances in his evenings and spare time, collects seventeenth-century editions of theology and history, studies Greek, and makes congregational calls. As a member of a religious group not normally eligible for an Oxford or Cambridge degree—indeed, physically and temperamentally unsuited to the university grind and with, therefore, little formal education—he presumes to rise to the surface of the literary pond with a bestseller. After a boyhood of almost passive submission to the First-Day and Fourth-Day silence of an unadorned Quaker meetinghouse, but with apparently little participation in the Quaker programs of philanthropy and missionary work, at twenty-seven he assumes an active congregational life as People's Warden in a ritualistic church with beautiful music and stained glass windows. Never embarrassingly wealthy, but always comfortably secure, he has no need to publish, as, for instance, Frances Trollope had, to feed a family, or, as William Hale White had, to supplement a meager wage. The question, then, to some reviewers seemed to be—to bend T. S. Eliot's phrase a little—why should he presume?

A cursory look at Shorthouse's background and antecedents will provide some sort of answer. If his birth into the Society of Friends can be considered an historical accident, it is not accidental that Shorthouse remained all his life in Birmingham when with only slight effort he might have sidled into the inner circle of London literati. After all, his family, his comfortable home, his business were in Birmingham.

But more significant surely was the Quaker ancestry which had settled his family in Birmingham. Members of the Society of Friends, "the People in Scorn called Quakers," [4] afflicted with frequent and heavy fines, their goods distrained, their bodies imprisoned for too punctilious observance of their "peculiarity" (oaths, tithes, dress, speech) since the days of George Fox (1624–91), were, in later generations, by what might legitimately be called an historical process, compressed into certain areas and certain occupations and almost accidentally into an affluence and therefore influence quite out of proportion to their numbers. (Accurate statistics are difficult to come by. In 1851 Quaker membership in Birmingham was three hundred and eighty in a population of almost two hundred thousand.) The Test Act (1673) which virtually kept them out of Oxford and Cambridge (but not out of Edinburgh, or Leyden, or Paris) was not repealed until 1863, and the religious subscription for graduation not until 1871. The Corporation Act of 1661 (not repealed until 1871) made it more than difficult for Quakers to enter many of the trades in a corporate town, so that they tended to gravitate from the corporate towns (where, for instance, they could not sue for debt) to noncorporate towns like Birmingham. The Corporation Act had not only required the taking of an oath of allegiance, but also that members of a corporation within one year take the Sacrament according to the rites of the established Church, something few Quakers were willing to do. Moreover, distraints for fines levied for refusal to pay the church-rate, or for failure to attend the Church, were frequently carried out by confiscation and sale, or sometimes destruction of merchandise, of household goods, or the working tools of tradesmen and small manufacturers. [5] A tradesman or manufacturer could painfully restock, but because the farmer sometimes could not he frequently moved from the land to the town. The occasionally heavy fines also caused a serious drain of capital which sometimes impoverished individuals who then needed the support of a sizeable group such as the one in Birmingham. (It is estimated that for the ten-year period 1820–29, i.e., just prior to Shorthouse's birth, over one hundred and forty-thousand pounds was taken from the members of the Society by distraint, "for Ecclesiastical purposes.")

Because of their "testimony" against luxuriance and extravagance in dress or household furnishings, many members of the Society, unwilling to compromise their principles (though others did), conscientiously refrained from making their living in the clothing and furniture trades, or made only a limited one in woollens, linen, or plain silk. Many therefore turned to the manufacture of useful objects. In the iron trade, Quaker views about war forbade the manufacture of cannon and arms, or even the participation in certain trades contributory to the manufacture of arms. But though, for those who could somehow square their belief with their action, good money was to be made in cannon, more was to be made in pots and pans and pokers, or in agricultural tools. An insatiable market in an expanding economy brought prosperity to the Friends—or at least to some of them.

Persecution and prosecution through two centuries had made the Friends anxious to demonstrate their integrity, with the result that their reputation for trustworthiness and fair dealing in business made their trade sought after; the sneer, "Quaker-dealing," lost its economic and social effectiveness, and became almost a term of respect. (It did not root out, naturally, "Thee, Thou, Quaker Cow" hurled by little boys at the backs of little Quaker girls.) The resulting accumulation of capital, consolidated and cemented by advantageous marriages, made possible the establishment of the Quaker banks which helped develop the iron works, the coal industries, the railways in which Quakers were already industrially engaged. As the "Yearly Meeting Minutes on Finance" periodically show, an indirect stimulus was given to Quaker economy by the attitude toward debt which was often considered by the Society as a misdemeanor rather than a misfortune.

But accumulating wealth and an inevitable participation in the affairs of the "world" induced tensions in the Society of Friends which some of its members eventually escaped by joining the more socially acceptable and less restrictive Church of England; or, if they remained with the Society, they arrived at a shaky compromise between the demands of their professed faith and the pressures of a world in which socially and economically they were unavoidably involved.

By the time Joseph Henry Shorthouse was born his family was prosperously established in Birmingham unto the third Quaker generation. The Shorthouse family tree bore mixed but hardy fruit. Before 1850, any who survived infancy ripened well into their eighties. Sarah Shorthouse (b. 12 September 1801) lived until 11 January 1902, a true centenarian. Almost without exception they seem to have founded a business, expanded a business, or married into a business. This record of health, industry, and acumen does not suggest a high incidence of literary production, but neither does it preclude the possibility that somewhere in the line there might have been a "mute inglorious Milton" or two.

To find the Quaker connection one needs go back only a hundred years from the birth of J. H. Shorthouse the novelist to the birth of another Shorthouse. Born in 1734, Thomas Shorthouse was "brought up in a laboratory" as an assistant in the chemical firm of the Morris family, Quakers, in Eachinghill, a village near Rugeley not far north of Birmingham.[6] His industry and integrity so recommended him to his employers that on the death of Moses Morris his son Joseph took Thomas Shorthouse into partnership. When the business later was given up, Thomas Shorthouse in 1761 set up his own small chemical business in Birmingham, started a household by his marriage with Hannah England of Rugeley who had connections with Friends at Tamworth, and took up residence in Edgbaston. Shortly after this, having for a time attended meetings of the Society, Thomas and Hannah formally joined the Society of Friends. Of their four children, William, the oldest, and his two sisters, "at the age of discretion" became active members of the Society. Thomas prospered sufficiently to expand his business, increase his property, and in 1805 to found the chemical works in Shadwell Street with which the name of Shorthouse was to be associated through three generations for more than a century. With his son William he expanded the business into export trade with America, prospering to such a degree that William (b. 29 December 1768), described later by his daughters as "a Radical and a disciple of Cobbett" [7] when he died in June 1838, though still comparatively young for a member of a hardy line, was already a wealthy man. (The story is told that on her wedding day he gave each of his three daughters, along with other settlements, a hundred guineas in gold.) On 31 May 1796 William had, at Wednesbury, married Rebecca Robinson, whose grandfather, as a young man near the end of the seventeenth century, had set up in Birmingham as a cooper. In this way William Shorthouse allied his business family with what was known to have been "a land-owning family in North Warwickshire in the last year of Queen Elizabeth." [8] Of their seven children three died in infancy of smallpox and scarlet fever. His elder son, Joseph, married Mary Ann Hawker whose grandfather, Isaac Hawker, had established the glass works in Birmingham in 1785. They had three sons, Joseph Henry the future novelist, John William, and Edmund. All entered the family business. All three died without issue, thus terminating the male line of the Shorthouse of Moseley and Birmingham family. But other branches of the tree continued to bear, for of William Shorthouse's surviving daughters, Sarah married Thomas Southall, pharmacist; Marianne married William Nicholson, a Cumberland farmer; and Hannah married William Nutter, tea and coffee merchant. Through three of the Southalls' daughters the Quaker names of Ransom, Dymond, and Evans were grafted to the tree. The Nicholsons, the largest family, with six surviving children, and the Nutters, the smallest with one daughter, added other names. The records of births, marriages and deaths of their descendants in China, Africa, Canada, and Florida indicate that they had moved beyond Birmingham to encompass the earth.

Though the business strain in the Shorthouses is strong, one can detect already in Rebecca Robinson Shorthouse (1765–1858), Joseph Henry's grandmother, evidence in the line of literary possibilities. She was not the plainest of the "plain," (conservative) nor the gayest of the "gay" (liberal) Friends. Herself well-read in more than Quaker literature, she had no aversion, as some of the more rigid Friends had, to "such literary publications as unprofitably elate the mind and give a disrelish for the purity of Gospel truths." She sat in the Ministers' Gallery as an Elder in the Friends' meetinghouse. As children, she and her sister Sarah, who later married Samuel Smith of Sheffield, founder of the ironworks there, had eagerly saved their pocket money to buy the first edition of the *Lyrical Ballads* and Wordsworth's later poems. She encouraged and stimulated her grandchildren in writing the "Moseley Pieces" and a "Family Magazine"—a literary game that went with the Thursday tea on what was known in this closeknit family as the "Moseley Days."

Shorthouse was no less fortunate in his father. "Quiet and gentle, but reserved [in his later years] almost to the point of frigidity, he was a man of much culture," says a writer in the *Friends' Quarterly Examiner* (1923, p. 16). Blessed with a tenacious memory and a powerful intellect, his mind crammed with the details of wide

reading and considerable foreign travel, he had an eagerness to
share with his sons his enthusiasm for old maps, military geography
and history, or travel books. Prosperous enough to support
indulgence of his tastes, he had accumulated a large library, and
encouraged his sons to enlarge it.

Of Shorthouse's mother his wife says: "She was always fond of
reading, and was herself a most charming and original letter writer.
Indeed both parents loved romance, and had the gift of imagination
which their son so largely inherited." [9] Shorthouse himself, writing
to George Bainton, remarks: "My interest in English literature
began very early, as my mother, who was an excellent reader,
spared no time or pains in reading to us, as we could understand
them, any of the best writers who she thought would be likely to
entertain or improve us. In this way we were familiar when very
little boys with the best parts of Sterne, Addison, Johnson, Cowper,
Mary Howitt, Mrs. Sherwood, etc. My father was also a man of
cultivated literary tastes." [10]

It is difficult to estimate, but it would be a mistake to minimize,
the contribution made to Shorthouse's development by the family
associations in the affectionate group of literary-minded uncles,
aunts, and cousins, among whom, as his favorite cousin Margaret
says, "Our cousin Henry Shorthouse was, by right of his genius, the
leading member." [11] The Thursday "Moseley Days" already alluded
to made for a convenient focusing of literary and other talent, such
as it was. Great readers all, some of them versifiers of sorts, young
and old stimulated each other in intellectual games and exercises. In
addition to Rebecca Shorthouse, the "genius of the wood," there
was Joseph Shorthouse, Shorthouse's widely-travelled father, who,
it was genially reported by a waggish fellow-traveller, "attended to
business when he had nothing else to do," [12] whose interest in
military geography had taken him and his brother-in-law William
Nutter to all the important battlefields of England and the
Continent, and whose memory for detail gave him an encyclopedic
knowledge. There was Shorthouse's uncle, Thomas Southall, a
pharmacist with a head full of astronomy, geology, meteorology,
ornithology, entomology, who "wrote and had printed a little book
explanatory of the rainbow, for his children's use." [13] Affluent
enough to afford an extensive holiday, he acquainted his family each
year with fauna and fossils of some new part of England or the
Continent, and two days before his death (12 January 1861) was still

sorting out his latest fossil acquisitions from Malvern, and worrying about his new telescope.

Thomas Southall's three print-consuming daughters were during his teens Shorthouse's most frequent companions. Together they went to the winter meetings of the Friends' Essay Society, often to the more weighty lectures at the meetinghouse, but most eagerly to those at the Philosophical Institution. They read and discussed the liberal churchmen, Charles Kingsley and Frederick Denison Maurice. Of a summer tour of the Scottish Lowlands in 1852, on which Shorthouse, then eighteen, accompanied them, his cousin remarks: ". . . we wandered, reading, drawing, talking, discussing. . . . We [sat] among the barley sheaves and read Tennyson." [14]

There was, first of the three, Anna Mary, sensitive, pensive, affectionate, the scholar, nine years older than Shorthouse, "with the pen of a ready writer," who had once seen Wordsworth "plain." There was Ellen, the shy one, eight years older, who set the literary tone of the household ["she did nothing but read"—travel, history, Dr. Arnold, Niebuhr, Grote] [15] who charmed her little boy cousins with her reading to them. There was Margaret, six years older than he, his favorite correspondent and critic in later years, and Isabel the roof-climber, who, like the rest of them, carved lines of poetry into the leads of the roof at Moseley and outlived almost all her sisters and cousins.

William Nutter—he was in tea and coffee—who had married Hannah Shorthouse in 1832, "had a fondness for Coleridge" when the others in this family circle "knew little of his writings." [16] As Joseph Shorthouse's frequent travel-companion he wrote "delightfully interesting" letters from abroad. Reading not so much as the others in the family, William Nutter read carefully—particularly French history—and was the acknowledged authority on "far-off things and battles long ago." A collector of engravings, he was an excellent linguist, fluent in French and Italian, who understood German, Spanish and Welsh, and had some knowledge of Latin and Greek, enough at least to enable him to get along with Herodotus and Thucydides. "He was neither horticulturist, botanist, or meteorologist," says his niece, "but he wandered in his garden as a poet." [17] Sarah Shorthouse Southall, his sister-in-law, Shorthouse's aunt, looking back from 1884, remarks about her daughters in the Moseley days: "They were also considerable readers, so that much literature of the past and present was known to them. Amongst those to whom they looked up with affectionate regard were their uncles Joseph Shorthouse and Wm. Nutter, whose extensive reading and intelligence with much conversational power rendered their company of great interest to the young people." [18]

But it was not all books and intellectual games at Moseley, for when their Cumberland cousins, the Nicholsons, several boys among them, joined the company, there was, in addition to the normal roof-climbing, some wall-walking, train-watching, and swinging in the barn before the evening program of literary excitement began.

Shorthouse's temperament drew him, of course, to art rather than to business. When at sixteen he took the perfectly normal step of entering the family business, sensitive, imaginative, vaguely dreamy, he was likely to attend dutifully and conscientiously to business, but suffer from the boredom of an unexciting routine and an aversion to the underfoot grittiness of the dirt-floored warehouse of Joseph Shorthouse and Sons. But, under an indulgent and unexacting father, when he was not occupied with uninteresting though unburdensome routine chores of the warehouse, he could ride the clouds of imagination and transmit his thoughts in office-letters to his cousins. He could breathe deeply the exhilarating air of the bookshops he frequented during his lunch hour. That the work was not exciting nor even demanding is clear from a classically succinct entry in his brother John's diary (30 March 1853), when Shorthouse was nineteen: "Went down to the Warehouse in the pm and helped H. to fold letters." There is evident not only a genially wry humor which is characteristic of Shorthouse, but also a warmth of repressed resentment which is not—in his designation of his father's office in New Market Street as "The Hole"—in the mid-day letters he wrote to Margaret, letters which, needless to say, make no mention of business. It says something about the reciprocal warmth of the relations with his cousins, whom he saw almost daily in those pretelephone days, that, chafing at unromantic surroundings, he should seek expression in those letters to Margaret for thoughts which could not be phrased in the stolid prose of invoices and inventories.

But a sensitive temperament in uncongenial circumstances was not necessarily enough to convert a manufacturer of chemicals into a writer of romance. Physical fragility, as he himself admitted, [19] made public life impossible. Treatment for the stammer which had afflicted him since early childhood was ineffectual.[20] The speaking from public platforms which participation in civic affairs required would have been too embarrassing to him and too painful for his audience to lure him into public life.[21] Shortly after his marriage the concussion suffered in the fall from a pony presumably brought on a succession of epileptic attacks which necessitated long periods of rest for recovery, and the worrying threat of their recurrence forced him to be contented with a careful, quiet life at home. Thus, more or less denied an exhausting public life, and sufficiently exhausted from his business life, he was confined to what he really enjoyed much more, a restful, private world of reading—and writing. One could say he was forced to find the time the writer needed.

III

"When I was a little girl between six and seven years of age," says Mrs. Shorthouse, "I remember walking one day with my mother in Edgbaston when we met a tall lady leading a little boy by the hand. . . . The little boy was about four years old, pale, dark-eyed, and handsome, and was dressed like most children of his age, in a dark-blue pelisse and cape, and large straw hat." [22] A year later she and the "timid, delicate, clever little boy" were at Miss Harris's school together, a school "attended by perhaps twenty little boys and girls from the best families in the neighborhood." "I do not think," she says, "that he or I could remember being harshly treated there ourselves, but we saw children punished, as we thought, severely, and it was a trial to me to be dressed differently, as a little Friend, from the other little girls." [23] Of how the little boy felt about his Quaker costume there is no record, but in the light of Shorthouse's later sartorial elegance it would be lack of imagination indeed to assume that he did not suffer. He developed a stammer. But though his parents quickly removed him from the environs of Miss Harris, the delicate, timid boy was in for more rugged exercises. At ten, after his convalescence from typhus, he attended as a day-pupil the Friends' school (largely concerned with the classics) conducted by William Lean, on George Street, a half-mile from his home. William Scarnell Lean, son of the master and eventually a scholar of some stature, years afterwards remembered Shorthouse only as a good classics scholar.[24] George Cadbury, another pupil, who remembered William Lean as a strict disciplinarian, could not help remembering also that Lean "seems to have

winked at the rough horseplay indulged by the boys. . . . One of
the methods of 'hardening' a new boy was to turn the boy's sleeves
up to the elbows and his trousers up to the knees, and then throw
him into a gorse bush . . . the pain of which he was to bear with
cheerful fortitude. Although a Friend, the master had a martial
spirit, and once a week took his pupils out into the fields for a game
of 'Attack and Defence' . . . a singular pastime, which must have
been the subject of much concern in the quietist households of the
young combatants." [25]

Though child of a tall father and a tall mother Shorthouse was
barely of average height, physically delicate, and temperamentally
unequipped for a struggle with the more muscular Christians. It is
not surprising, then, to read in his brother John's diary (1853): "Jan.
1—Went out a walk with Harry; Jan. 19—Some of the young men
had a game of football in the evening but we did not go; Feb. 17—I
and H. went to skate at Edgbaston Pool; May 2—H. and I went to
the field before breakfast . . . and had a good game of cricket;
June 28 [on holiday at Llandudno]—We all but H. went out for a
walk up the cliffs; July 20—Went to the field in the evening with
Edm. Harry came afterwards. Two or three of the worst of the
Clarendons came and played." It does come as a surprise, however,
in the *Life of George Cadbury* (p. 26) to find, without any reference
to the efficacy of William Lean's "Attack and Defence," Shorthouse
mentioned as a member of Richard Cadbury's prebreakfast football
and hockey teams.

On Shorthouse's death, someone identified only as a "very-well-
known Birmingham citizen," looking back to this period of
Shorthouse's young manhood, recalled:

I frequently met the author of 'John Inglesant' in 1853. It was in the days
when the 'Noah's Ark' cut of coat was in vogue. This coat was made to fit
well over the chest, and had very long skirts, reaching almost to the ankles;
two buttons were placed a little below the shoulder blades, and the skirts
were divided immediately below them. The coat was usually closely
buttoned as low as the bottom of the vest, and in windy weather the 'tails'
were somewhat unmanageable. The hat was somewhat of the 'Tom and
Jerry' pattern, slightly bell-topped, and with a brim dipping 'fore and aft,' as
sailors would say. A bright coloured necktie, straw-coloured kid gloves,
light-coloured trousers, tightly strapped down over bright boots of patent
leather, completed the walking-dress of the future celebrated author, while
in his hand he carried a smart gold-topped cane. Amongst his young Quaker
associates Mr. Shorthouse was known as 'Marquis,' from his somewhat

unQuakerly aristocratic bearing. In later years his sartorial equipment was a great contrast to that of his early manhood.[26]

Charles Linnell, the manager of Cornish Brothers, who knew him very well, has this portrait of the later Shorthouse:

His person, which was about the medium stature, was well-formed; his features had the general expression of kindness and simplicity, rendered more interesting by the hue of melancholy that pervaded them. For nearly twenty-five years Mr. Shorthouse paid a well-nigh daily visit to his bookseller's. There he would go for a midday chat, and there he would linger. It was interesting to watch the quiet and sober fashion in which he would peep into this book or look with some scorn into that. Mr. Shorthouse had a habit of 'communing' with himself. As he walked along these 'murmurings' could be heard. This tendency to talk to (or with) himself attracted the notice of many people. Mr. Shorthouse seemed to unite the characteristics of George Herbert and of Keble: the same modesty, the same purity of life, the same attachments to home and to literary pursuits, and the same love for the Church of England. Mr. Shorthouse cared not for the haunts of men; he loved solitude and retirement.[27]

James Bain, the London bookseller, met him at Macmillan's in London, May 1884. Writing to Mary L. Caley (20 May 1884) he reports his impression:

I met Mr. J. H. Shorthouse at Knapdale, Tooting, at dinner, with other distinguished people, on Saturday. I found Shorthouse and his wife extremely pleasant. He is a lively, humorous man, very different from his book. Of Jewish physiognomy, rather under the average height, loose black hair parted in the middle with the ends flapping into his eyes, receding forehead, projecting eyebrow, large nose, wide mouth, receding chin, suffers from occasional paroxysms of the larynx, which he relieves by clutching at his long pendant whiskers and stroking his agonized bosom.[28]

Shortly after the publication of "The Agnostic in Church" (April 1882) Dr. E. S. Talbot, Warden of Keble, invited Shorthouse to see "the inside of Oxford." Henry Scott Holland, years later, could enthusiastically recall that visit:

He was delightful to meet. In the first excitement, we eagerly invited him over to Oxford, and he came and talked metaphysics and religion with our 'gang.' He was disappointing in appearance; rather thick and short: with nothing notable about the face. And he had one of those terrific stammers which keep you in an agony of suspense lest something should give way, and he had the true stammerer's courage which fights its way through to the word it wants, and resolutely declines the hopelessly inadequate phrase offered it by pitying outsiders. But he never let this hinder his talk; and he never showed any selfconsciousness over it. He spoke freely: and earnestly: and was most winning.[29]

Edmund Gosse, biographer, poet and critic, met Shorthouse in 1883, and was Shorthouse's house guest whenever he lectured in Birmingham. Though he had offered advice and assistance to Mrs. Shorthouse in preparation of the manuscript, Gosse's review of her *Life, Letters, and Literary Remains* brought a protesting cry of pain from Mrs. Shorthouse,[30] for in the review—and one must be charitable here—he unconsciously permitted his pen to scratch rather deeply in describing "the impression which [Shorthouse's] very curious person made upon the few who knew him." On that matter he must be allowed to speak for himself:

Upon myself, who saw him first thirty years ago, when his energies were at their height, the effect then made was startling. I had vaguely anticipated something Quakerish or clerical, something faintly recalling the seventeenth century clergyman, with perhaps a touch of Little Gidding. Very elegant and colourless, one fancied him. . . . The exact opposite was the fact. J. H. Shorthouse was one of the most eighteenth-century-looking people who have been seen in our day. . . . To tell the truth, the instant and irresistible impression which he gave was that of a mask of 1750 suddenly revived out of some serious and romantic pastoral. . . . One almost expected him to take off his large artificial face, so much too big for his body, and reveal a living Shorthouse below. With this curious illusion of wearing a mask were connected his love of a discreet but unusual gaiety of colour in dress, and the movements of his soft, slightly prelatical hands. His extreme courtesy and his few and stereotyped but unusual gestures made it easy to think of a Shorthouse, scarcely changed at all, moving in the kaleidoscopic procession of figures in some Neapolitan festival. . . . It is perhaps not too fantastic to say that, in his intellectual character also, Shorthouse loved to wear a domino and fling a purple cloak across his shoulders. His mind went through life playing a grave and graceful part and his whole scheme of culture was a delicate sport or elaborate system of make-believe.[31]

If Gosse was perhaps playfully biting the "soft, slightly prelatical" hand, the prelatical eye of Boyd Carpenter, Bishop of Ripon, at

about the same period of Shorthouse's life, could see something less
artificial than what Gosse saw:

His genuine enjoyment of things beautiful and things humorous gave a
charm to his visits; he had none of the timid conventionality which lives in a
perpetual panic lest it should by accident lose its correct pose.[32]

Henry Sidgwick, the Oxford philosopher, who first met Shorthouse 5 October 1886, "found him unaffected and unspoiled by
fame, odd-looking, not exactly apt for conversation, highly nervous
and stammering in utterance. . . . His thoughts in talking seemed
to come slowly, and to be expressed with difficulty, though eagerly.
Altogether a singular product of Birmingham." [33]

Two years before he died, already wracked with pain, the sight of
one eye failing, Shorthouse wrote to Dr. E. S. Talbot (5 November
1901): "As a very little child I used to lie in the summer mornings
watching the fleeting clouds, and *feeling* God near. So it has ever
been. God always! God everywhere!" [34] "I have heard my husband
say," remarks his wife, after a lifetime of acquaintance, "that from
his earliest childhood he always regarded our Lord Jesus Christ as
the most loving and beautiful Being that ever walked this earth.
Throughout his life he never seemed to have entertained hard
thoughts of God. Every pleasure came direct from Him. And surely
not least was the gift of his own sweet, happy temperament. His
capacity for enjoyment made every simple pleasure a delight." [35]
The Greek text which underlines the title of *John Inglesant* is I John
3:2: "Beloved, now are we the sons of God, and it doth not yet
appear what we shall be." The inscription on his tombstone in the
churchyard of Edgbaston Old Church was of his own choosing, one
of his favorite texts: "The Spirit and the Bride say, Come."

Whatever the sophisticate of the 1970s, inured to violence and
regularly psychoanalyzed, may think of this kind of piety, nowhere—except in Gosse's lefthanded compliment—will he find any
denial of Shorthouse's sincerity, not in his own statements, not in
unguarded remarks of the people who knew him, nor even in the
sharper phrase of those who differed from him in belief. This
sincere, unaffected piety, like light through the stained glass
windows of the Church he was so fond of, colored everything he
wrote from his early adolescent essays for the Friends' Essay Society
to his last novel, *Blanche, Lady Falaise*, a book he claimed to favor
even above *John Inglesant*. Only Gosse, who had accepted his

hospitality during his lifetime, could, after Shorthouse's death, speak more cleverly than kindly of a "masquerade."

It is not exaggeration to suggest that the religiosity, (in a nonpejorative sense), of Shorthouse's temperament gave him that "great capacity for enjoyment, made every simple pleasure a delight," and even made an otherwise not-too-sympathetic reviewer admit admiringly that he was "as simple as a child."

From "God Always, God Everywhere," to a mystic communion with nature and the simple pleasures of eye and ear, of light on the waters and whispers in the reeds is a very short flight. On the rambles with his cousins, Shorthouse, never a great walker, "would sit in the sun," Margaret Evans says, "listening to the voice in which Nature spoke to him, eating of her bread, drinking of her cup, transmuting all to his own purposes." [36] "He was a dreamer," the same cousin says, "one whose imagination acted the part to himself of 'guide, philosopher, and friend'. This was the great interpreter of Nature, art, life and everything else. He was a poet born, idealizing everything. . . ." [37]

The pleasures of eye and ear may have been simple but, intense and insistent, they colored his writing. The flower garden was, one could almost say, the self-denying Quaker's commonest outlet in art. From his Quaker parents Shorthouse inherited his love of flowers much as D. H. Lawrence inherited his from his mother. The gardens at Moseley where he and his cousins spent their most delightful hours had been carefully, lovingly designed and created by his grandmother and his father. As children at Thimble Mill, his father's farm, he and his brothers worked "their little gardens." On their holiday trips he and his cousins were looking for flowers and fossils when they might have been robbing rooks' nests or torturing frogs. His letters, his essays, his novels proclaim this pleasure of the eye in the color, the delicacy, though never, except in a most general way, the scent of flowers, in eye-pleasing vistas of the manorial gardens that appear again and again in the novels.

The changing light and shade of nature fascinated him, the mists and the sunshine, the subtle light of day on water and cloud, yet he makes little of moonlight or solemn dark. "He responded to the moods of Nature," says his cousin Margaret, "with a sensitiveness that was natural to him, but it was her quiet aspects which most affected him. He was a native of 'the land where it is always afternoon'. There were certain scenes . . . which appealed to the poetic faculty within him, and deeply moved him—the bridge at

Eskdale Mill in the August heat, Wastdale Head by moonlight, the valley of the Duddon under a low sun on a hazy afternoon, and the old church at Seathwaite, with its everlasting dream of peace." [38] His dissatisfaction with the somberness of the Quaker costume he expressed in his own colorful apparel which gave him the sobriquet "Marquis" even among his own relatives. The richness of the pre-Raphaelite paintings which he and the Southalls were excited by in the gallery on Temple Row in Birmingham not only thrilled his eye but stirred his mind to romantic musings. And from the stained glass of Burne-Jones to an eye-filling and soul-filling pleasure in the "twilight saints" of the great cathedral windows was an easy journey and a logical one, if one considers the "dreary expanse of brick-work" [39] of the Quaker meetinghouse.

No less important was his ear. Training in music was not standard Quaker practice, and that he had no training in music he many times regretted. At Moseley, during his convalescence from typhus, he could not only watch the changing light on the park-land expanse beyond his window, but in this house with, as its owner said, "draughts enough in the living and sleeping rooms to turn a mill," [40] he could also hear the voices of the wind among the firs and the chimneypots. And, says his wife, "What the wind voices said to him here, and what the reed voices told him at his father's pool at Thimble Mill, he has recorded in his own beautiful language in *A Teacher of the Violin*." [41] Birmingham offered music enough to enable him to enjoy an occasional opera and, even better, the more frequent oratorio. He so much loved the rhythmic flow of the euphonious line that, despite his stammer, in "his own dreamy monotone" he read "The Lotos Eaters" to his cousins, or recited Longfellow's "Seaweed" against the sound of the sea at Conway. [42] Intense to him was the sound of silence, but more intense was his response on a quiet Sunday morning, as on his honeymoon at Scarborough, to the sound of church bells over some "wide-watered shore." The words and music of the church liturgy moved him inexpressibly, and therefore the church service, a feast for eye and ear, was his greatest simple pleasure. Two months before he died and when he was no longer able to write, he dictated a letter to his cousin Margaret (2 January 1903): "I tell everyone that I feel most clearly that my life—an exceptionally happy and sheltered one—would have been incomplete without this long period of suffering. But you must remember what I lose by not being able to attend the beautiful services of our Church. . . . When I used to hear such

services as that on Christmas morning, it seemed to me that I was
already in Paradise, or at any rate in heaven upon earth." [43]

IV

Shorthouse's secession from the Society of Friends is, therefore,
not altogether unintelligible. First of all, he was only one of the
many Friends who at mid-century, for reasons mainly economic or
social but also religious, were joining the Church of England.
Though Quakerism was changing in the nineteenth century,
Shorthouse was temperamentally out of tune with the cultural
restrictions of the Society. Every sect, once past the infancy stage of
imperative cohesiveness, adapts to the changing conditions of a
world in which it intends to survive; somehow by compromise it
alleviates the tensions between right and left wings, and enlightens
the moderates. Important, therefore, among the many changes in
Quaker attitude during the nineteenth century was a gradual
softening of the attitude toward the Fine Arts. By the time
Shorthouse was born a considerable number of adjustments had
been made, but not enough to satisfy him once he became conscious
of their limitations. Although there is little documentary evidence
from the life of Shorthouse beyond what one can read into his
brother John's diary, one need only go to the lives of his
contemporaries for evidence of restiveness among the younger
members of Birmingham Friends whose love of beauty in music, art
and culture could not be adequately satisfied by the cultivation of
gardens, glass manufacture, and by "edifying" reading.

Maria Cadbury, a few doors down Calthorpe Street from
Shorthouse, reminiscing about her brother Richard, suggests the
discomfort of the young under the confinements and prohibitions of
the Society, and how parents might—or might not—have alleviated
it:

Our natural longing for music was so far encouraged that we were allowed
to buy Jew's harps with our pocket money. These we thoroughly enjoyed,
having learned several Scotch airs from hearing our mother sing
them. . . . Our father had two musical boxes in a special drawer in the
bookcase. It was a great treat to us when he wound these up for our
pleasure. [44]

(But to the end of his days, one is tempted to add, George Cadbury
would not allow a piano in his house, though his brother Richard, no

less a Quaker, was intensely interested in music and art.) Margaret Southall, Shorthouse's cousin, six years older than he, speaking of her elder sister Ellen, remarks:

It was difficult for a mind like this to be limited within the bounds of a religious society in which we were brought up and as it then [1850] existed. Ellen disliked the peculiarities of Friends. Kingsley rose in her soul like a new day, the dawn of a wider faith. But under the influence of married life she accepted the restraints of Quakerism, as she had always done its principles of Christian morality, and the Oxford movement led her farther in the same direction.[45]

Walter Robson in "Some Quaker Characteristics of Seventy Years Ago" remembers:

I confess I was often glad when my Father and Grandmother shook hands and 'broke up'; but I think the training was useful, although frequently our thoughts wandered to picturing what the damp stains on the walls and the knots in the unvarnished wood of the dado might be made to represent.[46]

Mary Howitt, a schoolmate of Sarah Shorthouse, born and educated a Quaker, in her *Autobiography* (I, 50) makes a similar observation on the wandering minds of the young during the silence of the Quaker service. But writing from Nottingham to her sister in June 1830—seventeen years before she herself resigned from the Society of Friends—she is more severe:

Why, dear Anna, if thou feels the disadvantages and absurdities of Friends' peculiarities, dost thou not abandon them? William [her husband] has done so, and really I am glad. He is a good Christian and the change has made no difference in him, except for the better, as regards looks. I am amazed now how I could advocate the ungraceful cut of a Friend's coat; and if we [the two sisters] could do the same, we might find ourselves religiously no worse, whatever Friends might think.[47]

Anna, later Mrs. Harrison, remained with the Society of Friends; Mary, after a short flight of Spiritualism, settled in the Church of Rome (1882).

That the influences which incited a break with tradition were often early at work one can infer from Samuel Middleton Fox's observation:

When as a small boy, paying a timid visit, I saw a copy of Guido's "Aurora" hanging in the dining-room, bound copies of the *Athenaeum* on the shelves and knick-knacks from Rome on the table; when I heard the second part of Goethe's *Faust* discussed at the luncheon table under a print of Raphael's "Spozalizio della Madonna," a new world of wonder opened before me.[48]

Evidence of such leaven at work in the Shorthouse family is best indicated by Margaret Southall Evans's reminiscence on her youth:

We were made sharers in the stir of Birmingham politics, and educational opportunity of which we fully availed ourselves. We visited too at Fir Vale [her uncle Smith's], when Cobden and Bright were there so often, and Joseph Sturge exercised a magic influence over our young enthusiasm. So we grew political and very liberal. We hailed as hero Arthur O'Neill, just out of Wolverhampton Gaol. As well as the Saturday afternoon addresses by Dr. Icke, we attended the lectures at the Philosophical Institution, and heard Professor Maurice on Burke and Milton; Dr. Raphael on Hebrew Poetry; Lord, the American, on poetry in general; Louis Solgen, the Russian refugee; Thackeray on the Georges, in the Town Hall; and we attended several British Association Meetings. In addition to this, we were great readers of the writings of Liberal Churchmen, our dear father having given us Dr. Arnold's "Life and Sermons," and our Aunt Hunt, Myers' works on the Catholic Church and the Bible.[49]

They heard Newman deliver a course of Lectures on Protestantism at the Corn Exchange in High Street, a "tirade against Protestantism, the long sneer at the Faith he had so recently professed."[50] Speaking of the book which their father had given them, the *Life* of Dr. Arnold, she says: "We read that book, we re-read it, and we read it again. . . . We obtained and read the books referred to in his *Life*. . . . From that time Liberalism in the Church took its place in our estimation, by the side of Liberalism in the State, and some of us shed our old-fashioned Quakerism, though that which is the life of Quakerism still held its place, as it generally does when once it has taken root in the character."[51]

"Though by birth a member of the Society of Friends," says Mrs. Shorthouse of her husband, "their special tenets and peculiarities of dress and language had never been adopted by my husband from his own conviction. His tastes and sympathies made much that was of value to others uncongenial to him. His wide reading, especially of the older English divines, made the idea of an historic and national church peculiarly attractive to him."[52] Some of Shorthouse's thinking at this time is indicated by an undated letter to an unknown correspondent at Weston who had apparently remonstrated with him about his defection from the Society of Friends:

It is not my fault that Christians in all ages have agreed in the means and way of worship and communion with God which I desire to partake in, and that this worship has been the means of comfort and grace to millions of Christian people in England in all ages, and is now, and that, on the other hand, *primitive Quakerism* as a distinct sect is dead, *in which all agree*, and we are asked to join a new and untried sect simply because it *is* a sect, and not a *national*, if you will not call it the *true* church. . . . It is the duty of all Christians, as far as in them lies, to forward the time when the whole body of Christians shall be united, not only in a spiritual, but also, which has more to do with *this* life, in an outward and visible body of Christ. The great comfort and help of Christianity is its bodily form—that is, its sympathy with, and application to *men*; and as the body of Christ on earth was one, open and visible, so His Church should be *one*, open and visible too. We live in a constitution ordained by God which includes all visible things, and everything on earth, belonging to the original creation, both of the world and humanity, is divine and belonging to God. The Prayer-Book in this country is the only human ordinance (if it can be called a human ordinance, being nothing but the religion of the Bible arranged as a manual for daily use) that acknowledges this. As Maurice has often so clearly shown, it has preserved over and over again the most vital truths, which were entirely overlooked and forgotten even by those who professed to believe in, and use it.[53]

He found further comfort in F. D. Maurice's love of form and beauty and in his fear of the materialism and scepticism inherent in the new science.

Even geography is pertinent here, for in Edgbaston the Anglican St. John's was very close to his home, and the vicar a personal friend. The Friends' meetinghouse in Bull Street, Birmingham, was a mile and a half away. "More and more," says Mrs. Shorthouse, "my husband felt that he could only be happy as a baptized member of the Church of England.[54] Thus, Joseph Henry Shorthouse, bachelor, manufacturing chemist, formerly of 30 Calthorpe Street, Edgbaston, and Sarah Scott, formerly of 77 Wellington Road, both Quakers by birth, who had on 19 August 1857 been quietly married in the Friends' meetinghouse at Warwick to avoid the publicity of the larger Meeting at Birmingham, resigned their membership in the Society of Friends, December 1860, and were baptized together 14 August 1861 by their friend the Rev. Francis Morse of St. John's Ladywood, Edgbaston.

Though Shorthouse was temperamentally too sensitive, too courteous, too tolerant, and too kindly to drop, or even drift away from, his Quaker acquaintances, he moved thereafter in Anglican company. When health permitted he attended both the morning

and the evening services of St. John's or Old Parish Church in
Edgbaston and the special mid-day businessmen's Lenten services
at St. Philip's in downtown Birmingham. Wherever he was on
holiday he sought out a service to attend. He served a nine-year
term as People's Warden at St. John's Ladywood. His spidery hand
records the Sunday collection; his signature appears on congregational documents. He is host to visiting bishops on Confirmation
Sunday. After the publication of *John Inglesant* the Anglican circle
expanded beyond Birmingham to include by correspondence or
personal acquaintance many of the notable Anglicans of his day.
Though he might differ with them on particular interpretation of the
Thirty-nine Articles, he was united with them on the one
point—one he had continually emphasized—that in England, by
law established, with the sovereign at its head, and with an
unbroken tradition, the true church was the Church of England.
And when he had to retire from business, crippled by muscular
rheumatism, his greatest regret during the two years of invalidism
preceding his death, was not the pain but his inability "to attend the
beautiful services of our Church." On that gloomy March day when
with an Anglican service whose dignity would have pleased him he
was buried in the churchyard of Old Parish Church, Edgbaston,
among the many mourners were the workmen from his own
chemical works, the Quakers and Dissenters of the Birmingham
City Council, and other local dignitaries. Among the wreaths which
graced the simple casket were some from anonymous admirers of
John Inglesant and one from the Bishop of Ely.

CHAPTER 2

First Steps: Early Essays

ONE cannot properly consider Shorthouse's propulsion into what was at least contemporary fame on the publication of *John Inglesant* by Macmillan in 1881 without some observation of the route he travelled to get there. As the child of a liberal, cultured Quaker family, he was encouraged by his parents in his reading and writing. The opportunities for display of literary talent came early in the literary games of the "Moseley Days."

But if the "Moseley Pieces" can be considered the unimpressive flights of games which children play, the compositions for the Friends' Essay Society called for more serious and strenuous effort. Almost inevitably, as a "peculiar" people, more or less confined socially and culturally to their own religious group, often conscientiously denying themselves the satisfaction of theater, cards, and music, the Friends turned for artistic enjoyment and outlet to gardening and to that reading which consisted mostly of "improving books, often read aloud." The journals which many of them kept were a literary release as well as a record. In Birmingham, according to J. D. Hunter, they had in 1829 established the Friends' Reading Society (continued until 1963) to "provide sound and useful literature within the reach of all connected with the Society of Friends and the holding of First-Day Evenings for reading and conversation." (Novels, romances, political works were excluded.) Hunter goes on to explain the Reading Society's origin and function:

The [Friends' Reading] Society was born at a time when Friends were leaving behind the seclusion and quietism of the eighteenth century and becoming increasingly concerned with the world about them. In this case they approached the problem posed by the moral dangers threatening the growing number of young men attracted from all over the country to work in Birmingham through another more intimate concern—that for the spiritual welfare of the younger Friends of their own meeting. Thus the

growing conscience of nineteenth century Quakerism and the social
problems attending the adolescence of modern Birmingham became part of
one pattern.[1]

In 1829, listed among the thirty-one members of the Reading
Society are Shorthouse's grandfather, his father, and his uncles
Southall and Nutter. Originally membership was restricted to men,
but after 1832 an effort was made to attract female subscribers. It is
no surprise, therefore, that in 1840 Rebecca Shorthouse is also
listed as a member.

But it was really the Friends' Essay Society which provided
Shorthouse with the necessary writing practice. The heavy fog of
fading memory hangs over the origin of the Friends' Essay Society,
"the oldest social activity of the local Society of Friends," as it is
referred to in the remaining part of a letter dated 8 October 1952
which opens Volume 16 of the *Essays of the Friends' Essay Society*
in the Birmingham Reference Library. "Safe to say," says the same
source, that the founding of the Society was "not later than 1835."
Organized by Agatha Pearson and Arthur Albright, it was an
informal group, on invitation from a hostess, meeting at Highgate
during the winter months.[2] In 1847 the Society had "approximately
a dozen members." Apparently in 1851, when Shorthouse was
seventeen, the Society was reorganized into a more formal group
with a definite set of regulations. Members met at one another's
homes for tea, discussion of their essays, and supper. Shorthouse,
his two brothers, his three Southall cousins, and Sarah Scott whom
he later married, her sister and brother—almost a family compact—
were among the members of the Society which then had about
sixteen members. Shorthouse served for about fifteen years as
secretary of the Society and was, in the opinion of the members, its
most "distinguished and prolific contributor." At their monthly
meetings members were entertained by one or more papers on
topics sometimes set beforehand, sometimes freely chosen, sometimes deliberately controversial. "Anonymously laid on the table,"
after presentation by a selected member, the papers were circulated
among members, and brought back to the next meeting for
discussion. Each member was responsible for at least one essay,
"either literary or artistic," during the six meetings of the winter
months, with a fine of 2s. 6d. exacted for failure to contribute at
least one essay, and 10s. for neglect in two successive seasons—a
regulation which naturally was not endured without protest.

It is impossible to determine with any certainty the volume of

Shorthouse's apprentice pieces (about sixty at a guess). Mrs. Shorthouse, with the advice of George Macmillan the publisher, Edmund Gosse, and Rawdon Levett, Shorthouse's best friend, included in *Literary Remains* only what she considered her husband's best work. Several essays are known to have been excluded from *Literary Remains*, as Mrs. Shorthouse's correspondence with George Macmillan shows.[3] But there is another problem. The essays written by members of the Friends' Essay Society were assembled after 1873 and stitched into volumes of about six hundred handwritten pages each. Even the most cursory examination of the volumes warns against any assumption that all the essays written by the members were included in the bound volumes or that the essays are necessarily in chronological order. The essays were unsigned, always read at the meeting by one of the members present, never by the author. As the first volume is dated 1851–52, it is likely to include Shorthouse's adolescent pieces, but how many were not included in *Literary Remains* cannot—for that matter, need not—be known. Safely one can only say that several essays in the first volume seem to be in Shorthouse's hand—though he had more than one—or show his idiosyncratic punctuation. This is true also of later volumes. Though he resigned from the Society of Friends in 1860, Shorthouse seems to have continued with the Essay Society, for he did not resign as secretary of the Society until November 1867 after what seems to have been a long, unbroken term of office. Though no longer a Friend, he continued to contribute essays until at least 1870, by which time no doubt he was engrossed in writing *John Inglesant* which he had begun three years earlier. He was still on the "Circulation List" 23 April 1875 but not on the next list, 25 May. Only sheer perversity could induce one to make a doubtful point about Shorthouse's development during his literary apprenticeship in the Friends' Essay Society unless not only the number but also the chronological order of the essays could be firmly established.

Elfriede Rieger in her study of Shorthouse avails herself of an apt metaphor from physics to describe Shorthouse's literary work when she remarks that the rays perceptible in Shorthouse's early essays are brought into focus in *John Inglesant*, then are dispersed in the succeeding novels with decreasing intensity.[4] If the metaphor is even partially valid it helps to explain Shorthouse as *homo unius liber*, for what he was anxious to say it seems he said many times over with but slight variation in his essays and novels.

The essays which Mrs. Shorthouse in *Literary Remains* calls

"Early Essays" range all the way from "Books Versus Books" which
Shorthouse would have written when he was about seventeen or
eighteen, to "Ars Vitae" when he was about thirty-five or thirty-six,
when he had already resigned his membership in the Society of
Friends, and had by that time been at work on *John Inglesant* for
several years. Whatever their topic, his essays reveal a mind
early-laden with minutiae accumulated from a wide reading of
chroniclers and antiquarian travel literature (John Weever and
Thomas Pennant, for example); they reflect Shorthouse's love of a
past romanticized by his imagination into an exciting reality in
which the boundaries of time and space are indefinite, even
nonexistent, and the shapes move in a world of dream, of fantasy;
they show a mind reflective and philosophical—perhaps, more
properly, religious or mystical—rather than scientific, playing
rather than struggling with a few darling themes.

Thus, in "My Fever"—written when Shorthouse was about
twenty, and recalling doubtless his recovery from typhus fever
when he was eight—he constructs a beautiful, imaginative world of
delirium in which the limitations of the physical world have little
force and the world of the spirit is the satisfying reality. In the essay
he remarks on "the strange confusion with which you see before you
the actions of past ages, mixed up with what used to be your own
thoughts, together with the half-seen objects of the material world
which are moving around you. . . . "[5] Though the statement is
pertinent in the essay to his description of delirium one cannot fail
to note how often the "strange confusion" is operative in his other
essays, then later in his novels. In "The Ringing of the Bells,"
written possibly two years later, the same theme is touched on, this
time enlarged a little with the supernatural. Then, after another
three years, he replays the tune more resonantly in an essay "On
True and False Supernaturalism." Later, when he has experienced
the added distress of epileptic attacks, he works out the theme more
dramatically and powerfully in the Mintern scene (Ch. 16) and the
Montalcino scene (Ch. 21) in *John Inglesant.* An essay on "humor"
(1854?) he later reworked into a larger essay, "The Humorous in
Literature," which he published in *Macmillan's Magazine* (March
1883).

It is this "strange confusion" which later will mark Shorthouse as a
novelist of a particular kind. For in the essays he already reveals a
mind in which imaginatively the present is coincident with the past,
in which the physical world of the senses somehow unexpectedly

and inexplicably fuses with an "other" world of thought, or of dream
and hallucination and vision, or of foreboding. In "The Ringing of
the Bells" Edward Field, a drunken, atheistic squire has resolved
that the Sunday bells shall not be rung:

Suddenly, to their intense astonishment, there arose upon the air from the
steeple where the bells were, a peal louder, nearer, and more beautiful by
far than they had ever rung before. It swept over the fields and woods,
which were in their autumn foliage, ascended up joyfully into the blue sky.
Edward Field and his companions looked at each other with blank
dismay. . . . With a fierce exclamation Mr. Field put spurs to his horse
and . . . rode straight across the fields to the church. . . . The wonderful peal still continued. . . . The place was quite empty, the ropes hung
down motionless, and the bells above were quite still, but up in the steeple
where the bells were, there was a great ringing as of a most beautiful chime
or ring of bells. . . . And just then, the people being all assembled, the
ringing ceased of its own accord and the organ played solemn and grand
music and the morning service began.[6]

Later, in *John Inglesant* (Ch. 16) Shorthouse describes a state of
mind:

The confusion of mind which [Inglesant] suffered increased more and more
as he rode along, and the events of his past life came up before his eyes as
clearly and palpably as the objects through which he was riding, so that he
could not distinguish the real from the imaginary, the present from the past
which added extremely to his distress. He stood again amid the confusion
and carnage of Naseby field; once more he saw the throngs of heads, and
heard that terrible cry which welcomed him to the scaffold; again he looked
into the fatal crystal, and strange visions and ghostly shapes of death and
corruption came out from it, and walked to and fro along the hedgerows and
across the road before him, making terrible the familiar English fields; a
tolling of the passing bell rang continually in his ear, and his horse's footfalls
sounded strange and funereal to his diseased sense. He knew nothing of the
road, nor of what happened, as he rode along, nor what people he passed.

The "strange confusion" of Inglesant in Rome (Ch. 21) is possibly
magnified by Shorthouse's recollection of his own epileptic seizures:

His old disease, in fact, never entirely left him; he walked often as in a
dream, and when the fit was upon him could never discern the real and the
unreal. He knew that terrible feeling when the world and all its objects are
slipping away, when the brain reels, and seems only to be kept fixed and

steady by a violent exertion of the will; and the mind is confused and
perplexed with thoughts which it cannot grasp, and is full of fancies of vague
duties and acts which it cannot perform. . . .

What seems to be a preference for the supernatural over the
natural and for the strange over the familiar, shapes—if, indeed, it
does not provide the very subject of—such essays as "Fragilia" and
"The Ringing of the Bells." One may properly assume that this
preference comes from the same abundant vine as his interest in the
historical past. The past is interesting to him because it is remote,
no longer physically arrestable. And, because it is remote and not
immediate, the past can be imaginatively reconstituted with much
of its glitter and without some of its brutality to stimulate reverie,
reflection on the vagaries of life, and may possibly even provide
some instruction for the present. Thus, in a series of seven essays on
"Old Houses" he lets loose his imagination on bygone times and
people, on crimes and honors long forgotten, to applaud a departed,
cultured, aristocratic society as superior to the hustling, commercial, democratic one in which he moved. In the normal pattern of
his essays he fixes, through a *persona*, on some object of the past—a
person, a manorial hall, a tombstone, some interesting incident—
and allows his imagination to flit about it to form charming pictures,
to evoke nostalgic emotion, and then to drift toward an instructive
conclusion.

Though there is something about the writing that moves one to
think of the bright schoolboy armed with the *Encyclopaedia
Britannica*, there is nevertheless enough heavy quotation in the
essays to suggest a wide and honest but curious reading in his home
library or in the Birmingham Reference Library as well as a kind of
vicarious living in past centuries through books. His essays
"Literature" (ca. 1864), "Twenty Miles" (ca. 1854), and "An Essay
Which Is No Essay" (ca. 1856) illustrate his vicarious experience
through books. He has not only read Sir Thomas Browne (and
others); he has traced Browne's references and allusions. He has
read not only one of Thomas Pennant's tour books but several (for
he owned them). He is acquainted with contemporaries, like
William Morris, but his tributes go to Cervantes, Malory, LeSage.
That he was a Quaker on the way to Anglicanism is suggested even
in his earliest essays by his repeatedly unconcealed admiration for
old churches, a fond dwelling on their soothing architecture, and on
the aesthetic joy to be derived from their continued though

regrettably unattended services. In none of the essays does he mention the Quaker Meeting.

His essay "Vestigia" (ca. 1864)—he officially became an Anglican in 1861; he was to begin *John Inglesant* in 1867—is indicative of what is ahead:

It is not in books alone that the life and the England of the past must be studied, but in the life and the England of the present. The seventeenth century may be said to be the key of the nineteenth; and in more things than many would believe, our thoughts and actions and disputes are but a repetition of the thoughts and actions and disputes of two hundred years ago. We shall best understand our forefathers by standing in their footsteps, and by remembering that nothing happened to them but also is common to us: that they were touched by the same affections that we are, hoped the same things, and tried, many of them, to serve the same Master, and to do something to benefit that fellowship of humanity to which we and they alike belong.[7]

If later in *John Inglesant* Shorthouse draws together a love for the historical past nourished by wide reading in the seventeenth-century writers, a love of Anglican ritual, a half-worship of feudal lordship, and an implied parallel between the seventeenth century and the nineteenth, the reader has been forewarned by the essays he wrote for the Friends' Essay Society between 1851 and 1867, the year in which he began to write *John Inglesant*.

CHAPTER 3

Summit: John Inglesant

THE man who was born a Quaker in 1834 and baptized in the
Church of England in 1861, the amateur scholar interested in
the Civil Wars and theological disputes of seventeenth-century
England, published in 1880—at his own expense—a "philosophical
romance," *John Inglesant*. In it he reviewed and weighed the
Roman Catholic, Anglican, and Puritan claims to men's allegiance in
matters of individual belief. He concluded that the Church best
entitled to that allegiance was the Church of England by law
established. He also wrote himself into the book. By means of the
seventeenth-century Inglesant, his fictional representative, Shorthouse threads his way through the religious confusion of the
nineteenth century to an assured belief in Anglicanism. *John
Inglesant*, then, is in fictional form the journal of a man in quest of a
satisfying faith. It is also an oblique record of Shorthouse's own
deliberations as he found his way from Quakerism into the congenial
atmosphere of the Church of England. Within the novel Inglesant
rejects Quakerism (with whose tenets and restrictions Shorthouse
had never been in sympathy) and he rejects the Church of Rome in
which some of Shorthouse's Quaker contemporaries had found
refuge. Though Shorthouse drew his livelihood from business, he
derived his greatest enjoyment from religion. *John Inglesant* is an
exposition of Shorthouse's inner life, the life beneath and behind his
domestic, social, and business life. Writing to Francis A. Jones (18
June 1891), apparently in reply to a question about which he
considered "the finest" of his novels, Shorthouse remarked: " 'John
Inglesant' is, of course, the work into which I put my life, and I can
never write such a book again." [1] He was referring not only to the
nine-and-a-half years devoted to the writing of the book but to the
distillation in *John Inglesant* of his thoughts on the actuating force of
his life—religion.

I

"I should so like to write a book; if it was only quite a little book which nobody read, I should like to write one," Shorthouse often remarked to his wife, and he continued his reading and note-taking until he could announce: "I am quite ready to begin a book, only I want a plot." [2] Eventually he found the beginnings of a plot while reading in "an old book" of a returning Crusader who forgave the murderer of his brother. In a letter (8 April 1888) written several years after *John Inglesant* had made him famous, Shorthouse describes this discovery:

Many years ago I met with a few lines in an old book of anecdotes narrating the fact of a Florentine gentleman named Gualberto, giving up his sword upon the altar instead of using it against the murderer of his brother. This struck me immensely at the time, and around it the whole of *John Inglesant* may be said to have formed itself. It was not till after publication of the book that I knew anything more of the story. I believe that in no version of it, is there any mention of the result of Gualberto's action upon the murderer. [3]

He amplifies slightly in a letter to his friend Levett, six years later (28 May 1894):

The hero of the sword story was a certain Giovanni Gualberto, a gentleman of Florence, and the church where it was deposited was that of San Miniato. . . . Two hundred years ago a crucifix was shown there, with the head bowed in the attitude which it assumed when it accepted the sword. I took the story from a few lines of a very old book and it was only long afterwards that I found that it was a well-known guidebook story. I am quite justified in saying that *John Inglesant* was written to lead up expressly to this one incident, and I do not think it would have been written if I had not chanced upon this beautiful story. [4]

Early in 1867 he began. For the next nine years he worked at intervals on his story, reading to his wife what he had written in the evening, until the novel was completed during the family holiday at Llandudno in September 1876. His friend William Peveril Turnbull, one of the very few friends who had read passages of the manuscript, recommended him to two publishers—anonymous so far—neither of whom would risk publication of an unknown author. Shorthouse had just purchased "Lansdowne," the house at 60 Wellington Road where he was to reside until his death, and had found that the cost of renovating the house prohibited his publishing *John Inglesant* at his own expense. The manuscript rested in a drawer for four years.

However, early in 1880, when Shorthouse was financially able to undertake private publication, his brother Edmund recommended him to Rickman King, a member of the Society of Friends, the printer for Cornish Brothers, and on 11 February 1880 he took his manuscript to the printer. He received the first copy of his novel on 1 July. Only one hundred copies, elegantly bound in vellum, were printed. Review copies were given to the two Birmingham morning papers (*Daily Gazette* and *Daily Post*), to the *Athenaeum*, and to the *Guardian*; two copies were donated to the Birmingham public libraries, and about seventy were presented to friends and relatives. The remaining copies were sold by Cornish at a guinea each.

Though favored recipients of the presentation copies expressed more than polite approval, and the reviews in the Birmingham papers were favorable, there were no loud huzzahs from the public. On the urging of Charles Linnell of Cornish Brothers Shorthouse submitted a copy of the novel (not the manuscript) to Smith, Elder and Company. Their reader, novelist James Payn, turned it down on the score that it was unlikely to prove a good publishing risk—an act which seems to have given Payn more enduring fame of a sort than his own novels.

The rest of the story has been often told (with the normal variations, of course). In January 1881 the Reverend Jamson Smith, one of Shorthouse's friends among the masters of King Edward's School, Birmingham, sent the copy he had received to the Oxford don, Arthur Johnson of All Souls', who in turn recommended it to Matthew Arnold's niece, Mary Augusta [Mrs. Humphry] Ward. Impressed with the novel, she recommended it to Alexander Macmillan on a visit the following week to Macmillan in London. Macmillan, who, like Shorthouse, was a lover of Plato and F. D. Maurice, had already seen the favorable review in the *Guardian* and envinced an interest in publishing the novel. With becoming promptness Shorthouse responded to this piece of good fortune. He wrote to Macmillan (20 January 1881):

Mr. A. H. Johnson, of All Souls College, Oxford, tells me that Mrs. T. H. Ward, of Oxford, has spoken to you about a philosophical romance of which I have printed one hundred copies for private distribution, and that you have kindly expressed a wish to see the book. I have told Messrs. Cornish of

Birmingham to send you the last copy they have (I have only two or three left myself), which I hope you will receive safely.

My chief desire is to get the book published *as it is*. I have not adopted the form and manner of the work without consideration, and the book as it stands, with all its peculiarities, is just what I intended it to be! To alter it, therefore, and to turn it into something quite different (such as an ordinary romance), would be to render useless all the labour I have expended upon it, and would deprive it of its sole claim to public notice. Of course there are several passages . . . which might be altered to advantage, but even there the peculiarities are not without intention.[5]

By this time Macmillan had himself read *John Inglesant*. Though impressed by the book, he had with publisher's caution referred it to a reader for confirmation. On 18 February he wrote to Shorthouse offering to publish the novel, and on 21 February 1881 Shorthouse accepted Macmillan's offer, again with the stipulation "that the book shall be printed as I wrote it." [6] On 17 March he received the first proofs and on 1 July the first copy of *John Inglesant* in the two-volume edition of which only seven hundred and fifty copies were printed. Macmillan's reader (in this instance, possibly, George Macmillan) had worded his recommendation rather warily: "This is a romance which is certainly very much out of the common run . . . ; the style is not quite bright enough nor vivid enough, but it is the style of literature. . . . What the writer lacks is geniality of touch. . . . It is interesting and romantic but strikes no chord. . . . It is rather a remarkable sort of book, for all that—but I believe it just possible that it might fall stone-dead." [7]

Although the reception by reviewers was generally favorable, a happy accident helped to launch the novel on a conveniently rising tide of approval. William Ewart Gladstone, one of the more prominent admirers of the book, not a bishop but a prime minister and a known indefatigable reader, was constant and generous in his praise, was even photographed at Hawarden, asleep in his garden with the second volume of *John Inglesant*, the title clearly visible.[8] One can only guess at the effect of this unpremeditated publicity. The sales of *John Inglesant* necessitated such rapid reprintings of the novel that by July 1882 ten thousand copies had been printed—a thousand were taken by Mudie's—and Macmillan could risk a limited two-volume edition of two hundred and fifty copies in handmade paper. In the same year G. G. Munro, in New York, ever alert, brought out a pirated paperback edition in his Seaside Library. Bernard Tauchnitz, in Leipzig, arranged with Macmillan for the inclusion of *John Inglesant* in his Collection of British Authors series.

In February 1883, Macmillan, stimulated by the steady sales of the book, issued four thousand copies of the popular one-volume edition which was reprinted quarterly, and sometimes monthly, until by 1929 a total of over fifty thousand copies was reached. The Sixpenny Edition of 1901 was issued with thirty thousand copies, and its reprint in 1907 added another thirty thousand.

A few months before Shorthouse's death, a De Luxe Edition in three volumes, limited to five hundred and ten copies, was issued by Macmillan, November 1902. Shorthouse's death, 4 March 1903, revived an interest in *John Inglesant* which had been waning, and Macmillan reissued the novel (in the Illustrated Pocket Classics series) which was published simultaneously with *Life, Letters, and Literary Remains of J. H. Shorthouse*, edited by his wife, April 1905. It began with a cautious initial run of two thousand, but reprintings eventually pushed the figure to thirty-eight thousand by December 1929. Macmillan's ventured only once more with an issue of ten thousand copies in the Cottage Library series, February 1933.

In 1961, under the title *John Inglesant in England*, the SCM Press printed three thousand copies (with a preface by the Archbishop of Canterbury) of an eviscerated edition of *John Inglesant* from which the Italian section had been subtracted. Only fifteen hundred copies were sold; the remaining copies were destroyed in 1964. The recent reprint boom has produced *John Inglesant: A Romance (1900)* by the Scholarly Press, in 1970; a microfilm of the three-volume 1902 edition; a microfilm of the New York 1886 issue; and most recently a reprint by the Garland Publishing Inc. of the first, the 1880 Birmingham edition of *John Inglesant*, as Number 33 in their series called *Victorian Fiction: Novels of Faith and Doubt*, edited by Professor Robert Lee Wolff.

II

It is possibly a testimony of the merit of *John Inglesant*—Paul Elmer More has called it "the nearest approach in English to a religious novel of universal significance" [9]—that it resists easy summary. In one sentence, *John Inglesant* is a dramatization (as one chooses) of the quest for a faith, the record of a spiritual journey, the "biography of a soul." [10] an illustration of the war between flesh and spirit. Against the background of seventeenth-century England,

France, and Italy, Shorthouse hurries John Inglesant, a sensitive, refined, even saintly, half-mystic courtier of near-Catholic family background, through a buffeting sea of conflicting philosophic and religious views until, all his doubts resolved, he drops his anchor in the quiet waters of the Church of England.

Born in 1622, the younger of twin sons, John Inglesant is left because of his frail health to a lonely boyhood at Westacre Priory, south of Malmesbury, Wiltshire, an estate which had been granted to his great-grandfather a century earlier as a reward for service in Henry VIII's suppression of the lesser monasteries. Meanwhile, his brother Eustace, the heir, similar to John in appearance but different in temperament, is maintained by his Catholic father as a page at Court. At Westacre, John, a silent, dreamy child inclined to mysticism, absorbs a mixture of piety and superstition from his grandfather, the servants, and country folk; he acquires a desultory and heterogeneous education—catechism, classics, Platonism, Rosicrucianism, mystical philosophy—from a succession of local clergymen who arouse in him "obstinate questionings" to which he can find no satisfactory answers.

When he is fourteen, he is entrusted by his father for two years to a Jesuit, Father St. Clare (Hall), who is to shape him into an obedient, useful, political agent in the ambiguous attempts at reconciliation of the Church of England with the Church of Rome. In August 1637 he is removed from his seclusion and thrust into the life of the Court, first in London, and later in Oxford. At first excited by the glitter, but increasingly unsettled by the politics of the Court, Inglesant intermittently finds relief from the glare in the "dim religious light" of Nicholas Ferrar's "Protestant Nunnery" at Little Gidding in Huntingdonshire. As a courtier and a soldier attached to the royal cause in the Civil Wars he becomes the agent of the King on a diplomatic mission to Scotland and a trusted observer at the trial of Archbishop Laud. However, the task for which he has been specifically trained by the Jesuit—a delicate mission to obtain Irish aid for the relief of Chester—miscarries. Loyally silent, he is betrayed by the King, and only through the machinations of Father St. Clare does he escape the scaffold. The execution of the King, January 1649, frees Inglesant from responsibility to an affable but ineffectual royal master, in fact makes him redundant. The cause for which he has been trained no longer exists—the early reconciliation of the Church of England with the Church of Rome.

Shortly after Inglesant's release from prison, his brother Eustace

is murdered by Malvolti, an Italian intriguer, who escapes to the
Continent. During his long, rather haphazard search for Malvolti,
Inglesant is disturbed in his own mind by the incompatibility of a
desire for religious calm and a desire for vengeance. Inclined to the
Church of Rome since childhood, he is drawn successively to a
number of conflicting philosophies. In Paris he is drawn to the
asceticism of Hugh de Cressy (an Anglican turned Benedictine in
1646); in Rome he is attracted both to the Italian Cardinal's pagan
humanism and to the quietism of Miguel Molinos (a Spanish priest
who had been sent to Rome in 1663 and had subsequently attracted
a large following). He fails, however, to arrive at a satisfactory
religion of his own. Drawn to the Church of Rome by the
venerability of its tradition and the beauty of its service, he is
repelled by what he sees in Italy of ecclesiastical mismanagement
and corruption. He is even more repelled by what he considers an
unacceptable limitation of individual freedom imposed on its
adherents by the Church of Rome.

After a few narrow escapes from attempted assassinations,
Inglesant is convinced that he is not a free agent in his passage
through life. When, in a lonely mountain pass, he finally confronts
Malvolti, his brother's murderer, in a moment of illumination he
forgives him, and as a token of self-abnegation lays the sword of
vengeance on the altar of a nearby chapel, thus leaving vengeance to
God.

Subsequently, he plays a major role in an intrigue to secure the
estates of the Duke of Umbria for the Papal See, and a minor role in
a papal election. He marries, he loses his wife and child in the
plague. He retires to a monastery, then emerges to support Molinos
against the Jesuits in his plea for access to the sacrament without
confession. For his honest but politically injudicious plainspeaking
in defense of Molinos he is advised to leave Italy or face
imprisonment by the Order which since boyhood he has obediently
served. He is last seen in the precincts of Worcester Cathedral as "a
gentleman lately come from Italy." All his doubts dissipated and
apprehensions allayed, he has become a champion of the Church of
England by law established.

III

But even a long summary can only indistinctly trace the narrative
line of *John Inglesant*, and can only hint at the contents of the book.

For the operatic narrative—with solos long and short, recitatives, Italian villain, wicked Jesuit, worldly prelates—is only the skeleton over which Shorthouse has stretched a skin of history. To give his hero the religious experiences necessary to the argument of the book, he has then fleshed the narrative skeleton with a miscellaneous assortment: sketches of personalities; philosophical discourses small and large; detailed pictures of places; historical, biographical, and bibliographical minutiae; tidbits of out-of-the-way learning accumulated from years of reading. And permeating the mass is a religiosity (in the best sense of the word) which holds everything together. Such power as the novel possesses originates not from its linear dimensions but from the complicated religious explorations of Inglesant, explorations for which the plot is only a fragile vehicle.

When Shorthouse first got the desire to write a book is not—and need not be—known, but by the time he was in his teens "Henry's book" had already become a goodnatured joke among his Southall cousins. His urge to write may be explained by his possible desire to enlarge on some of his favorite exercises in the Essay Society. But the kind of book he was likely to write—if he was ever to write one, for he was thirty-three when he began—was determined by his reading interests in history, romance, the seventeenth-century divines, philosophy, George Herbert, Wordsworth, and Keble.

He was by temperament a dreamer rather than an accountant, a man in whose mind the real and the unreal were not distinctly separated. Religio-aesthetical (or aesthetically religious) in outlook, he needed some powerful stimulus to prompt the ordering of a mind crammed with the minutiae of miscellaneous reading. That stimulus probably came from his own religious problem—the inevitable strain resulting from his resignation from the Society of Friends and his baptism in the Church of England. The anonymous author of *Quakerism, or, the Story of My life* (1852)—Shorthouse would have been eighteen then—describes her agony when she abandoned the Society of Friends for the Anglican communion:

Nobody unless they have passed through the ordeal, can conceive how very painful it is to feel one's-self cast off from all earthly communion with the Church—branded as unfit to worship God in the society of those who were one's fellows,—disowned by them, as one guilty of a crime which mortals might not forgive—slighted in public, and repulsed in private—banished from their company on earth, and clearly given to understand, that into that heaven which is prepared for Friends, I had no chance of being received. I sought for admission into the Church of England and Ireland; and there, with all my family about me, found a ready entrance. Six children, husband and wife, were all baptised together—eight persons.

Very early Shorthouse had shown an uneasiness about the restrictions of the Society of Friends and an increasing inclination toward the less restrictive Church of England, an inclination which was aided by his study of the seventeenth-century divines. But when the break with the Society in which he had been brought up actually came, he possibly felt self-conscious about his defection. Even though there was no resulting unpleasantness with his own liberally-minded family, one may reasonably conjecture that he was unconsciously driven to justify the religious position he had taken. He needed to write his *Apologia*. When he withdrew from the Society of Friends, why had he joined the Anglican communion and not the Church of Rome as some Friends had? Or, as other Friends did, why did he not find satisfaction in one of the dissenting Nonconformist Protestant groups outside the Church of England— Baptists, Methodists, Presbyterians, Unitarians, Plymouth Brethren? And as an Anglican was he to consider himself "High Church" (ritualist), "Low Church" (evangelical), or "Broad Church" (latitudinarian)—especially when there were no clear dividing lines among these parties. One may therefore take Shorthouse at his word when he stated that *John Inglesant* was a private book not written for publication, and that he had never aimed at popularity as a novelist. Edmund Gosse, from his eminence among the London critics, may, of course, be right when he asserts that Shorthouse conceived of himself as a man with a mission to preach salvation.[11] But it is more likely that this sense of mission, if it is not a Gossean misapprehension—for Gosse did not make Shorthouse's acquaintance until 1883—is a Shorthousean afterthought which might more easily account for his later novels than for the writing of *John Inglesant*. During the ten-year silence when *John Inglesant* was composed only his wife knew and only a very few of his closest friends were dimly aware that he was writing a book. The silence does not suggest missionary zeal so much as self-consciousness.

What, then, mission or no mission, might one expect from a religious minded, literarily inclined graduate of the Friends' Essay Society? One can be fairly certain that in the preface to *John Inglesant* (1882) Shorthouse's statements about his intentions in the

novel are evidence after the fact. It was only after the 1880 edition of
John Inglesant had been given the approval of his friends and had
had a favorable review or two (which satisfied him at the time), that
he was willing to push the novel more prominently into public view.
In fact, it was not until after the Macmillan edition (1881) had been
auspiciously set afloat and the reviews were not all favorable that he
became entangled in a net of correspondence in which he began a
piecemeal statement of what his aims had been.

He writes to Macmillan (14 October 1881): "I have written a short
preface with which I am tolerably satisfied. You will see what you
think of it." [12] The preface was added to the New Edition (1882)
and became the official formulation of his aim, an aim which had
solidified from his discussions with his Birmingham friends and
relatives, his new correspondents, and his reading of the reviews
which Macmillan faithfully sent him.

To his cousin Margaret he writes, 17 July, two weeks after
publication, when he sent her a copy of *John Inglesant*: "I have left
the book to tell its own tale and read its own lesson to everyone
according to their own liking, but I may tell *you* that my *own*
reading of the book is that God prefers culture to fanaticism." [13] On
28 August, when she had read the book, he writes again somewhat
more defensively: "The book is a protest of culture of every kind
against fanaticism and superstition in every form. It is, in fact,
totally opposed to the popular ideas of religion (or the popular
religions of the day); had I sympathized with the popular religions of
the day it would never have been written." [14] And he repeats the
observation in a cautionary postscript later in the year (7 December
1880) when sending a copy of *John Inglesant* to Professor W. Knight
whose acquaintance he had made the week before.[15] In November,
writing to Edwin A. Abbott, author of the religious novel
Philocristus (1878), he adds a new twist: "Perhaps the chief object
[of *John Inglesant*] is to promote culture at the expense of
fanaticism, including the fanaticism of *work*; to exalt the unpopular
doctrine that the end of existence is not the good of one's neighbour,
but one's own culture." [16]

In October 1881, when he was writing his preface, he was
presenting in more orderly form what had only been sporadic in his
correspondence. After stating at the beginning of the preface that
his novel is a "philosophical romance" in which "fiction is used
expressly for the purpose of introducing philosophy," he concludes:

Nevertheless this may be said for it [*John Inglesant*], that it is an attempt, and an honest one, to blend together these three in one philosophy—the memory of the dead—the life of thought—the life of each one of us alone. Amid the tangled web of a life's story I have endeavoured to trace some distinct threads—the conflict between Culture and Fanaticism—the analysis and character of Sin—the subjective influence of the Christian Mythos. I have ventured to depict the Cavalier as not invariably a drunken brute, and spiritual life and growth as not exclusively the possession of Puritans and Ascetics. I feel the responsibility of introducing real historical characters and orders of men into a work of this kind. My general defence must be that I have written nothing which I should not equally have set down in an historical or a controversial work.

A tall order indeed for an amateur aiming at a unified work of art on his first flight. But, after all, he had not presumed to call *John Inglesant* a work of art, only "a work of this kind."

Fortunately, Shorthouse's choice of the romance form for "a work of this kind"—quite apart from his constitutional modes of thought which made the choice inevitable—released him as a craftsman from the shackles of careful plot-structure or the burden of detailed characterization appropriate to a realistic novel. The romance form enabled him to roam "among the most serious thoughts and speculations which have stirred mankind." If philosophy was to predominate, everything else must be subordinate, and the characters, therefore, are "only introduced for a set purpose, and having fulfilled this purpose—were it only to speak a dozen words—they vanish from the stage." Thus, in this "philosophical romance" characters and incidents, real and fictional, are selected and manipulated "with a philosophical intent" to support the argument of the book. Characters fictional and real, then, became mouthpieces for particular doctrines or religious attitudes, and events fictional and real merely provide the stimulus or the occasion for the expression of the doctrine. The characters need not be rigidly confined by space and time. The shifts from the physical to the spiritual to the supernatural need not be imperilled by sober logic. The real and the unreal can be juxtaposed, or even mixed, without violent lament from the reader whose disbelief has not been quite suspended.

By availing himself of the old device of the narrator as editor of newly discovered manuscripts—thereby making *John Inglesant* a memoir—Shorthouse not only sets the episodic form of the narrative but enables the novelist to extricate himself from any trap he might find he has inadvertently stepped into. With a brief comment, therefore, on the imperfections of the hypothetical manuscript, he can wave his character on to the next episode and a new experience. One of his Quaker acquaintances, Rachel King, reminiscently remarks: "I remember his telling me how long he was delayed in *John Inglesant* by his characters having got into a castle and refusing to come out." [17]

But in order to combine "real life and philosophy with *vraisemblance*" (he loved the word) Shorthouse characteristically selected seventeenth-century England and Italy for the setting of his novel. The seventeenth was in many respects similar to his own century, particularly in its doubts and perplexities and in its groping struggle for stability, but even more particularly in its conflicts between Protestant and Catholic and in the internecine war in the Church of England. Of all the centuries of English experience it was the seventeenth he knew best, and he was not alone in thinking that of all centuries it was the most significant.

IV

"I feel the responsibility of introducing real historical characters and orders of men into a work of this kind," he says in the preface, and so his fictional characters are made to move among historical figures and events. The fictional hero of the romance, John Inglesant, wavering between Protestantism and Catholicism, moves from Protestant England to Catholic Italy and back again. While he is in England, his experience is regulated by the space and time of the Civil Wars, but once he has left England, after an indeterminate period in Paris, his adventures in Italy have few precise dates to fix them in time. And so, relying on an accurate memory for detail (an inheritance from his father), and on his memory of places seen or read about (not to mention the aid of a large print collection) Shorthouse proceeded to furnish and populate his stage, cautiously limiting himself by English history and geography, English calendar time and English space.

In what he calls an introductory chapter he sets up Geoffrey Monk, the purported editor of the memoirs of John Inglesant at Lydiard "on the borders of Shropshire towards Wales." He sketches in the details of a familiar landscape to the West, sloping up to the Malvern Hills, as he himself could see them still in his time from his own home in suburban Edgbaston. To this landscape he adds "an old and very picturesque house, jumbled together with the additions of many centuries," which he remembers from a visit to Malvern in the summer of 1862 when he was recovering from the first of his epileptic attacks. Borrowing from Anthony à Wood's *Athenae Oxonienses* a few details such as the name "Lydiard" and the inscription on Inglesant's tomb, he completes the external setting for what is the end, not the beginning, of the story.

"I had the Berrington's [*sic*] house, Little Malvern Court, in my mind when I wrote the description of Lydiard," writes Shorthouse to his cousin Isabel Southall (29 March 1881), "but as I was never *inside* the house I cannot say how far the description is exact." [18] But for the interior of the "picturesque house" he provides a library with a four-hundred-year accumulation of "scarce literature of the sixteenth century," "a large collection of Roman Catholic works and pamphlets," "reports of trials," and other papers which make the writing of the memoir possible for Geoffrey Monk—a library curiously similar to Shorthouse's own. Among the family portraits in the diningroom he places the portrait of John Inglesant, "a young man with a tonsured head, in what appeared . . . to be a very simple monk's dress," and in the drawingroom a "Vandyke" of John's brother Eustace in the costume of a Cavalier. With his two portraits of the twin brothers, the expression of two sides of the same personality—the saintly cavalier—the stage is set and all props in place. [19]

In order to set his main character in relation to the movements of his time, to provide for him a varied religious and cultural experience, Shorthouse accommodates him with a large and varied stage: Protestant England and Catholic Italy. In the English portion of the novel, geography and events of the Civil Wars more or less determine the rapid sequence of scenes. The first scene, in the "old and very picturesque house" at Lydiard—either a prelude or postlude, depending on how one considers it—is followed (Ch. 1) by a flashback scene to Westacre in Wiltshire (1539) during the time of the suppression of the lesser monasteries, where Inglesant's antecedents are established; then the scene is refurnished for the period of Inglesant's solitary childhood a century later (Ch. 2). When Inglesant is sixteen, the scene shifts to the Court in London and to Little Gidding in Huntingdonshire (Ch. 4), then to York (Ch. 6). Following this, as King's messenger, Inglesant travels north as far as the Grampians. He returns to London, revisits Little Gidding, participates in the Battle of Edgehill, and moves with the Court to

Oxford (Ch. 8). The movement of the King's army and the king's
business determine the order of the following scenes set alternately
in and out of Oxford, until the scene shifts briefly to Ireland, then to
Chester (Ch. 12). After the failure of the Irish mission the scene
shifts again to London, at first to St. James's Palace, then to the
Tower. On Inglesant's release from the Tower at the end of January
1650 the scene shifts to the southwest counties again (Ch. 16). Time
and place in the English scenes are neatly governed by the progress
of the Civil Wars.

The series of scenes on the Continent is modelled after the
seventeenth-century tourist route, partially at least on John
Evelyn's tour of France and Italy in 1644—Paris, Genoa, Sienna,
Florence, Modena, Mantua, Verona, Ferrara, Rome, Naples—with
Rome occupying the same focal position as Oxford does in the
English scenes. The English scenes are set in manors, palaces, and
battlefields; the Italian scenes are in the churches, the theaters, the
galleries and museums, the streets, and the mountain passes.

Though in the first part of the novel Shorthouse patches together
characters and scenes from a variety of seventeenth-century
sources, he nevertheless confines the characters on his stage to the
timetable of the Civil Wars. Thus the dates are precise. Inglesant is
born in 1622; he enters London 2 August 1637; he is at York in
August 1640; he is at the Battle of Edgehill 23 October 1642.[20] But
in the Italian scenes, though places are geographically precise, time
is not. Once Inglesant has left Paris in May 1651 few dates regulate
his wanderings in Italy, and few episodes are anchored to dates.
Inglesant spends "some time" at Genoa and "some time" at Sienna,
"many days" here and "forty days" there, with little to indicate the
passing of seasons or even of years. In fact six papacies are
telescoped into one for the purposes of the story. One can assume
that Shorthouse's familiarity with the history of the Civil Wars not
only facilitated his writing of the English portion but also prevented
his taking liberties with the English history which readers of *John
Inglesant* might well know. In the Italian section he was himself on
less familiar ground and might also have assumed that the English
reader would not be disconcerted by mangled Italian history.

V

"I feel the responsibility," Shorthouse says at the conclusion of his
preface, "of introducing real historical characters and orders of men

into a of this kind," and he adds, with a rather careless firmness,
"My general defence must be that I have written nothing which I
would not equally have set down in an historical or controversial
work." In order to achieve what earlier in the preface he had called
vraisemblance he extracted from his library the historical characters
which were to give a sense of reality to his fiction, and reconstructed
the events which were to reveal the religious tensions and political
antagonisms among which his fictional hero was to move. As a
devoted royalist and longtime but not blind admirer of Charles I,
Shorthouse, as one might expect, went to royalist sources, then
painted with tender care the portrait of the unlucky monarch and
the victims of his political ineptitude, Strafford and Laud. Thereby
he not only gives a picture of the times, but, more importantly,
gives added stature to his fictional hero, Inglesant, who is also a
victim of royal betrayal. But in his recreation of men and events he
was capable of readings and distortions suitable to the demands of
his novel, distortions of sufficient magnitude to provoke from
Samuel Gardiner, the historian of the Civil Wars, who had
otherwise liked *John Inglesant*, the comment that Shorthouse was
"playing ducks and drakes with history." Similarly, Lord Acton, the
Catholic historian, in letters to his favorite correspondent,
Gladstone's daughter Mary, expressed his dissatisfaction in a
lengthy itemization of what to him were annoying historical
discrepancies in *John Inglesant*.[21]

Shorthouse's method of re-creating, as distinguished from creating, characters and events is exemplified by the episode of Charles I
at Edgehill (Ch. 8). With fragments from Sir Richard Bulstrode's
Memoirs and Reflections (1725), Clarendon's *History of the
Rebellion* (1707), and Anthony à Wood's *Athenae Oxonienses*
(1691-2) rearranged and neatly fastened into place with sentences of
his own, Shorthouse creates a vividly interesting mosaic of
characters and scenes. However, in his reconstruction of Oxford life
immediately following (Ch. 9) his method is slightly different. He
arranges fragments mined from Robert Burton's *Anatomy of
Melancholy* (1621), Lady Anne Fanshawe's *Memoirs* (1829), Richard
Ward's *Life of Henry More* (1710), the *Rawdon Papers*, and from his
favorite quarry, John Aubrey. He retains the names of Isabella
Thynne and Dr. Henry More, but unaccountably alters Ann
Harrison to Ann Harris, Richard Fanshawe to Richard Fentham,
and Lady Conway to Lady Cardiff. Later, inexplicably, the
historical Lady Conway (Cardiff) is married to fictional Eustace

Inglesant (Ch. 9). The startled reader can only surmise that the change of Lady Conway's name is merely a subterfuge to legitimatize the marriage of a real with a fictional character. Lady Conway's real home at Ragley, Warwickshire, is moved to Dorset and given the name of the home of one of Shorthouse's favorite authors, George Borrow—Oulton in Sussex. To muddy the waters of confusion even further one might add that in the 1880 edition of *John Inglesant*, which Shorthouse saw through the press himself, More's name appears consistently as *Mole*. Certainly in this instance typographical error or faulty proofreading must be ruled out as explanation.

The historical figures who represent a succession of religious views Shorthouse had little trouble with. Thomas Hobbes he resurrected from Aubrey, adding only a bit of *Leviathan* (which had not yet been written); Henry More the Platonist he pieced together from Richard Ward's *The Life of the Learned and Pious Dr. Henry More* (1710). For Hugh de Cressy he drew on Aubrey and à Wood. But the most elaborate patchwork and the most effective is the picture of Nicholas Ferrar and the Little Gidding community (Ch. 4). Drawing his detail mostly from Peter Peckard's *Life of Nicholas Ferrar* (1793), but also from Samuel Jebb's and John Ferrar's,[22] and by slightly rearranging the details, he created a compelling picture of the "Protestant Nunnery"—for many readers the finest section of the book.[23]

Unlike Lady Conway, who lost her name, Mary Collet is allowed to retain hers as well as other characteristics attributed to her by Peckard and by Jebb. But Shorthouse makes a major alteration of the figure he found in his source.[24] The historical Mary Collet was never in Paris and did not die young (she lived to the respectable age of eighty). However, functionally, in *John Inglesant* she is the embodiment of religious faith and of divine love which knows no body, in contrast to Lauretta, the Italian aristocrat Inglesant later marries, who is the embodiment of sensual or earthly love. It is fictionally convenient in the novel that Mary Collet die beautifully young. Yet, though there is historical distortion here, Shorthouse cannot be accused of having deliberately manufactured a Victorian tear-jerker by dwelling on the death of Mary Collet in Paris. She is needed in the novel for vivifying an important moment in Inglesant's life, and having done that she is allowed to die in a scene which has exaltation but no tears. Lauretta, Inglesant's other love, although a fictional character, also dies young, victim of the plague, one of the uncontrollable accidents of human life. The deaths of Mary and Lauretta release Inglesant from personal obligations, just as the execution of his king had freed him from political ones earlier. Henceforward he may move untrammeled in his quest for a faith.

In creating his fictional Jesuit, "Father Sancta Clara, as he was called, of an English family named St. Clare, a Jesuit missionary priest, who travelled in England under the name of Hall" (Ch. 2), an agent busy in the delicate maneuvering of parties attempting to reconcile the Church of England with the Church of Rome, Shorthouse avails himself of a real historical figure. A Franciscan scholar, Christopher Davenport (1598-1660), known to his contemporaries as Franciscus a Sancta Clara, was for fifty years during the Civil Wars and Commonwealth active in this attempt at reconciliation. One of the chaplains of Queen Henrietta Maria, he was also a friend of John Aubrey and Anthony à Wood. Plucking Davenport out of Berington's *Memoirs of Gregorio Panzani* (1793), which Shorthouse admits he "made great use of in *John Inglesant*," [25] he adds a touch from à Wood who notes the alias of Davenport: "Francis a S. Clara, Francis Hunt, or Francis Coventry; for by each of these names was he known." [26] For a Jesuit and another alias Shorthouse turns to Aubrey who speaks of Father Franciscus Linus, i.e. Hall, "a Jesuit scholar who had great skills in the optiques and was an excellent philosopher and mathematician and a person of exceeding suavity, goodness and piety." [27] This Jesuit, like Shorthouse's, was known to Sir Kenelm Digby. Thus the Franciscan Davenport drops his own alias "Hunt" (from à Wood), picks up an echo perhaps from Father Holt in *Henry Esmond* and becomes the Jesuit Hall (from Aubrey) busy in the Franciscan Davenport's occupation.

Among the purely fictional characters, Geoffrey Monk, the purported editor of the memoir, and Valentine Lee, the writer of the information-laden letter at the end of *John Inglesant*, are purely functional characters and call for no comment, no more than do the transient historical figures like Milton, Crashaw, Montrose, Saumeurs the tennis player in Paris, Febur [Febus] the chemist in Padua, and Van Helmont, to name only a few of many who appear only briefly. Having done their stint they disappear. Some fictional characters, like the fanatic in Padua, the vielle-player who tells his tale, and Zecca the Boccalini-quoting doctor, are allowed a little more space, a little more time, but are also more or less functional, excite no interest as people, and are merely purveyors of ideas which either reveal the limitations of their views or show the strength of Inglesant's.

Inglesant's twin brother Eustace, another fictional character, though slightly (and somewhat unconvincingly) drawn, appears only three times, but he is nevertheless important in Shorthouse's scheme of the novel. When he is onstage, either by parallel or by contrast he emphasizes Inglesant; when Eustace is offstage the reader is not allowed to forget him. In one sense Eustace represents the worldly cavalier; in another, he is the expression of Inglesant's *alter ego*, that part of his nature which is at war with the spirit. His murder is the motivation of Inglesant's experiences on the Continent. The twin brothers, so alike in appearance yet so different in temperament, can be said to represent between them the best of the Cavalier as Shorthouse saw him—the cultured Christian gentleman, scholarly, refined, pure in spirit, not exempt from temptations of the flesh but capable of mastering them.

Shorthouse's pro-Cavalier sentiment could provoke some of his finest language, but his anti-Puritan bias, more frequently than his anti-Jesuit bias, could lead him at times into what, surprisingly for him, were lapses curious, shrill and warm with displeasure.[28] What seems to him to have been most reprehensible about the Puritans was not that they were narrow in their views but that they were not gentlemen. It is something to Shorthouse's credit, then, that the fictional Thorne, Inglesant's Puritan rival for the love of Mary Collet, is drawn as fairly as he is. Though he shows up badly in contrast with Inglesant at Little Gidding (Ch. 2), is even reduced in stature by Shorthouse's borrowing of one of Thorne's big speeches from the diary of Milton's Quaker friend Thomas Ellwood, Thorne is allowed a scene of holy dying at Gosford Bridge (Ch. 10) where he is a noble figure among the crude, less forgiving, Puritan soldiery. However, though Thorne is appropriately named for his role, Shorthouse provides for him in his dying moments the shelter of "an old thorn tree"—not once, but twice—and almost wipes out with ineptitude any respect for Thorne one might earlier have had from observing the favorable contrast between him and other Puritans.

For the arch-villain of his piece he created Malvolti, an operatic stock figure, the familiar Italian intriguer, dark, treacherous, dagger-happy, and incorrigibly dissolute. He is a character who eventually has to be seen in the novel as the incarnation of evil, the devil in human form, a real, powerful, inexplicable force in human affairs which threatens the good because they are good and can, if

vanquishable at all, be vanquished only by Christian love or divine
benevolence. Reviewers rather heartlessly and needlessly pounced
on Shorthouse's delinquent French and Italian in his novels, but he
seems to have remembered enough Italian to give the reader the
first hint about the function of his villain in the name Malvolti, a
combination of the word for evil (*male*) and the verb meaning to
will, mean, or desire (*volere*). The name explains what seems to be
Malvolti's unexplainable conduct—the senseless murder of Eustace
Inglesant, the repeated attempts on Inglesant's life. It explains—
almost—one of the chief puzzles of the novel, Inglesant's pursuit of
a murderer whose appearance he does not know and Malvolti's
attempts on Inglesant's life because he resembles his twin brother.
It explains even the climactic scene in the mountain pass where
Inglesant, as if by divine revelation, recognizes Malvolti—whom he
has never seen—and forgives him. Thereafter, Shorthouse manipulates Malvolti to emphasize the point about the miracle of Christian
forgiveness which he has made in the scene. After a brief respite
from evil chores, Malvolti reappears as a blind, half-mad friar,
selflessly toiling among the plague-stricken poor, but nevertheless
burning with a desire to revenge himself on the seducer of his sister.
When he (with Inglesant) eventually finds him dying of the plague,
Malvolti forgives his sister's seducer as Inglesant earlier had
forgiven his brother's murderer. Thus by the parallel of similar
conduct in contrasting characters Shorthouse emphasizes the
triumph of good over evil. Shorthouse could perhaps honestly feel
the satisfaction he expressed to Levett when commenting on his use
of "the hint" from the unidentified "old book": "I have never been
able to find, except in the *Memoirs of John Inglesant*, the slightest
hint as to what became of the murderer of the brother." [29] Even
Nathaniel Hawthorne may have had a finger in the creation of
Malvolti. Reviewers were ready enough to suggest that Shorthouse
had borrowed heavily from *The Marble Faun*, but none seems to
have fastened on what Shorthouse (since youth a lover of Hawthorne) really made most use of—the sinister, unredeemable
Capuchin. A symbol of unrelenting, inexplicable evil in *The Marble
Faun*, he turns a moral somersault and in *John Inglesant* comes up
as the regenerated Malvolti, Capuchin.

VI

But as a piece of character creation John Inglesant himself
deserves the most careful scrutiny. Certainly Inglesant embodies

some of Shorthouse's own qualities: modesty, courtesy, genuine piety, intellectual curiosity, love of art and sacred music. In Inglesant Shorthouse could have envisioned himself born into another class and another age. And it is not unlikely that he conceived of Inglesant as an attainable ideal of manhood in nineteenth-century England. Through Inglesant the various strands of the argument in the book (as Shorthouse outlined them in his preface) are drawn. For a reflection of the religious tensions of the seventeenth century—Roman, Anglican, Puritan—as they might have affected a sensitive contemporary mind Shorthouse chose to give Inglesant an ideal rather than a real character, responsive negatively and positively to various religious and philosophical views of his time. By birth and training a Cavalier, by nature a half-mystic, by taste an aesthete, "the glass of fashion and the mould of form," Inglesant is the ideal Cavalier as Shorthouse saw him—as he also viewed Falkland, Clarendon, and such—a combination of courtier, scholar, soldier, and priest, and therefore a suitable medium for his purpose in the novel. Professor Robert Lee Wolff recently has advanced the convincing suggestion that Shorthouse intended in the name "Inglesant" to express the idea of "English saint." [30] Certainly this interpretation of the symbolical significance of Inglesant's name makes unnecessary any further philological wrestling with *Ingle, Engel, Ingelsant, Inglissent, Ingilsind.* Moreover, Shorthouse had no need to invent the name, for, as some one has shown, he could have found it in the *Leicester Post Office Directory.*[31]

If one considers the importance of the Little Gidding scenes in the pattern of *John Inglesant*, it is easy to suspect that Shorthouse got his first hints for the character of Inglesant from the life and character of two of his favorite poets, Richard Crashaw (1612–49) and George Herbert (1593–1633), both in their different ways closely connected with Nicholas Ferrar and the Anglican retreat which he had set up at Little Gidding in 1625. After a fashion the lives of Crashaw and Herbert represent alternatives which are continually before Inglesant in his religious indecision. Crashaw, musical, saintly, of Puritan family, observing the church spoliation and the persecution of the Anglican Church by the Puritan party, was drawn gradually, perhaps despairingly, but almost inevitably, to the discipline, order, and beautiful ceremonial of the Church of Rome. He was eventually to die in Italy as Canon of Loretto. Herbert, equally as saintly, but of aristocratic family, eschewed the courtly and' political ambitions of his class for the Anglican priesthood at Bemerton near Little Gidding. Though, like Crashaw, he is drawn to the Church of Rome, Inglesant finally finds his place with Herbert, if not at Bemerton at least at nearby Worcester. His alternatives of faith and action are represented also by Hugh de Cressy, an Anglican who became a Benedictine, and by Nicholas Ferrar, who, though a near-Catholic, remained Anglican. One could add also the example of Christopher Davenport, mentioned earlier, an Anglican whose brother John became "a noted Puritan" while he himself took the road to Douay into the Order of Franciscans.

With a pat here and there from John Aubrey, the boy John Inglesant, born in 1622 at Westacre near Malmesbury, delicate, isolated, lonely, absorbing the superstitions of the countryside and the oral history of the area from his grandfather and the countryfolk, apparently formed as a character in Shorthouse's mind. For John Aubrey (b. 1626) was, like Inglesant, also born near Malmesbury, "being weak and like to die," and "got not strength till [he] was 11 or 12 years old," spent "an Eremiticall Solitude" "bred up in a kind of Parke far from Neighbours and no Child to converse withall," but able to listen to "old women and mayds to tell fabulous stories nightimes, of Sprights and walking of Ghosts," hearing from his grandfather Lyte "of the old tyme, the Roodloft, etc., ceremonies of the Priory, etc." [32]

When it came to showing the formation of Inglesant's mind, Shorthouse heard Aubrey whispering again. Aubrey, looking back on his own youth, remarks: "I had apprehension enough, but my memorie not tenacious; so that then was a promising morne enough of an inventive and philosophical head. . . . I was exceeding mild of spirit; mightily susceptible of fascination." In like manner, Inglesant, viewed by one of his early teachers, is an "apt pupil, an apprehensive and inquisitive boy, mild of spirit and very susceptible of fascination, strongly given to superstition and romance; of an inventive imagination though not a retentive memory; given to day-dreaming, and . . . metaphysical speculation (Ch. 2)."

Aubrey gives further assistance, less directly, in the development of this young mind, for Inglesant's first teacher, the old curate of the Chapel, bears some resemblance to Thomas Hobbes's father as noted by Aubrey, "vicar of Westport juxta Malmesbury," one of the "many ignorant Sir Johns of Queen Elizabeth's time," who "could only read the prayers of the Church and the homilies." And it was

Aubrey's grandfather Lyte who had had the teacher who taught in the church which Camden had visited.

When the curate dies, Inglesant acquires more of Aubrey's education at Blandford St. Mary's in Dorset that "was the most eminent Schoole for the education of Gentlemen in the West of England." Later he sits under the teacher of both Aubrey and Hobbes, "Robert Latimer, Rector of Leigh-de-la-Mere," who had "an easie way of teaching." Add to all this Aubrey's comment about Hobbes, that "when he was a Boy he was playsome enough, but withall he had even then a contemplative Melancholiness," [32] and young Inglesant becomes recognizable.

But though Shorthouse got more hints from Aubrey than can conveniently be discussed here, it is interesting that the character of Inglesant as it develops, though inheriting a little from Aubrey and something from Hobbes as noted by Aubrey, is also quite a bit of neither. He is not so much a mixture as an amalgam resulting from something Shorthouse has added in the creation, something of himself, his religious concern and the royalism, Anglicanism, and veneration for the Sacrament which he shared with John Evelyn. For on this base from Aubrey Shorthouse builds his half-mystic courtier, well-dressed, well-spoken, impeccable in manner, constantly searching for religious certainty though seldom assured, intermittently wracked by doubt or lifted to exaltation, stumbling and groping in a world either too dimly lit or too glaring for his satisfaction.

The groundwork of Inglesant's character laid, Shorthouse sends him on his way in quest of a faith, which, as it turns out, he finds only after many vicissitudes. But the quest for a faith is also a search for culture, and Inglesant's observation and examination of men, events, and ideas is not only religious and philosophical but aesthetic as well. The religious *Via Media*—the mean between Roman Catholicism and Protestant Puritanism—is eventually not distinguishable from the *Via Media* of life. Culture, as Shorthouse viewed it in the best Cavaliers, represented the mean, a proper balance of the world and the spirit, of freedom and authority, of self-denial and self-fulfilment.

Step by step—with an occasional false step—Inglesant yearningly moves from a child's openminded curiosity, through doubt raised by experience of men and affairs, past alternatives momentarily attractive, to certainty. The sediment of legend, superstition, and romance from his Westacre boyhood will, stirred a little, periodi-

cally darken his thought; the fascination with the past will keep his
eye on the attractiveness of an historic church; the awareness of the
supernatural, the gnawing discontent with the present and the real
will alternately torture and uplift him.

Shorthouse indicates early in the novel the direction of Inglesant's journey and the eventual destination. Having given
Inglesant near-Catholic antecedents he puts up the first obstacle on
the road to Rome, Inglesant's first teacher, who innocently plants in
his pupil "some faint prejudice" against the Church of Rome.
Later, not so innocently, Father St. Clare "prepare[s] his pupil to
receive in after years . . . that kindly love of humanity; that
sympathy with its smallest interests; that toleration of its errors, and
of its conflicting opinions; that interest in local and familiar affairs, in
which the highest culture is at one with the unlearned rustic mind"
(Ch. 3). "He even [takes] pains to prevent his becoming attached to
Popery" (Ch. 3). By the introduction of Inglesant to Hobbes (Ch. 5)
another fingerpost is erected, not very distinct but discernible.
Hobbes's "attractive materialism" will stir doubt in Inglesant's mind
for some time to come, but Hobbes, having unburdened himself of
anti-Roman feeling, points out: "I take the sacrament in the English
Church, which I call in England the Holy Church, and believe that
its statutes are the true Christian Faith" Ch. 5). Though at Little
Gidding Crashaw is drifting Romewards, Nicholas Ferrar, standing
steadily at the brink, is assured that he himself will not fall over. He
cautions Inglesant that before joining the Roman communion he
should make a tour abroad, if possible to Rome itself (Ch. 4).

Much later, in Italy, though drawn by the beauties of landscape
and art, the beauty of the churches and the church services,
Inglesant is deterred from joining the Church of Rome by his
observation of corruption in ecclesiastical administration, by the
silencing of Molinos, by a growing consciousness that that balance of
freedom and authority which is necessary to culture can be found
only in the Church of England, by law established, historically
based, but a *national* church with the sovereign as its head. Only in
such an organization can there be room enough and assurance for a
free English spirit led by the "Inner Voice," guided by the "Divine
Light."

Though at times faint, the yearning for the Divine Light never
leaves Inglesant. One of his early teachers (Ch. 2) had at parting
planted the idea in his mind:

Hear what all men say but follow no man: there is nothing in the world of any value but the Divine Light—follow it. What it is no man can tell you . . . it is not here nor there . . . it will reveal itself when the time shall come. . . . If you go to the Court . . . attach yourself wholly to the King and the Church Party, the foundations of whose power are in the Divine Will. . . . I have never told you to act freely in this world—you are not placed here to reason . . . but to obey. Remember it is the very seal of a gentleman—to obey. . . . Whenever—and in whatever place—the Divine Light shall appear to you, be assured it will never teach you anything contrary to this.

The first real crisis in Inglesant's life comes at the age of sixteen after his reading of the seventeenth-century biography of St. Teresa, *The Flaming Heart*: [33] "A great deal of it was so strange to Inglesant that he was repelled by it . . . but running through all the book, the great doctrine of Divine Illumination fascinated him. . . . What must this be but the Divine Light of which his old master had so often told him he was ignorant but whose certain coming he had led him to expect" (Ch. 3)? His experience with *The Flaming Heart* sharpens in Inglesant an awareness of a vague longing for some kind of authority or guide and the conflicting desire for a mind which can remain unfettered by dogma or by any institutional authority such as church or priest.

Henceforth he is a seeker wavering between desire for authority and desire for freedom from authority, between the desire to submit to the spirit and the inclination to rebel against the spirit, between the saving necessity of self-denial and the attractiveness of self-fulfilment. The alternatives remain the same, extremes: the Church of Rome to which he is drawn by its tradition, by beauty of music, ceremonial, and imposing edifice, and the "Other Way," the lonely pathway of the soul, spiritual self-fulfilment unimpeded by human institutions. He will find relief from the world of politics in the calm of Little Gidding but return dutifully to the world of action. At war with himself he will turn from the glory of God he experiences at Mary Collet's deathbed, and, self-willed, he will also turn from de Cressey's asceticism to plunge into the excitement of Rome. He will vengefully pursue his brother's murderer, then surrender the sword of vengeance to God. Drawn ever nearer to an authoritative Church of Rome he will nevertheless defend Molinos in his insistence on the individual's right to the Sacrament without confession. And the struggle is over. Having examined men and institutions he makes his choice—the Church of England by law established, the Church which represents both authority and freedom, restraint and culture, and which offers the Sacrament for all who come. A long time and a long journey since his first visit to Little Gidding when during the Sacrament "he was lost in a sense of rapture, and earth and all that surrounded him faded away" (Ch. 4).

VII

It is unlikely that Shorthouse conceived of *John Inglesant* in the shape which the novel eventually took. If one can assume that *John Inglesant* traces the progress of a soul from its vague groping for light, through a series of experiences with contradictory philosophies, until it reaches spiritual contentment in Anglicanism, the episodic structure of the novel can be readily accounted for. To provide the variety of worldly and spiritual experience necessary for Inglesant, Shorthouse moves him through chronologically consecutive scenes of varying length, casually (and geographically or spatially) rather than causally related. Particularly helpful to Shorthouse in the achievement of an easily manageable pattern was his adoption of the memoir convention, for it not only made unnecessary the causal connection of episodes but also made possible easy extrication of the hero from difficulties his creator might inadvertently have written him into. Thus by use of hiatus Shorthouse periodically breaks his narrative thread; at other times, when it is necessary to move Inglesant on to a new experience, he allows the presumed editor, Geoffrey Monk, to comment on the inadequacy of the "papers" when the jump is made. This method enables Shorthouse also to change the pace of the movement by insertion of miniatures or enlargements, or of interesting, explanatory (but sometimes self-indulgently erudite) paddings which accelerate, but more frequently slow down, the movement of characters and events.

In attempting to account for the near indefinable power of the novel, however, one needs a point of view which is undimmed by the fiercely partisan praise and blame distinguishing contemporary comment on the novel. For though *John Inglesant* shows the passage of a Cavalier from the uncertainties of youth to the assurance of age, what gives universality to the Cavalier's experience is Shorthouse's employment of an underlying and unifying assumption, the age-old concept of the warfare between flesh and spirit, the eternal debate over body and soul. In a letter to his friend Levett (28 May 1894) Shorthouse remarks that "John Inglesant was written to lead up expressly to this one incident," that is, Inglesant's meeting with Malvolti in the mountain pass (Ch. 32).[34] To Margaret Evans he writes (28 August 1880): "One of the principal objects of the book is to show that to the children of God, *i.e.* to those who have listened to the heavenly call, for existence commences with a response to the Divine Voice, there is no temptation without a way of escape." [35] Viewed thus, the novel can be seen as organized, after a fashion, around three focal points: the temptation of the world, the temptation of the flesh, the temptation of the devil. Inglesant turns reluctantly from Hugh de Cressy's asceticism because the temptation of the world is too strong (Ch. 19); he subdues the yearnings of the flesh in the journey with Lauretta to Pistoia (Ch. 29); he triumphs over the temptation of the devil when, with his brother's murderer in his power, he forgoes the satisfaction of vengeance, forgives him, and lays his sword upon the altar as a symbol of sacrificial surrender (Ch. 32). If this pattern is accepted, other important episodes in the novel become subsidiary and contributory to the underlying idea of temptation, an idea Shorthouse was to use again in *The Countess Eve.* The Little Gidding scenes, including the death of Mary Collet in Paris, almost sufficient unto themselves, focus on an exaltation of the spirit, on a calmness in contrast with the urgings of the eager flesh. The Civil War scenes and the Italian scenes, in differing ways, show the manysidedness of the world's impingement on the spirit and accentuate the fierceness of the warfare of flesh and spirit. These three focal points, then, mark the stages in the progression from a defeat of the spirit by the flesh, to a victory of the spirit over the flesh, and finally to a soul-saving triumph over evil.

VIII

Shining through *John Inglesant* are bright threads of meaning— some more distinct than others, some scarcely distinguishable from each other—which are at the end gathered into one fast, almost surprising knot, a statement of religious belief in what Shorthouse called in a letter to a friend "Broad Church Sacramentalism." [36]

His conception of the English gentleman, his constant concern about culture and self-culture, his interest in art, his partially aesthetic, partially mystical, religious inclination are combined with an interest in the historic past, a respect for its venerability, and a belief in the validity of its pattern.

Most distinct, perhaps, is his idea of the gentleman. Most obvious, of course, in the presentation of that idea are the character and deportment of Inglesant. He is the "Compleat Gentleman." Though gentle, soft-spoken, moderate, sensitive, refined, careful of appearance, he is also manly, active, athletic, firm. Well-descended from ancient landed gentry, he has the assurance of blood and breeding. Courtier, scholar, and soldier, he can move with ease, untarnished, among prelates and kings. A lover of the arts, he responds like a delicate instrument to all the beauties of landscape, the beauties of ritual, the beauty of stained glass. Shorthouse describes Inglesant, aged twenty-one (Ch. 9):

He was sincerely and vitally religious, though his religion might appear to be kept in subordination to his taste, and he had formed for himself, from various sources, an ideal of purity, which in his mind connected earth to heaven. . . . The circumstances of his early youth and training . . . acting upon a constitution in which the mental power dominated, rendered self-restraint natural to him. . . . It is one of the glories of that age that it produced such men as he was, and that not a few; men who combined qualities such as, perhaps, no after age ever saw united; men like George Herbert, Nicholas Ferrar, Falkland. . . . He was a sincere believer in a holy life . . . but he was not capable of a sacrifice of his tastes or his training. On the other hand, as a courtier and man of the world, he was profoundly tolerant of error and even of vice (providing the latter did not entail suffering on an innocent victim), looking upon it as a natural incident in human affairs. This quality had its good side, in making him equally tolerant of religious differences. . . . He was acutely sensitive to ridicule, and would as soon have thought of going to Court in an improper dress as speaking of religion in a mixed company, or of offering any advice or reproof to any one.

But the qualities of the gentleman exemplified by Inglesant are craftily emphasized periodically by other characters in the novel who somehow are not gentlemen (at least not by Shorthouse's definition). There is, for instance, Thorne, Inglesant's rival for the love of Mary Collet, "possessed of considerable property" but without benefit of rank, honest but narrow in his views, who, dying nobly in a mistaken cause, though he is superior to the coarse, intolerant soldiery about him, is, for all that, the "Incompleat Gentleman." There is Inglesant's brother Eustace, well-born but unstable, his brother-in-law di Guardino, well-born but unscrupulous, the fanatic virtuoso in Umbria, "born of a good but poor family," but unbalanced. And, of course, there is Malvolti, who has neither noble birth, nor stability, nor scruple. All are "incompleat" when viewed beside Inglesant.

The idea of the gentleman is further forced upon the reader's mind by cautionary, infelicitous authorial intrusions concerning the qualities of Falkland, Herbert, Ferrar. As he traces the progress of Inglesant, Shorthouse inserts casual epithets, such as "a finished and attractive lover," to underline the gentlemanliness of his hero. After the miscarriage of Inglesant's Irish mission the abusiveness of the parliament men is contrasted with Inglesant's dignified poise and restraint (Ch. 13). More inclusive and subtly eloquent (Ch. 14) is the authorial comment on the execution of the King: "A revolting coarseness marks every detail of the tragic story; the flower of England on either side was beneath the turf or beyond the sea, and the management of affairs was left in the hands of butchers and brewers."

Twined inseparably with the idea of the gentleman is the idea of culture: culture in the sense of civilization; culture in the sense of desirable attainment or accumulation of the best that has been thought and said and done; culture in the sense of self-improvement, the practice of which Shorthouse considered the most important duty of man. Shortly after the publication of *John Inglesant*, in a letter to Edwin A. Abbot, Headmaster of the City of London School and also a writer of religious novels, he remarks that one of his intentions in the book was "to exalt the unpopular doctrine that the end of existence is not the good of one's neighbor but one's own culture." [37]

The idea of culture, then, in its various meanings gleams through *John Inglesant*. From an observation of the culture of England and Italy as manifested in people, institutions, politics, social practice, Shorthouse forces the reader to observe culture in its narrower sense as an affection for the arts and learning and in its most restrictive sense as self-development (as distinguished from self-indulgence). And he forces the reader also to consider the idea of life as an art, and, by corollary, the idea of the gentleman as a work of art. The gentleman who is by accident of birth a product of a culture in the widest sense moves in his milieu, acquiring an agreeable balance of admirable qualities, physical, intellectual, artistic, and moral. He is a "man of culture" who by an assiduous artistic self-interest emerges as the epitome of a civilization. Clarendon (a favorite of Shorthouse's) speaking of the uncorruptible Falkland (another favorite) puts the stamp on the type: "He was superior to all those passions and affections which attend vulgar minds, and was guilty of no other ambition than knowledge and to be reputed a lover of all good men." [38]

The Little Gidding scenes afford good instances of Shorthouse's manner of combining the various meanings of culture in a single episode. The Little Gidding community is a particular form of an English institution, the Church; the members of the community—notably Nicholas Ferrar—are not only unswervingly loyal to a temporal and imperfect sovereign, and devoted to a "Heavenly King," but they are also sensitive, scholarly, artistic. Though normally engaged in good works, they find, in a happy union of asceticism with a sense of beauty, their greatest satisfaction while kneeling for the sacrament in a tastefully restored chapel.

Whether religion is a necessary part of a gentleman's culture or whether culture is a necessary part of a gentleman's religion Shorthouse never really makes clear. John Inglesant at one point (Ch. 4) is described as one who in spite of his Jesuitical and court training was "naturally modest, and whose sense of religion made him perfectly well-bred." If, positively, balance, or, negatively, an avoidance of extremes, is necessary for culture, it is equally necessary for religion. Hence Shorthouse implicitly condemns fanaticism—the one extremity self-denial, the other self-indulgence. Inglesant's passage through life is disturbed by the opposing desires of his own nature, on the one hand a yearning to lose himself in the divine ecstasy and on the other to rejoice in the flesh. "I have left the book to tell its own tale and read its own lesson to everyone according to their liking," says Shorthouse, writing to his cousin Margaret when he sent her one of the first copies of *John Inglesant* (17 July 1880), "but I may tell *you* that my *own* reading of the book is that God prefers culture to fanaticism." [39] The following November, writing to E. A. Abbott, he notes: "Perhaps the chief object [of *John Inglesant*] is to promote culture at the expense of fanaticism, including the *fanaticism of work*." [40] What he meant by "fanaticism of work" Shorthouse never explains. Perhaps he is expressing his opposition to the Carlylean gospel which he so much disliked; perhaps he is protesting against the accelerating bustle of developing industry and commerce and of the men engaged therein; perhaps he is even protesting against the idea of self-improvement with a financial end in view, the school of Samuel Smiles; and no doubt he is also decrying Puritan (or Quaker) busyness contrived to thwart the devil from finding work for idle hands.

But political, and particularly religious, fanaticism is another matter. And in this matter Shorthouse obliquely condemns the religious and social restrictions of the Society of Friends under which he had been brought up. Though Thorne is distinguished as superior to the crude soldiery and the rude parliament men, Shorthouse puts all Puritans into the same basket—earnest, but narrow, rude, crude, and fanatical. Lady Cardiff, a convert to Quakerism, is guilty of "lavish almsgiving and other vagaries." The Quakers are disposed of by Dr. More: "They have indeed many excellent points, and very nobly Christian, which I wish they would disencumber from such things as make them seem so uncouth and ridiculous" (Ch. 17). The Duke of Umbria is made the executioner of the Lutherans: "I have heard from a Lutheran a system of religion that makes my blood run cold, the more as it commends itself to my calmer reason" (Ch. 26). The fanatic in the duchy of Umbria challenges his company "to tread the life of painful self-denial" (Ch. 27). Mary Collet's spiritual self-sufficiency exalts Inglesant, but he turns away knowing that it is not for him. De Cressy's asceticism is too confining; the Italian Cardinal's humanism too unconfining. Thus by his support of Molinos (Ch. 37) Inglesant is arguing in Shorthouse's name only for an acceptable, desirable balance of individual freedom and necessary authority, as opposed to the unquestioning acceptance by the individual of unlimited authority, or tyranny, whether it is represented by a Roman pope, an Anglican hierarchy, or the elders of the Quaker Meeting.

The anti-Roman thread in the fabric of the novel becomes visible intermittently, particularly in the last quarter of *John Inglesant*. Though Inglesant is steadily attracted to the Church of Rome and rather tentatively puts one foot over the threshold several times, he repeatedly draws himself back from what he concludes are only external charms encrusting an iniquitous ecclesiastical system. Shorthouse is careful to show that the Jesuit Hall, though a man of culture, charm and rare attainments, is an obedient tool of his order, a schemer. Though Hall enlarges Inglesant's mind, he also clouds it. He dissuades him, as a useful agent in a delicate business, from joining the Church of Rome for what, in essence, are treasonous ends—the disaffection of Englishmen from their sovereign and their subjection to a foreign authority. Nicholas Ferrar is anti-Roman in a most gentlemanly way; a near-Catholic, he remains Anglican; he does not attempt to dissuade Inglesant from following Crashaw but cautions him to see Rome before he makes up his mind (Ch. 4). It seems more than chance that Hobbes, early in the novel (Ch. 5) with the aid of Chapter 37 of his *Leviathan* (still to be written), is made the hangman of Jesuitry and Romanism. Inglesant may be permitted to enjoy the intoxication of worship in the great churches, to luxuriate in the sense of an historical past, but as pupil of the Jesuits he is made a political agent in a dubious affair to acquire the Duke of Umbria's estates for the Papal See. He is even given a walk-on part so that he can observe the slippery politics of a papal election; he is forced either through his own observations or by the reports of others to view the mismanagement of the Papal States. And in the Molinos episode, with Gilbert Burnet's "Three Letters" to aid him, Shorthouse sprinkles about such toxic phrases as "tyranny which they [priests] exercise over the spiritual life of men," "pernicious influence of the clergy upon all ranks of society." [41] Then, in the closing pages of the novel he puts the case unequivocally in favor of Anglicanism.

In his report on *John Inglesant*, April 1881, though he recommended publication of the novel, Macmillan's reader remarked: "The tone is rather sombre, the stroke is not rapid, the air is heavy. There is much also, & too much of mysticism of a curious kind." [42] Fond as he is of the word "mystic," Shorthouse never makes clear his understanding of the term. But if one can consider mysticism to mean a belief in an inexplicable attainment of insight into mysteries transcending normal human experience or, perhaps, more narrowly, as a belief in the possibility of a direct union of the soul with God, then it is not difficult to trace the thread of mysticism, somewhat thicker and more subtly colored than the other threads, in the fabric of the novel. And if one proceeds on the assumption that Inglesant's career is one long search for an acceptable authority, the mysticism in the novel becomes almost intelligible to the nonmystical reader. While Inglesant would have been willing to recognize the validity of the Puritan's desire for communion with God without intermediary priest, the authority of the Bible, as it was accepted by some Puritans, he would have resisted as too narrow. Inglesant, in fact, seems to have no perceptible knowledge of the Bible and his mysticism therefore cannot be attributed to a study of the Pauline epistles. The authority of the Church of Rome he eventually rejects because he considers compulsory confession before communion a denial of personal freedom; the authority of official doctrine, or of priest, is to him repugnantly confining. He searches fairly steadily for an authority which will satisfy his own nature, the authority of the mystic's "experience," independent, unexplainable, but authentic, a transcendence of the mundane to a perception of the divine—what amounts to special revelation. There is in Inglesant a willingness, even eagerness, to lose his life by finding it in the mystic experience, yet somehow, paradoxically, to retain his identity. For such a nature satisfaction should have been possible through the "Inner Light" of the Quakers among whom Shorthouse had grown up, but a reliance on the authority of the Inner Light made unnecessary such church rites as the Lord's Supper, discouraged the aid of the senses in worship, and encouraged a formlessness amounting almost to a sort of spiritual anarchy. Whatever else he might have wanted, Inglesant (and Shorthouse) wanted form. And so Quakerism is hardly touched on in the novel. Lady Cardiff's conversion to Quakerism is less important than her association with Dr. Henry More, for it is More's criticism of Quaker practice which diverts Inglesant from Quakerism and prompts him to seek authority elsewhere.

The boy Inglesant, introspective, dreamy, gets from his first teacher the "facts," that is, the catechism and Latin grammar. But it is another teacher, the one with the "easy and attractive way of teaching," the Greek scholar, Platonist, Rosicrucian, believer in alchemy and astrology, who takes Inglesant a step ahead by acquainting him with his "theories of spiritual existences" and the "Divine Light"—"the Light that shineth from the hill of God"—which is to be obeyed if and when it appears (Ch. 2). When, at sixteen, Inglesant reads *The Flaming Heart*, "the great doctrine of Divine Illumination fascinate[s] him" (Ch. 3), but his enthusiasm is cooled by the recommended obedience and entire submission to a "spiritual guide," a priest. Puzzled, Inglesant visits one of his old masters, and though he gets from him no really satisfying answer, he moves another step ahead in his search. "God forbid [says the vicar quoting from Synesius] that we should think that if God dwell in us, He should dwell in any other part of us than that which is rational, which is His own proper temple" (Ch. 3). Is the spiritual guide, then, to be reason?

If to Inglesant the Inner Light's lack of form was unsatisfactory, equally unsatisfactory was an overemphasis on form. He could get

no help therefore from the ritualist country parson who "evidently
looked on forms and ceremonies with the greatest reverence, and
was totally incapable of telling his visitor [i.e., Inglesant] anything of
that mystical life he was so anxious to realize" (Ch. 3). Form he must
have but form alone is not enough. When next in his search
Inglesant turns again to a former schoolmaster (Ch. 3) he listens
eagerly:

The more and the oftener [says the old man] we recognize the supernatural
in our ordinary life, and not only expect and find it in those rare and short
moments of devotion and prayer, the more, surely, the rays of the Divine
Light will shine through the dark glass of this outward form of life, and the
more our own spirit will be enlightened and purified by it until we come to
that likeness of the Divine Nature, and that purity of heart to which a share
of the Beatific Vision is promised, and which, as some teach, can be attained
by being abstract from the body and the bodily life.

The Beatific Vision, the Divine Illumination, the Divine Light, all
can come, then, only to the pure in heart.

Inglesant achieves the mystic experience at Little Gidding (Ch. 4)
when, during the sacrament, sense, form, symbol, freedom and
authority, natural and supernatural, fuse indistinguishably into one:

Above the altar, which was profusely bedecked with flowers, the antique
glass of the east window, which had been carefully repaired, contained a
figure of the Saviour of an early and severe type. The form was gracious yet
commanding, having a brilliant halo around the head, and being clothed in
a long and apparently seamless coat; the two fore-fingers of the right hand
were held up to bless. Kneeling upon the half-pace, as he received the
sacred bread and tasted the Holy wine, this gracious figure entered into
Inglesant's soul, and stillness and peace unspeakable, and life, and light,
and sweetness filled his mind. He was lost in a sense of rapture, and earth
and all that surrounded him faded away.

Dr. More, at Oulton (Ch. 17), strengthens the mystic thread by
addition of the world of sense:

I can read, discourse, or think nowhere so well as in some arbour, where
the cool air rustles through the moving leaves; and what a rapture of mind
does such a scene as this always inspire within me! To a free and divine
spirit how lovely, how magnificent, is this state for the soul of man, when,
the life of God inactuating her, she travels through heaven and earth, and
unites with, and after a sort feels herself the light and soul of this whole
world, even as God!

And he adds:

This divine body should be cultivated as well as the divine life. . . . You
have only to consider that the oracle of God is not to be heard but in His
holy temple, that is to say, in a good and holy man, thoroughly sanctified in
spirit, soul, and body.

Shortly thereafter, then, at the deathbed of Mary Collet (Ch. 18),
Inglesant, though without the visible form of the sacrament, can
renew his Little Gidding experience in terms close to More's:

The old familiar glamour that shed such a holy radiance on the woods and
fields of Gidding, now, to Inglesant's senses, filled the little convent room.
The light that entered the open window with the perfume of the hawthorn
was lost in the divine radiance, that shone from this girl's face into the
depths of his being, and bathed the place where she was in light. His heart
ceased to beat, and he lay, as in a trance, to behold the glory of God.

Later, in Italy, Molinos (Ch. 25) speaks of that "act of devotion,
which [is] called the contemplative state, in which the will is so
united to God and overcome by that union that it adores and loves
and resigns itself to Him, and, not exposed to the waverings of mere
fancy, nor wearied by a succession of formal acts of a dry religion, it
enters into the life of God, into the heavenly places of Jesus Christ,
with an indescribable and secret joy."

The frontiers of reality and unreality, natural and supernatural,
are frequently blurred in the novel by reference to trance, to dream
or near-dream states, to mist, to carnival pantomimes, to Inglesant's
vague forebodings, to his enjoyment of the music in church or
theater. The frontiers are crossed in some instances: the "certainty"
of "second-sight" (Ch. 6) which is a kind of foreshadowing of
Inglesant's reading of the astrologer's crystal (Ch. 15); the appearance of Strafford's ghost (Ch. 6); the vielle-player's story (Ch. 22);
the ominous "peculiarly twisted cord" which Inglesant first sees in
imagination and then in reality (Ch. 21). But the frontiers remain
undefined through Shorthouse's monotonously repetitive "strange,"
"fantastic," and "mystic," words whose suggestiveness is hindered
as often as aided by the vagueness with which they are used.

Though in the rapturous state natural and supernatural are
indistinguishable, the natural sensory world is ever-present, somehow remaining itself. The light of day, if it cannot be considered
symbolic of the Divine Light, the spiritual guide, is at least a
constant subtle *reminder* of the Divine Light. The light streaming

through the windows of the Little Gidding chapel clothes the kneeling worshippers. The light floods the convent room of the dying Mary Collet. The light is "already brilliant and intense" when Inglesant meets and forgives Malvolti in the mountain pass. In the forest pavilion scene the "forest seemed transfigured in the moonlight and the stillness into an unreal landscape of the dead" until, Inglesant's temptation over, "the deadly glamour of the moonlight faded suddenly, a calm pale solemn light settled over the forest" (Ch. 29). On his last visit to Little Gidding, during prayers, "at the words 'Lighten our darkness,' [Inglesant] look[s] up at some noise, and [sees] the sunlight from the west window shining into the Church upon Mary Collet and the kneeling women, and, beyond them, standing in the dark shadow under the window, the messenger of the Jesuit" (Ch. 11) summoning him to the world of political intrigue.

The organs and choirs of the great churches, the sound of wind among the leaves, the sound of water rushing near or murmuring from afar, elevate the spirit to the contemplative state; the distant sounds, like churchbells breaking the silence of a Sunday morning, are the reminders, the messengers, the suggestive influences. But it is in the silence that the soul waits for the Divine Light, and listens for the inner voice; in the contemplative state the soul prepares for the rapture.

IX

The last chapter of *John Inglesant* has been damned often enough as an example of artistic ineptitude to invite a sympathetic defence. It has been argued that the chapter is unnecessary, that in a true work of art the meaning should be implicit and not thrust at the reader in an appendix. There is no reliable evidence in the correspondence of Shorthouse to indicate that he had anything in mind more complicated than what has been suggested above. In a novel in which he was explaining to himself and to any who might listen why he had abandoned Quakerism for Anglicanism, the last chapter pulls together the threads intermittently seen running through the novel—the idea of the Christian gentleman, the idea of culture as a desirable adjunct, the idea of authority historically justified by law, freedom within the authority for the use of reason, the possibility and validity of the mystic experience—and joins them firmly into a statement of Shorthouse's own religious position, of a Quaker who had become an Anglican but an Anglican of a particular kind—a Broad Church sacramentalist.

"In reply to your letter I am a devoted adherent of the Church of England *by law* established; more particularly I should call myself a 'Broad Church Sacramentalist,' " says Shorthouse in a letter to W. A. Wickham (5 October 1883) published by the *Guardian* (18 March 1903) two weeks after Shorthouse's death. Just how "Broad" and how "Sacramentalist" still need to be determined. The Society of Friends in which he had been brought up of course rejected the sacraments of Baptism and the Eucharist. At twenty-seven, in 1861, Shorthouse felt himself sufficiently convinced about sacraments to be baptized in the Church of England and thereafter to find spiritual satisfaction in the frequent celebration of the Eucharist. John Inglesant for all his "craving after the sacrifice of the Mass" balks really on only one point, the denial of access to the supernatural (Eucharist, Mass) without preliminary confession. Shorthouse, like Inglesant, wishes within an authoritative structure to exercise freedom of belief and action, and that puts him into the Broad Church. He is a freethinker (in the literal sense of the word) under the flexible, protecting umbrella of the "Thirty-Nine Articles."

Shorthouse's sacramentalism (as he called it), or sacramentarianism (as others called it), is difficult to label neatly. It is distinguished by what amounts to an ultra-emphasis on the efficacy of the Eucharist, which, is, first of all, different from the Low Church symbolic celebration and, second, goes beyond what was officially High Church. The sense of "communion" with the Divine or supernatural in the Quaker worship might have been sufficient for him had he not required a visible form and found it in the Eucharist as administered by the "authorized representative of Christ" in the Church of England. Another step took him to the position he expressed to Dr. Talbot (17 December 1882): "The Sacrament and Christ feel to me as one and the same. At least the Sacrament seems to me the means by which God reveals himself to us, through the medium of that, as I call it, 'the idea of Christ—the forces that *are* Christ, not *were*'." [43] Somewhat later in an undated letter to a Mrs. Moller, he elaborates: "Communion with God is given to those who seek it diligently, not to those who despise or pass it lightly by; in this respect it is like all other scientific truths. It is entirely independent of all dogma, but the history of thought, of the world, of the individual experience has conclusively proved that the reception of the *idea of Christ* has been the most efficacious means of proving this intimate communion with God. . . . The man who lives consistently and continually in communion with this idea cannot fail to be very different from the man who does not." [44] Near the end of *John Inglesant* Shorthouse puts into Inglesant's mouth these words: "The English Church, as established by the law of England, offers the supernatural to all who choose to come. . . . Upon the altars of the Church the divine presence hovers. . . . It is barred by no confession, no human priest."

The power of the book—the "potential," as reviewers and stockbrokers are now so fond of saying—is undeniable to the receptive reader, but difficult to explain to the doubter, for *John Inglesant* has diverting weaknesses aplenty to irritate even the charitable reader: improbabilities, characters who are not people, speeches too studied, too long, and sometimes vaporish, a monotonous overuse of favorite words like "mystic," a seriousness without relieving humor, infelicities of phrase which make one suspect a bad ear, sentences which do not quite mesh with each other, and erudite authorial intrusions. But rich compensation for such peccadilloes is the gallery of memorable portraits and scenes: foremost, the Little Gidding scenes; then, the dramatic scene in which Strafford's ghost appears to the King, Inglesant's tensely vivid moments on the scaffold, the ominous meeting with the astrologer in Lambeth Marsh, the church scenes in Rome, and the plague scenes in   Naples.

Shorthouse's normally cautious, languorous, almost pedestrian, prose can sometimes jog briskly, as in the capsule summaries and swiftly sketched miniatures, or can break out with nervous, emotional energy when he touches matters which affect him deeply, such as the execution of the King (Ch. 14). He has the skill to evoke a variety of moods: calmness particularly, and exaltation, mental stress and strain, foreboding and ominousness. Witness Inglesant's visit to the unfinished St. Peter's (Ch. 24):

But when, having traversed the length of the nave without uttering a word, he passed from under the gilded roofs, and the spacious dome, lofty as a firmament, expanded itself above him in the sky, covered with tracery of the celestial glories, and brilliant with mosaic and stars of gold . . . when beneath this vast work and finished effort of man's devotion, he saw the high altar, brilliant with lights, surmounted and enthroned by its panoply of clustering columns and towering cross; when, all around him, he was conscious of the hush and calmness of worship, and felt in his inmost being the sense of vastness, of splendour, and of awe;—he may be pardoned if, kneeling upon the polished floor, he conceived for the moment that this was the house of God, and that the gate of heaven was here.

Shorthouse's description of Inglesant in the Church of the Sancta Chiara (Ch. 35) is a representative example of that quiet intensity which he was capable of conveying in carefully wrought sentences which surge up frequently from the level of the narrative:

Inglesant passed up the Church towards the high altar, before which he knelt; and as he did so, a procession carrying the Sacrament, entered by another door, and advanced to the altar. . . . The low, melancholy miserere—half entreating, half desponding—spoke to the heart of man a language like its own; and as the theme was taken up by one of the organs, the builder's art and the musician's melted into one—in tier after tier of carved imagery, wave after wave of mystic sound. All conscious thought and striving seemed to fade from the heart, and before the altar and amid the swell of sound the soul lost itself, and lay silent and passive on the Eternal Love.[45]

More important, despite all its shortcomings as a novel judged in normal terms, *John Inglesant* is pervaded by a refreshing sincerity. There can be little doubt that Shorthouse, with the barriers of time and space removed, saw himself as the Inglesant he might have been, rejoicing in the beauty of the temporal world but honestly concerned with matters eternal. Not least of the gifts of *John Inglesant* to the reader is a sense of the attractiveness and rarefied pleasure of high thought and of the devout and noble life. In nineteenth-century, commercial Birmingham Shorthouse himself wanted to live such a life, and in some measure he succeeded.

Though the reluctant reader may protest that here is not "God's Plenty," he will nevertheless find "loaves and fishes" adequate for the needs of the day. The only piece of safe critical ground was pointed out by the assessor who remarked that *John Inglesant* is "a book of strange and rare quality, unreadable by some people, to others one of major importance." [46] John Ruskin wrote to Miss Beever that he found *John Inglesant* "harder than real history and of no mortal use—I couldn't read four pages of it." [47] Andrew Lang remarked that "by very considerable exertions I managed to avoid perusal of 'John Inglesant.' " [48] Samuel Butler was "seldom more displeased with any book." [49] However, many felt otherwise. By 1880 the impact of eighteenth-century Methodism which flowered into the Evangelical movement was evident from an increase in the number and size of the dissenting church bodies and in the development of a vocal Evangelical party in the Church of England. The Catholic Emancipation Bill (1829) and the appointment of Cardinal Wiseman as Catholic Archbishop of Westminster (1850) aroused in Roman Catholics hopes of expanding influence. But in Anglicans and Dissenters the same events excited an apprehension of possible Catholic domination. The mid-century Oxford movement by precipitating the ritualist debate had been divisive in effect. The embittered parties, fearing Roman Catholic encroachment, viewed with alarm the loss of prominent Anglicans like John Henry Newman to the Church of Rome.

Certainly in the supercharged atmosphere of 1880 *John Inglesant* could find favor, for it touched on a matter even more important to the Victorians than a healthy economy, an expanding merchant marine, or an enlarging empire. It examined their religion. In the tumult of grieved and angry voices Shorthouse's quiet voice spoke out for a traditional church, but, above all, for an *English* church. Herbert Hensley Henson speaks for many when he recalls the reception of *John Inglesant* in the 1880s: "I read the literature of the Oxford Movement and shared the general enthusiasm for *John Inglesant*. The conception of a National Church, Catholic and free, appealed to my historic sense, to my patriotism and to my local loyalty. I became an ardent advocate of the Establishment." [50]

Until Mrs. Humphry Ward's *Robert Elsmere* (1888) no novel of its kind was to provoke so much animated discussion, so much affection and hostility, as *John Inglesant*.

CHAPTER 4

Descent: The Later Novels

S HORTHOUSE evidently felt that he had not been able to say all he wanted to say in *John Inglesant*, for the novels which followed are what nowadays would be called spinoffs, dilations of ideas which had been touched on or suggested but not adequately developed in *John Inglesant*. In the later novels he forsook the large canvas of *John Inglesant* and daubed daintily on smaller areas with paler colors.

I The Little Schoolmaster Mark
(1883–85)

Shorthouse wrote to George Macmillan (10 February 1883): "I am much interested by what you tell me about the new magazine [*English Illustrated Magazine*]. I have an idea for a German story in my head which I think a 'great genius' might make something very good of. I fear I shall not be equal to it but if I succeed you shall have the offer of it." [1] On holiday in April, writing to Macmillan from Exmouth, he indicates his progress with the tale: "I am trying my hand at what I first meant to be a magazine philosophical tale but what I think I will probably develop into a book of, perhaps, the size of The Beleaguered City. I do not know if I can manage it, and at any rate it will take all my time for some months. . . ." [2] But by the end of August the tale must have been completed or so far advanced that he could cautiously agree with Frederick Macmillan: "I shall not object to my tale appearing in the new magazine as you wish it so much. . . . It *must* however appear as a *whole*. It would not bear breaking up. Its effect would be utterly spoiled. I am very glad that you like it. I am very well satisfied with it myself." [3] Macmillan agreed with him. The story was of such a nature and such a length that, like the seamless robe, it could not without damage be divided into instalments. In October 1883 Macmillan published ten thousand copies of the "philosophical tale," and it did appear intact in the contemporary (November) issue of Macmillan's *English Illustrated Magazine*. The lovers of *John Inglesant* must have been eager for more from Shorthouse's pen, for *The Little Schoolmaster Mark* sold rapidly. Another five thousand copies were printed in December.

The public reception of the tale was rather mixed, comment ranging all the way from the *Academy's* almost reckless "such a story as the Little Schoolmaster Mark is worth a dozen first rate novels" [4] to the *Westminster Review's* ruthlessly blunt "to poor mundane critics like ourselves it has the effect of being 'some such thing to no such purpose.'" [5] But Vernon Lee [Violet Paget], who earlier had not liked *John Inglesant*, and still refused to be charmed, unbent sufficiently to give little Mark a friendly pat. Canon Alfred Ainger, who earlier had liked *John Inglesant*, was inspired to preach a sermon on little Mark. When he sent Shorthouse an extract from the sermon, a cheerful interpretation of the tale, an exchange of letters ensued between author and interpreter about the meaning of the story. Canon Boyd Carpenter's enthusiasm carried him even further than Ainger's, for he wrote a continuation of the tale which he sent to Shorthouse (7 March 1884). Another exchange of letters resulted. Mrs. Russell Gurney, whom Shorthouse had met on one of his holidays at Malvern, sent him a detailed allegorical interpretation which must have startled the author. [6] It can be safely said, then, that the tale was neither universally honored nor consistently interpreted. But it was not ignored, and when after Shorthouse's death all his work was reviewed *Part I* of *The Little Schoolmaster Mark* was assigned a place next to *John Inglesant*.

If Shorthouse was satisfied with *The Little Schoolmaster Mark*, the correspondence must have roused some misgivings in his mind about his effectiveness to communicate. He was tolerant enough to admit that a work of art might be variously interpreted, but naturally would have preferred that he should be clearly understood. He must, however, have had doubts (or plans) from the beginning, for shortly after the publication of *The Little Schoolmaster Mark* (and the resulting correspondence) he informed Macmillan that he was "dimly groping after a second part of Little Mark." [7] In fact, a week or so earlier he had expressed to Boyd Carpenter a desire to clarify the meaning of the tale by writing a second part. [8] The correspondence which developed from the publication of *The Little Schoolmaster Mark* seems to have been helpful to the groper, for on 18 December 1883 he modestly comments to Lady Welby: "I am beginning to feel my way dimly towards a second part, if by any help or insight I can get from others I should be able to do it," [9] and writing to Edmund Gosse, also in December, he twice mentions that he is still groping.[10] By July 1884 he was able to write to Frederick Macmillan: "I have completed the second part of 'Little Schoolmaster Mark'. . . . It is not quite as long as the first part. I do not know whether you will think it best to publish it separately or to add it to the sheets already printed for the first part. I should think the latter would be best. I think it will be a much better book." [11] *Part II* of *The Little Schoolmaster Mark* was published by Macmillan, with an initial issue of two thousand copies, December 1884. In March 1885 parts *I* and *II* were issued in one volume only slightly shorter in length than Mrs. Oliphant's *A Beleaguered City* (1879).[12] But whether by pursuing Part I with Part II Shorthouse got "a much better book" was not so easily demonstrable.

Mark is a tailor's son, village-bred and educated, physically delicate, emotionally sensitive, imaginative, even dreamy, inordinately pious in a simple, childlike way, and teacher of the village children. In April 1750, at fifteen, he is wrenched from his restricted but congenial surroundings, and, as tutor to the Prince's children, thrust into a new and for him terrifying world, the Italianate court of a German princeling. He is leaving behind, as he thinks, "all that is fair and beautiful, and going to that which is false and garish and unkind" (15).[13] Although not unkindly treated, in his few weeks at the court Mark is shaken by the "falseness and frivolity" about him; he is oppressed by unaccustomed doubts; he is tortured by a perplexity incomprehensible to him. Unhappy himself, he gradually becomes aware nonetheless that among the court actors and the "actors of the Court" none is happy. He is anxious to return to his village. While despondently wandering in the palace garden, he is uncomprehendingly caught up in an extempore play devised as a diversion for the bored Princess. Terrified, he accidentally falls from the platform to his death on the ground below. So ends *Part I* of *The Little Schoolmaster Mark*.

Shorthouse subtitled the tale "A Spiritual Romance." The faint, romantic narrative line can indicate little of the spiritual freight he apparently meant the tale to carry. Inglesant's inconclusive conversation with the Cardinal in *John Inglesant* (Ch. 23) had touched on "life as a fine art," "life as a game of cards," "life as a spectacle in 'theatro ludus,' " "life as a rehearsal." Scattered through the Italian section of *John Inglesant*, the theater scenes, the carnival crowds, and the masquers in "the brilliant phantasia of life" obligingly performed their limited functions in the pattern of the novel but left some important questions only suggested or half-answered. In *The Little Schoolmaster Mark* Shorthouse attempted to answer them. Whether or not he felt that the sprawling narrative of *John Inglesant* had made impossible a sharp focus on these questions is beyond proof. But in *The Little Schoolmaster Mark*, some ideas extracted from *John Inglesant* are condensed into a single theme. Use of a central metaphor—theater: reality and unreality—enabled him to focus on the problem: "What is the relation of religion and art?" and on its extension, the relation of religion to the art of life, "noble living."

Against the backdrop of the "theater of the court" and the court theater he manipulates rather simply a handful of sharply differentiated characters, artists of sorts, actors of sorts but all expressing a variety of attitudes toward life, art, and religion: Mark, an embodiment of simple faith, unspoiled piety, unworldliness; Ferdinand the Prince, "a beautiful soul manqué," a German dilettante with Italianate tastes, who views religion aesthetically; the Prince's sister Isoline who "*is* such a [beautiful] soul" ascetically devoted to good works; the Prince's wife Adelaide, "not a good woman," aggressively and emotionally antireligious and worldly; the Count, *cavaliere servente* of Adelaide, a more urbane expression of her worldliness but exhibiting a rationalistic worldliness of his own; the music master and his pupil Faustina Banti, a promising young singer; and Carricchio and his gay-sad troupe of travelling court players.

At the court innocent Mark is successively placed in contrast with the "un-innocent" world, and in scene after scene the clues to the direction and meaning of the tale are laid. First, on Mark's arrival at court the domestics strip him of his village homespun and array him uncomfortably in court attire, thus making him outwardly attractive but leaving him inwardly apprehensive. A little later, in the scene with Faustina, Mark is introduced to the world of art, as the voice of the talented young singer reveals to his unaccustomed ear the disturbing glories of music beyond the solemn measures of the Lutheran hymns he has been accustomed to (22). In the same scene two further clues are given: the death of her canary immediately and strangely brings something new into Faustina's singing; a little later, referring to the court play, she says to Mark, "You shall come on yourself sometime, just as you are" (31). In the scene which follows, Mark is further disturbed by the Prince's sophisticated theory of "noble living" and "necessary suffering." Implicit in the next scene, the scene with the actors, is the contrast between what Mark believes to be reality and the world of make-believe he witnesses. Again, as in the scene with Faustina, he is told: "If you would take a part [in the play] and keep your character throughout, it would be magnificent" (50–51). Carricchio, the actor-manager of the strolling players, expands the Prince's idea of "noble living": "There is no art without life and no life without art. . . . There must be a higher art that surpasses the realism of life—a divine art which is not life but fashions life" (54–55). But the acting terrifies Mark and the secular music disturbs him, fills him with a sense of evil he feels he must escape from. His simple, unreasoned faith shattered by vague and gnawing doubt, he escapes to the forest where he accidentally meets Isoline whose idea of "noble living" (in contrast to her brother's) is the life of self-denial. "The good are not happy," she reflects sadly, "and the happy are not good" (73). The "good" Mark, unhappy, discovers that the "good" Isoline also is unhappy, that her self-denial and self-righteous devotion to good works cannot assure happiness. Mark wishes desperately to return to his village, but Isoline tells him return is impossible: "All are changed somewhat since you came. . . . You have passed as you say, the golden gates into an enchanted world; you have known good and evil; you have tasted of the fruit of the so-called Tree of Life; you cannot go back to the village. . . . Do not be afraid to die. Instead of your form and voice there will be remembrance and remorse. . . . The body of the sown grain is transfigured into the flower of a spiritual life, and from the dust is raised a mystic presence that can never fade. Do not be afraid to die" (79–80). Gethsemane Redux.

Mark reluctantly returns to the court. In the scene with the Prince's wife Mark is assailed by antireligious intellectualism as she, Adelaide, viciously attacks his faith "infected with the superstitions of the past" (87) and sneers at his belief in God, heaven and hell. The Count follows her assault with a more urbane attack on Mark's belief in the existence and nature of God. Mark, unable to retaliate with satisfactory intellectual arguments for his faith, feels so "emptied and vacant, he [can] not even think of God" (94). From the Prince's mouth, however, comes eloquently the refutation which Mark is incapable of uttering, but which Shorthouse evidently felt had to be made.

In the concluding chapter, the play scene, which culminates in the death of Mark, draws together the tagged strings from the previous scenes. The "actors of the Court" are masked observers of the court actors' theatrical spectacle of symbolical sacrificial suffering and death. Into this scene Mark is thrust to suffer and die. The court unmasks; the play is over.

A twentieth-century reader trained to find the Christ figure in unlikely places should be able to complain only that Shorthouse planted the figure too obviously. "All are changed somewhat since you came," Isoline had said earlier. Mark's death is sacrificial; through his death many are saved. Shorthouse in this tale seems to be arguing none too clearly that there is a significant distinction between religious and unreligious art, that there is necessarily a distinction between artistic and inartistic religion, and there should therefore be a desirable, cohesive relationship among art, religion ,and life. He seems to conclude that the "noble life," the "divine art," the highest achievement of man, must not only include religion but must be dominated by it. Writing to Boyd Carpenter (15 September 1883) he states the view as a question: "Is religion always to be a stranger and alien from life's Feast?" [14] Writing to Alfred Ainger two months later and using the same metaphor he is more expansive: "May it not be a mission—as it is to show what life *may* be—to show what religion *might* be?—not as an outcast or alien from life's feast, but as the honored and presiding guest." [15] Religion, then, is not only a part of life, not an adjunct, but the *presiding*, the dominating, the shaping force of life.

Shorthouse's normal manner of character creation has some pertinence here. Although the character of Mark is really quite different from that of the eighteenth-century German pietist Heinrich Jung-Stilling (1740–1817), Shorthouse in *The Little Schoolmaster Mark* drew generously on Stilling's *Autobiography* for some details of scene and character. [16] What seems to have been unnoticed by his critics—the ones who deplore his borrowings—is the significance of Stilling's reputation as a healer, a specialist in cataract operations, a man who restores sight. It is only a step from Stilling to Mark whose death clears the vision of the court. It is only another step, and an easy one, from Mark to that great Healer of the blind whom Mark can be said to represent.

In a slightly different manner, by combining a hint from Vernon Lee's *Studies of the Eighteenth Century in Italy* (1880) [17] with a hint from the life of Faustina Hasse-Bordoni, the Venetian soprano,

Shorthouse gives significance to the fictional character he created in Faustina Banti, the first to be redeemed by the death of Mark. The promising young cafe singer whom he found in Vernon Lee's *Studies* he combined with the nobly born Faustina Bordoni (1700–81), a favorite of the Viennese Court, by some considered the greatest soprano of the eighteenth century. Though there are no known dead canaries in Faustina Bordoni's background what was important for Shorthouse's purpose in the novel was not so much the quantity as the kind of acclaim Faustina Bordoni received. Of her London debut, 5 May 1726, Dr. Burney says, "She, in a manner, invented a new kind of singing. . . ." Another [Arteaga] speaks of her "new and brilliant passages of embellishment." [18] In *The Little Schoolmaster Mark* the death of the canary brings something inexplicably new into Faustina Banti's singing; the death of Mark does even more.

It does not greatly matter how much detail Shorthouse got from Vernon Lee for creating Carricchio and his travelling troupe—and he got quite a bit—but it is quite possible that it is really the theatrical group in Goethe's *Wilhelm Meister* which gives significance to the central metaphor (theater) in *The Little Schoolmaster Mark*. From *Wilhelm Meister* Shorthouse extracts a thematic idea, "noble living," which he works out through the metaphor of theater. "The theatre," Goethe says (in *Book I*, Chapter 16) "has often been at variance with the pulpit; they ought not, I think, to quarrel. How much is it to be wished, that in both the celebration of nature and of God were entrusted to none but men of noble minds." He continues in the next chapter: "Each man has his fortune in his hands as an artist has a piece of rude matter which he is to fashion to a certain shape. But the art of living is like all arts: the capacity alone is born with us; it must be learned and practised with incessant care." It can be inferred from *The Little Schoolmaster Mark* that "the art of living" "learned and practised with incessant care" is achievable only "by men of noble mind." Religion and art are not mutually exclusive; they supplement and complement each other.

Though they are very different from each other in many ways *John Inglesant* and *The Little Schoolmaster Mark* touch on one point. In neither are the characters three-dimensional, and are probably not intended to be. In *John Inglesant* they are bright two-dimensional figures in a rich tapestry; in *The Little Schoolmaster Mark* they are shadowy forms behind a gauze curtain. They are real only insofar as their voices are real—or believable. Their bodies

do not matter except as the shells for "walking ideas." The mood
pieces of *John Inglesant* were only part of a larger whole; *The Little
Schoolmaster Mark* is itself a mood piece, suggestive, breathing an
old-world charm. But occasionally one cannot escape the impression
that the author, listening to his own music, intent on euphony, has
allowed the meaning to evaporate.

In *Part II* Mark is dead but his influence persists. Standing
remorseful over the body of Mark, Prince Ferdinand and his sister
Isoline realize that neither the aesthetic life nor the ascetic life is
enough, "nothing profits save the Divine Humanity, which,
through the mystery of Sacrifice, has entered the unseen" (128).
Ferdinand rouses himself to an interest in affairs of state; Isoline
disbands her religious house; Adelaide is urged to take belated
interest in her husband and children. Faustina's singing "improves
day by day." The Maestro is inspired to compose his masterpiece,
an opera based on the death of Mark, with Faustina in the leading
role. Even the cynical Carricchio becomes wholesomely cheerful.

Thus, in the first two chapters of *Part II* the point implicit in *Part
I* has been reemphasized, but Shorthouse struggles on for another
seven chapters. The Maestro, depressed when his opera is pushed
off the boards, wishes to leave the spiritually deadening court so
that he may search for a city where his music will be valued.
Faustina, who has fallen in love with him, loyally insists on
accompanying him. The Prince, in love with Faustina, bribes the
Maestro to reject her and even invites aid from the cynically wise
Carricchio who warns him: "Let her alone. . . . She alone of all of
us . . . has solved the riddle which that boy, whom we killed, was
sent to teach us. She alone has made her life an art, for she alone has
found that art is capable of sacrifice. She alone of all of us has based
her art upon nature and upon love" (183). The Prince nevertheless
tries to persuade Faustina to remain at court, but "her splendid eyes
expanded to their full orbit [as Daisy Ashford, the nine-year-old
author of *The Young Visiters*, might say] flashed upon the Prince
with a look of astonishment and reproach" and she utters "but one
word—'Prince!' " The word and tone strike "upon the conscience
and cultured taste of the Prince" and he realizes he has "tarnished
the fair dream of finished art which he had conceived it possible to
perfect" (213). Faustina after "some time in a sort of swoon,"
wanders into a palace chamber where she finds Isoline playing
Mark's Lutheran hymn on the harpsichord. On hearing Faustina's
tale of her encounter with the Prince, Isoline soothes her:

He [Mark] was truly a wonderful child. A very Christchild . . . in his simple life and death. . . . The lives of all of us seem different for his life—changed since his death. As for me, since his life crossed my path I have seen more . . . of the mercy of God and of Christ working in paths and among lives where I never thought to look for it before. . . . Do you not see . . . the blessing it has been to my brother . . . for the desire that he felt, surely a noble one, to refine the life of art by the sacred touch of religion—the effort that he made, though it seemed a failure—has tonight proved his own salvation through you. . . . You alone possessed the perfect gift of nature—the untainted well-spring of natural life—which assimilated Mark's spirit, and reproduced his life within your own. . . . Your little brother that died was not without his work, and the canary even was the type of a nobler life, even as Mark's death was the type of a nobler death. In strange and unlooked-for ways the mission of sacrifice and love fulfils itself and . . . we can never realize the blessing we have derived, the changed aspect of the race we have inherited from the Cross of Christ. (217–20)

The following evening at the court ball the Princess is informed that her husband has disappeared. Returning to her suite she comes upon her weeping children who tell her that they "both dreamed the same dream" of Mark's leading them through a garden, a burial ground, and to a Calvary where they see their parents dead. Mark vanishes, Christ descends from the Cross, the parents are resurrected, and Christ, too, vanishes. Princess Adelaide gets a "sense of strange forces and influences," a sense of "how poor and bare her life ha[s] been . . . how unblessed by the purest, the truest art—the art of pathos and of love" (232). She joins Faustina and Isoline at mass. After mass she receives a note from her missing husband saying that he has joined the religious community of Count Zinzendorf at Herrnhuth: "We have been dead, and laid upon a bier; but we will, please God, live hereafter for the children and the Christ" (238).

Only the most intrepid reader will thread this maze of art and religion. And only devotion to Shorthouse will prompt him to repeat the adventure. What was unclear, but at least suggestive, in *Part I*, becomes confusing, even murky, in *Part II*. If, as he said, Shorthouse in *Part II* was "groping," he apparently did not notice that he was falling over his pen. To Lady Welby he could confidently remark (23 November 1884) that Parts I and II "should be read together to be understood." [19] A year later he can say to Gosse (20 October 1885): "I don't think that *Little Mark* is sufficiently appreciated and am inclined to wait till people wake up

to estimate that work." [20] Inexplicably, Gosse seems to have agreed
with him.

II   Sir Percival: A Story of the Past
and of the Present
(1886)

In the interval between *John Inglesant* and *The Little Schoolmaster Mark* Shorthouse had written "The Agnostic at Church" for the
Nineteenth Century (April 1882), an introductory essay to George
Herbert's *The Temple* (1882), and a short preface to a selection from
Molinos's *Spiritual Guide* (1883). He had also written a number of
short stories for *Macmillan's Magazine* and had begun a "romance of
the Italian Renaissance." To Macmillan he writes (14 December
1884); "I *had* a copy of Bocalioni [sic] when I was writing *John
Inglesant*, and had read it with some care. . . . I had also a copy of
Castiglione's *Cortegiano*, which I also read, though, as far as I
remember, it is a dull, stupid book. I do not think I shall want either
for my *Romance of the Renaissance*, which . . . has made a
beginning, and is already in some shape. I have plenty of
materials—too many in fact. . . . My tale will be very *difficult* and
take a long time, but we must not despair." [21] Two months later (15
February 1885) he postscripts his compliment to Lady Welby on her
Echo of Larger Life: "I am working at a romance of the period of the
later Italian Renaissance; whether it will ever come to anything I do
not know, but I find it immensely interesting. The conflicting
aspects of thought and feeling are wonderfully various and
graphic." [22] The following month, writing again to Macmillan (17
March 1885), apropos of having sent a copy of *The Little
Schoolmaster Mark* to John Addington Symonds at Davos, he
remarks: "I hope to get some help from him [Symonds] as to the
Renaissance Romance, which he is kind enough to take an interest
in, but I cannot say that I get on so well in it as I had hoped; it is a
very complicated subject." [23] Seven months later, replying to
Edmund Gosse (20 October 1885) he says somewhat gloomily: "You
are very kind to ask about my work. I got some way into a romance
of the later Renaissance, 1490 to 1510, just before the French and
Germans broke in upon Italy, and had got the characters pretty well
in hand, but became oppressed by the greatness of the subject, and
it is laid by indefinitely. It interested me very much, and I had some
very nice letters from J. Addington Symonds." [24] Then there is

silence, but evidently "with things going on in it," for he suddenly announces (25 June 1886): "*Sir Percival* is quite ready, and I will send the MS up when I have gone through it once more." [25] How far Shorthouse had progressed in his "romance of the Renaissance," or precisely what difficulties he encountered in its construction is not known; presumably it was snuffed out by something more pressing or more manageable in *Sir Percival*, which was published in September 1886 (thirty-five hundred copies), with two quick reprints in October (four thousand) and December (four thousand) before the year was out; it was reprinted the next year and at intervals until 1910.

Shorthouse had dedicated *John Inglesant*, not to his wife as one might have expected, but to Rawdon Levett, his longtime best friend in Birmingham; *The Little Schoolmaster Mark* he had dedicated to Lady Alwyne Compton, aristocratic wife of the Bishop of Ely whose acquaintance he had made in 1882. *Sir Percival* was dedicated to Canon Francis Morse who had baptized Shorthouse and his wife in 1861—rather belatedly as it turned out, for Morse, whom he considered his "spiritual father," had died in mid-September before *Sir Percival* was off the press. Nevertheless, the dedication of the book to Morse is some indication of the seriousness with which Shorthouse regarded his latest creation.

Though there was the normal amount of favorable comment such as the *Westminster Review*'s (January 1887) kindly "quintessence of purity and delicacy of thought and sentiment," [26] the reception of *Sir Percival*, despite healthy sales, must have been a test of Shorthouse's cultured calm. The writer of the *Saturday Review* (27 November 1886) spoke for many of the other reviewers, in sentences of alternate praise and blame, when he remarked that *Sir Percival* was "an imperfect and undigested book . . . containing indeed some passages of great beauty and animated by a noble and admirable spirit, but not artistically conceived, much less artistically finished." [27] The *Academy* (13 November 1886) had already two weeks earlier fearlessly damned the book as "decidedly silly and decidedly dull," [28] and was supported the following month by *Blackwood*'s (December 1886) with an indignant protest that "it is a kind of insult to the public, which has been so appreciative of his efforts, to present them with such a mystic piece of false sentiment and monkish religiousness as this." [29] But Shorthouse had some consolation. He wrote to Maurice Macmillan:

I am very glad to hear of the successful sale. I did not expect the Reviewers to be in sympathy with 'Sir Percival.' I receive every day most gratifying letters from all parts of the country from entire strangers to me. We thought the 'Pall Mall' very clever and amusing. "Vernon Lee" in the Academy was disappointing; she began well but afterwards was deficient in originality and staying powers. The Athenaeum was the most wretched. No one can guess what is meant by 'an effort after minute accuracy of detail almost equal to Father Holt's in Esmond, with a want of success even more conspicuous than that of the worthy Jesuit'. Such a sentence as this on the first page of the Athenaeum. . . . Most of the reviewers [sic] are misstatements. The things found fault with are not in the book at all. One man evidently never heard of the Bourbon Restoration 1815–30.[30]

When he sent the manuscript of *Sir Percival* to Macmillan (25 June) Shorthouse had added a cautionary note: "I decidedly *object* to its first appearing in the magazine [*English Illustrated Magazine*]; you will see for yourself that it would be quite unsuitable. It is, in fact, almost a devotional book, and contains a complete sermon."[31] And after publication of *Sir Percival* in September, writing to Canon Ainger, he remarks with a somewhat defensive obscurity: "Except in those parts where *art* is impossible in a novel with a purpose, as all my books are, I take it that *Sir Percival* is *too* good art. It would have been understood better in some quarters if the art had been more openly shown."[32]

The narrator in *Sir Percival*, Constance Lisle, early-orphaned, deeply religious, grows up in quiet old Kingswood with her great-aunt and uncle, the Duke and Duchess of Cressy and de la Pole. When she is about twenty-two, a cousin, Percival Massareen, an instinctive gentleman, heir to "several millions," arrives, and she falls in love with him. Shortly thereafter when another cousin arrives, Virginia Clare—an alarmingly energetic, freethinking socialist glowing aggressively with ideas for social reform—Percival falls in love with her. Virginia dies a few weeks later of a fever contracted while nursing a woman deserted by plague-fearing villagers. When, after Virginia's death, Percival offers marriage to Constance she refuses him. He goes to Africa, distinguishes himself as a soldier, and dies in an unsuccessful attempt to rescue an English bishop from hostile natives.

Again the slight story line suggests little of the real quality of the novel. Padded with careful pictures of manorial halls, literary tidbits from Malory and the poets, and a lengthy sermon, the tale has considerably more weight than the skeleton promises to bear.

Concealed art (as he thought) was less likely to have accounted for the lack of popularity of *Sir Percival* than Shorthouse's failure to deal with the narrative problems which he had encountered in its construction. Sending a copy of *Sir Percival* to Lady Welby (5 November 1886) Shorthouse remarks: "*Sir Percival* is perhaps as bold a venture as a writer ever wished. The effort to describe a conscious existence within the grace of God is perhaps an impossible one." [33] If he considered *Sir Percival* a bold venture and the task he had set himself an impossible one, he complicated matters almost enough to assure miscarriage. The subtitle "A Story of the Past and of the Present" suggests a difficulty he may or may not have foreseen. *John Inglesant* had been a story of the seventeenth century with implications for the nineteenth in which it was written and in which the purported editor of the memoir is speaking, but it is a straightforward narrative. *The Little Schoolmaster Mark* is a mood-piece set in the eighteenth century with unbelievable characters but a believable social setting. In *Sir Percival* the narrator is presumably an old lady writing in 1920 of events which had been contemporary in 1885, but which had distinctly medieval overtones (or undertones). In fairness to Shorthouse it can be reasonably supposed that he hoped with this telescoping to suggest the timelessness of "existence within the grace of God," to point to something permanent in the human condition. He could have had no notion, despite the rapid changes in his own time, of the proximity of 1920 to the atomic age. Therefore in *Sir Percival* Shorthouse's thrusting of Malory into a modern setting was bound to be bothersome to the nineteenth-century reader already familiar with "Idylls of the King." It is even more bothersome to the reader of the twentieth, who though aware of the periodic revival and refurbishing of Arthurian materials in his own time, can find in *Sir Percival* neither romance nor reality.

In *John Inglesant*, Geoffrey Monk, the editor-narrator, though an obvious narrative device, is credible as a sort of character rather sketchily drawn because he is telling someone else's story. In *Sir Percival* Shorthouse took a miscalculated risk in funneling Percival's story through Constance, for Constance, though appropriately named for her role, is at a disadvantage from the beginning. She is telling her own story rather than Percival's. She is the channel of grace through which Percival is led to sight of the Grail. Her function as narrator is clear enough in the epigraph from Malory which graces the title-page: "[So God help me sayd Sir Percivale] I sawe a damoysel as me thoughte, alle in whyte with a vessel in both handes, and forth with al I was hole." Constance is the "damoysel" and represents even the Grail itself, the vision of which makes Percival "hole." To force Constance, the instrument of Percival's salvation, to tell the story with ladylike reticence and without egotism and conceit pushes her unfairly to the brink of priggishness. Even her appropriately Victorian feminine self-effacement, "I am only a woman and my opinion is of little worth" (15), is insufficient to save her. In an unenviable position, covertly revealing, overtly concealing, Constance fails to convince the reader of her reality; an irritating self-consciousness does not prevent her from being too remotely wraithlike for comprehension. By contrasting her with Virginia Clare, her freethinking cousin and rival for Percival's love, Shorthouse intended no doubt to show Constance to advantage—he was always a bit condescending about female agnostics, socialists and dissenters—but somehow in juxtaposition to Virginia's forth-rightness, energy, and moral fervor, the nerveless piety of Constance seems pale and ineffectual. Constance, the "beautiful soul" (a kind of half-sister to Isoline in *The Little Schoolmaster Mark*) sacrifices her love that Percival "should become a great and a good man" (259), that he might be made "hole," "a knight of the Holy Fellowship of the Table, not of Arthur, but of Christ" (267). Virginia, the agnostic, sacrifices her life in an act of humanitarian service at a sickbed, an act which Constance nobly commends, admitting with a faint smugness that in death Virginia has "gone to that God whom she died serving, though she fancied that she did not know Him" (259). Though very different from each other, both Virginia and Constance admonish Percival in similar manner, "Only be true" (260). Percival as good as lost to her, Constance says generously to Virginia, "He is another man since he loved you. It was just what was wanted to draw him upwards" (195). Later, dying in delirium, Percival has difficulty separating the figures of Constance and Virginia, and it is Constance, who, unconvincing as she is, is given the stage to herself: "Who is this seated in her saddle beneath the rustling branches of the oak? She turns her head towards me—Virginia? No, it is Constance—Constance with the pleading eyes" (298). Virginia had elevated Percival with her love, but Constance leads him to the Grail.

By setting up Percival Massareen as a nineteenth-century counterpart of Malory's Sir Percivale, Shorthouse managed by constant suggestion of the parallel to impose a moderate greatness on what is otherwise a commonplace character. Impressive most for his lack of vices, Percival, silent, but supposedly thoughtful, languishes between two women who in their different ways uplift him to be "one of the best knightes of the world that at that time was, and in whome the veray feythe stood moost in" (98). He arrives at Kingswood as a handsome boy, with no ideas of consequence and no promise of greatness, but protected from well-meant blundering by the poise of his "class." Shorthouse may, however, be pardoned, despite the obscurity and self-satisfaction of his remark, for having said that *Sir Percival* was "*too* good art," for the reader finds that the end of the novel has been forecast from the beginning, and that Percival Massareen has been carefully built from a very ordinary young man into a modern knight, and that what he does makes the greatest Shorthousean sense. Long before Percival appears in the novel, what first strikes the reader as an unnecessary bit of imperial drumbeating and a lingering on the virtues of the "thin red line," a pride in "the class of England . . . without whom the world's victories would never have been won" (16) turns out to be one of the pieces that fall into place in the final pages of the novel. Early in the novel the reader is invited to the little church in which there is a "small east window" with its "Parcivale," "one of a series of which it is the sole survivor" (33). Though they have other functions in the novel, the allusions to the seventeenth-century Jansenist community of Port-Royal near Paris tirelessly emphasize the ideal of the "gentleman and saint" and repeatedly insist on the efficacy of frequent communion. Charles Simeon, at Cambridge, so important in the life of De Lys,[34] is "a remarkable instance of the combination of religion with high breeding." Repeated snatches from Malory gradually encrust the unpromising Percival with enough armor to make him as gentleman and saint a modern knight "not of Arthur, but of Christ," a sort of John Inglesant without Inglesant's intellect. In light of all this, the death scene at the end of the novel, which has so often been ridiculed by hurried reviewers, is quite logical within the pattern of the novel. Percival and the Bishop, both doomed, take their last communion together. They have no wine. They resort to "a tradition of the Middle Ages . . . that if a man was dying on a field of battle, and if he eat three blades of grass with intention, he received the sacrament though other priest there were none" (294). The sacramentalism of *John Inglesant* was one of the strands unobtrusively tied into the final statement. In *Sir Percival* it is part of the climax—as if both novels had been directed to the same end.

Though he did not have sacramentalism in mind, one reviewer sensed the kinship: *"John Inglesant* is the development of a conviction. *Sir Percival* is the consummation of the same conviction." [35]

The plot, if one can speak of a plot, unwinds slowly, almost lethargically, with a serene monotony appropriate to a novel in which the narrative line is merely a device for holding together a number of Shorthouse's favorite ideas. The pace is kept at a slow walk by the insertion of long, careful descriptions of manorial gardens, churches, ruins; illustrative anecdotes and anecdotes within anecdotes; frequent and occasionally long, supportive quotations from Malory, Keble, Arnold, Mrs. Hemans; excerpts from Handel's *Messiah*; and near the end of the novel a fifteen-page sermon. Though all these are effectively used in creation of mood, they discourage any briskness of pace.

But it is with the setting—which is not only a stage for the characters—that Shorthouse has taken the greatest pains. The setting is not so much a place as a force which shapes the characters. Shorthouse's devotion to "old houses," as exhibited by some of his unpublished essays written for the Friends' Essay Society, is no mere romanticizing about departed glories. It expresses a belief in the "spirit of place." The emphasis in the description of old Kingswood is intentionally on the "quiet and holy influence of the place" (263), and the characters thrust into this setting are influenced by it—the Duke and Duchess by habit, Constance by inclination, Percival and Virginia in spite of themselves. The clock seems to have stopped at "ten to three," and only what is timeless seems to matter. The old Duke, with the reminders of the past about him, lives on as his ancestors did, conscious of the obligations of rank and culture but not much interested in the world without. Constance, though a dependent, develops a spiritual security. Percival is stirred to a consciousness of mission. Even Virginia's iconoclastic views of class and privilege are absorbed by the place and negated by her "noble" sacrifice.

But it is not the pace of the novel, nor the imperfect realization of its characters, nor even a lack of sympathy with the idea underlying the novel which most discourages the reader from taking a second look at *Sir Percival*. The bulk of *John Inglesant* made possible easy burial of impertinent material; the brevity of *The Little Schoolmaster Mark, Part I* made impossible retention of such material without damage to the gauzy fabric. But *Sir Percival* was just long enough to permit a bit of authorial self-indulgence without great harm. Though the ideas are expressed through the mouths of characters, the voice is Shorthouse's, sometimes playful, sometimes dogmatic. Thus Constance comments gratuitously on the snobbery about "restored" armor, on the merits and demerits of Montaigne, Pascal, Scott, and G. P. R. James, on the history of Arthurian romance, on the dangers of horseback riding, and on the psychology of knitting. And by the following comment on education one is reminded that in the year previous to the publication of *Sir Percival* Shorthouse had for a fortnight allowed his name to stand for School Board election with the "Bible Eight" on the platform of "freedom for the teacher to teach the Bible as any other book": ". . . the fact was fully proved that it is only where religion sanctifies and purifies the heart and life that anything worthy of the name of education—that dare call itself the highest achievement of learning—can exist" (37). It is the voice of the man who wrote letters to the Birmingham papers on the same subject. The sermon which De Lys preaches in chapter 9 is only a variant of the Prince's speech in *The Little Schoolmaster Mark* (95). It is an unnecessary excursion, unless one can assume rather arbitrarily that Shorthouse felt he had made Virginia Clare too attractive and therefore had to insert the sermon as a gentlemanly refutation of all agnostics, female or otherwise. But Virginia Clare is also a Shelley-reading socialist, and therefore socialism—before she has even arrived—is treated like agnosticism, as a mere whimsicality. "It is impossible," says Lord Clare (only one of the numerous lords in the novels), "for a noble to lead a democracy. The moment you begin to reason and argue with people you may as well be a socialist at once" (113). It seems almost incomprehensible that a nineteenth-century novelist could dismiss agnosticism and socialism as if they were children's games which adults did not play.

One cannot avoid the conclusion that Shorthouse's muse was "in heav'n yclept" Euphonia, for he seems always to have written with one ear straining for sound. Even when he is most closely following his sources the textual changes he makes are usually not for accuracy's but for euphony's sake. Normally, his sentences move with a careful dignity and even beauty. Only a sleepy muse can account, however, for infelicities which destroy a character or scene. His fondness for the word "mystic," which is spattered through all the novels, in *Sir Percival* wearies the reader. There is an "awful and mystic apartment" (11), a "mystic depth of light and shadow" (31), a room with "mystic depths of shadow" (99), a "mystic sky-line in the distant south" (105), a "tone of mystical rhythm" (213), a "mystic doorway in the wall" (265). And Percival can never recover from the blow dealt him by one of his own remarks: "I am glad he [Malory's Sir Percivale] was so good a fellow as that. It is well to have a fellow like that of your name to follow."

III   A Teacher of the Violin and Other Tales
(1888)

In the postscript of a letter to Canon Ainger (2 October 1884) Shorthouse says: "The action and re-action of feeling on musical tone has long been a subject of interest to me. I am certain that some time a *great musical tale* will be written by someone, and will be a revelation to all of us." [36] He closes his letter to Edmund Gosse the following year with "Some day a great musical and art novel will be written which will be a revelation to mankind; I want the technical knowledge to do it." [37] Complimenting Mrs. Humphry Ward on her *Miss Bretherton* (1884), he remarks, "I have always believed that some great romance (my instinct shows me a *musical* Romance) but at any rate, some great art Romance, will be written, which will be a revelation to mankind. Such books as 'Miss Bretherton' are delightful as means and incentives towards this much to be desired end." [38] But writing to Gosse five years later (20 July 1890) apropos of *Dominant Seventh*, a musical story, he indicates that he is still "always on the lookout for *the* great *Musical Romance*." [39]

However, in the meantime, he must have tried his pen at shaping into a novel the idea of "action and re-action of feeling on musical tone." If his tale did not turn out to be the musical romance which was to be a "revelation to mankind," he could nevertheless write to Maurice Macmillan (27 July 1887) with becoming modesty: "I have finished a little German tale on the violin with which I am fairly well satisfied. It would be suitable, I think, either for the old magazine or for the English Illustrated and if either of the Editors like it I shall be glad to send it. I think it is worth £75. These things are not easy to write and it is impossible to write many of them." But he added, "I should be very glad if you would see your way afterwards to print it, with the two novelettes that appeared in *Macmillan's* in a little book. I am so constantly having inquiries about these latter." [40] The following January he wrote again to Maurice Macmillan:

I send you the three tales from *Macmillan*. My wife wishes me to suggest to you that we should publish "Ellie" with them. We printed 500 copies which have all been sold at Bazaars, etc.—and we are often asked for it—it would make up for the shortness of the Marquis story which is much shorter than the other two: but I shall be quite satisfied with whatever you decide to do. My friend Rawdon Levett, whom you know, wishes me to reprint the *Apologue*. . . . I leave the decision in this case, also, entirely to you. I expect to have some verbal alterations to make in the *Teacher of the Violin* but these will be only slight, and can be done in proof. Hallam Tennyson will let me dedicate the book to him.[41]

"A Teacher of the Violin" appeared in *Macmillan's Magazine* November 1887. Shorthouse's wish to have his stories reprinted was fulfilled in March 1888 by Macmillan's accommodating but cautious issue of three thousand copies of *A Teacher of the Violin and Other Tales*, which was reissued only once more (in August 1891), with another two thousand copies. The "other tales" were "The Marquis Jeanne Hyacinthe de St. Palaye" (*Macmillan's Magazine* July 1882), a longer and better story, "The Baroness Helena von Saarfeld" (*Macmillan's Magazine* August 1882)—both swiftly pirated by G. G. Munro in New York—a slight tale, "Ellie: A Story of a Boy and Girl" (printed in Birmingham for private circulation, 1883), and a shorter piece, "An Apologue" from the *Nineteenth Century* (July 1882). The book was dedicated to the Hon. Hallam Tennyson.

In "A Teacher of the Violin," Otto, son of an eighteenth-century Bavarian village pastor, "from a little child . . . profoundly impressed by the sounds of nature" (7), begins "early to recognize the mysterious connection between sound and human feeling" (9). An aging countess to whom his father is chaplain takes a fancy to him and he becomes her adopted son, Otto von Saale, his future thus assured. She sends him to the university where under the tutelage of Veitch,[42] "teacher of the violin," and his pupil Adelheid, a professor's daughter who is reader and musical tutor of the Princess Cynthia, Otto becomes proficient on the violin. Adelheid falls in love with him; he falls in love with the Princess Cynthia. At a court performance Otto's inspired playing entrances the Princess with its "alluring lawlessness" (63), but also with "a sense of restraining, abiding, cultured harmony" (86). Disappointed and jealous when the Princess is betrothed to Prince von Schöngau, Otto wilfully neglects his music. But when the Princess tells him "you have taught me what I am, and you have shown me what I may become. You yourself will not fail," Otto offers himself to Adelheid and apparently lives happily ever after "a life that is in tune with the melodies of heaven, in tune because it is guided by a purer life, inspired by a loftier purpose than its own" (110). The music-enlightened Princess, later Queen, also does not fail; true to her rank, in the absence of her husband she saves the capital city from destruction by the Napoleonic army.

A summary, however, does not reveal much of the actual content of the story; it merely reveals its weaknesses. Shorthouse probably did not delude himself that he was writing the great "musical romance" which would "resolve the mysteries of life." In *John Inglesant* he had periodically taken short flights in which he tried to express the reasons for the effect of music on the human spirit, but somehow his thoughts on music were submerged in the mass of the book. In *The Little Schoolmaster Mark* he had ventured again on a small scale by narrowing the focus on a particular character. In "A Teacher of the Violin" he devotes the whole tale to an examination of the influence of music but suffocates the central idea by wrapping it into a love story. Such plot as the tale has is merely a device for holding together some random thoughts on music rather than a structure for organizing them into an effective and intelligible pattern.

He begins promisingly enough by imposing on the main character his own boyhood fascination with and fantasizing about the wind in the chimneypots at Moseley and the whispers in the reeds at Thimble Mill, his father's farm. So to Otto "the sounds of nature" become "a passion, a fascination, a haunting presence, and even a dread" (7)—one hears Shorthouse-the-lover-of-Wordsworth speaking. But there is something insufficient about the "untutored sounds of Nature," (13) so Otto is moved toward the organized sound of art. He is helped along by a flash of insight, "like a message from above," to the concept of "the true music which is not only heard by the spirit-born but is born of the spirit itself" (17). When he learns to play the violin, he concludes: "I delighted only in the fancy that I was a mere automaton, and that the pervading spirit that inspires man and breathes in Nature—was playing through my spirit upon the obedient strings" (26). But there is still something missing. That his "*forte* is expression" is pointed out repeatedly in the tale. It is, however, group-playing which is to be considered the real artistic expression, not the single note but the harmonious chord in which each note is in suitable relation to the other. And so, near the end of the tale, when, after a futile love for Cynthia, Otto has been long married to Adelheid, he can remark: "In the sustained and perfect harmonies that result from concord of full, pure, true notes, there is rest and peace for the wearied and troubled brain; and the harmonies of life, that absorb and hush the discord of the world, are heard only in the private walks and daily seclusion in which love and Christian purity delight. Both harmonies came to me through a teacher of the violin" (110–11). One may presume, then, that music was not the subject matter after all, but a metaphor; for, apart from the deliberately sly ambiguity of "teacher" (Veitch or Adelheid) the "violin" here is synonymous with Otto's heart.

In an article "The Humorous in Literature" which he had written for *Macmillan's Magazine* (March 1883), Shorthouse had praised Jean Paul Richter (1763–1825) as "the greatest and most perfect humorist." It is not surprising, therefore, that in the creation of the main character in "A Teacher of the Violin" he should have started with some nuggets mined from Jean Paul's *Autobiography* which prefaced the *Life of Jean Paul Richter*, a book Shorthouse owned. In "A Teacher of the Violin" the speaker in the two autobiographical chapters which flank the central chapter is Otto von Saale, who is, like Jean Paul, the music-loving son of a Lutheran clergyman. The surname of Jean Paul's friend and critic, Christian Otto, provides a properly Bavarian first name for Shorthouse's character. The surname "von Saale" he gets from the river Saale near Jean Paul's home. Otto's patron, the old Grafin von Wetstein to whom his father is chaplain, is the Baroness von Plotho to whom Jean Paul's father was chaplain. Otto's first visit to his future patron is similar to Jean Paul's visit to Zedwitz with his father. Jean Paul, too, in his university days in Leipzig, like Otto, lodged at the "Three Roses in the Peterstrasse."

On this base Shorthouse proceeds to build. He starts with himself, for Otto's meditation about "the wailing of the wind at night through the crevices of the high-pitched roof and panelled walls of the old parsonage" (10) is surely Shorthouse's memory of the nights at Moseley when he was recovering from typhus. Jean Paul's "to music was my soul, like my father's, everywhere open, and had for it a hundred Argus ears" [43] when it is applied to Otto's love of the sounds of nature, is given a Wordsworthian twist by Shorthouse and becomes "The sounds of nature were more even than this: they became a passion, a fascination, a haunting presence, and even a dread" (7).

From that point, Otto is on his own and one can detect

Shorthouse only in the language faintly reminiscent of the "musical passages" in *John Inglesant* and *The Little Schoolmaster Mark*. However, he does rather strangely exert himself at the beginning and the end of the tale by the use of some fragments from Falk's *Characteristics of Goethe*[44] (which Shorthouse also owned), for when Otto is theorizing on sound (11) he illustrates with an anecdote about Goethe's dislike of barking dogs. In the context of the *Characteristics* the anecdote is an interruption in a discussion on the immortality of the soul. In "A Teacher of the Violin" the dog anecdote is used to illustrate the irritation of continued noise, but Shorthouse, in fitting the anecdote almost verbatim into his narrative, neglects to omit some irrelevant matter. One can only suspect that pedantry blinded him to his own ineptitude. He fared better with the Princess Cynthia, whom he also borrowed from the *Characteristics*. The Grand-Duchess Louisa of Saxony-Weimar described by Falk in the *Characteristics* becomes the Princess Cynthia in "A Teacher of the Violin." Shorthouse uses her to give his tale a dramatic, well-executed ending; through her, too, he is able to emphasize the importance of rank in human affairs. As Princess Cynthia she had become conscious through Otto's music of the obligations of rank; as Queen she behaves in a crisis with the serene dignity of all Shorthousean aristocrats. If the text for *John Inglesant* and *The Little Schoolmaster Mark* has been changed, the sermon has not.

The "other tales" in the title of *A Teacher of the Violin and Other Tales* are "The Marquis Jeanne Hyacinthe de St. Palaye" and "The Baroness Helena von Saarfeld," for "Ellie" is too slight even for a tale and "An Apologue" is a mere sketch (a *jeu d'esprit*, he called it). "I send by this post," says Shorthouse writing to Macmillan (3 June 1882), "the mss. of the 'Two Tales.' In reading them over to my wife we both think it doubtful whether they had better be published just now. They differ so much from *John Inglesant* in that they have no moral purpose but are mere descriptions of life under certain forms." Six weeks later (23 July 1882) he remarks: "I have been rather nervous about these two tales which I let the *Magazine* have because Mr. Macmillan and Mr. Grove wished it. I take the first tale to illustrate the culture which comes from rank; the second, in August, that which comes from intellect."[45] "The Marquis Jeanne Hyacinthe de St. Palaye" was published in *Macmillan's Magazine* July 1882; "The Baroness Helena von Saarfeld" followed in August.

"The Marquis Jeanne Hyacinthe de St. Palaye" has "no moral

purpose," then, and is only a description of "life under certain forms
[here eighteenth-century French]." But echoes from *John Inglesant*
have "rolled from soul to soul" and in the narrower compass of "The
Marquis Jeanne Hyacinthe de St. Palaye" have grown to such an
extent that they repeat only the themes of rank and culture, an
emphasis which might have caused an imbalance within the
framework of the earlier work.[46]

Madeleine de Frontenac, on the day before papers are signed
affiancing her to the Marquis, is interrupted by the Marquis in her
clandestine meeting with the Chevalier de Grissolles, her lover
since childhood. With admirable poise the Marquis sends the
Chevalier on his way, speaks to Madeleine only of the obligations of
rank, and later says nothing to her father who has always opposed
her attachment to the Chevalier. Next day the documents are
formally signed. Shortly thereafter the father receives information
of another rendezvous. Allowing the father to storm ahead on a false
scent, the Marquis confronts the guilty pair alone, warns off the
Chevalier, convinces Madeleine of the futility of opposing her
destiny as a titled lady. The family moves to Paris, the Marquis
accompanying them. In Paris the Chevalier manages several
meetings with Madeleine but finds her changed. His valet drops
hints about suitable ways of eliminating a rival. The Marquis, with a
presentiment of the future, alters his will to settle fifty thousand
louis d'or on the Chevalier. At a boar hunt the Chevalier
"accidentally" murders the Marquis. The dying Marquis, looking up
at his befuddled murderer, expires on an overwhelmingly gracious
note, "Ah, Chevalier, that was scarcely fair."

What is important in the tale is not the plot but the idea. The
Marquis is merely what John Inglesant might have been in another
time, another society—completely poised, imperturbable, beyond
anything so trivial as passion, by virtue of his rank a force for good,
an expression of culture, an example of "noble living." The
Chevalier is only another of the "incompleat" gentlemen, and
Madeleine with her common sense, if she is not so spiritual as Mary
Collet nor so vigorously rebellious as Virginia Clare, has an affinity
with Constance Lisle.

"The Marquis Jeanne Hyacinthe de St. Palaye" may, as Shorthouse averred, have illustrated "culture which comes from rank,"
but if "The Baroness Helena von Saarfeld" was intended to illustrate
the "culture which comes from intellect," it is difficult to see how,
unless one can naively assume that a French setting illustrates

"culture which comes from rank" and a German setting "culture which comes from intellect."

It is well-nigh impossible to summarize "The Baroness Helena von Saarfeld." On the peg of an anonymous narrator Shorthouse hangs the first-person narrative of Richter (echo of Jean Paul), an aging actor whose father had wished him to be a printer. He recounts his successful theatrical career, the offer of marriage from an "emancipated" Baroness Helena and his noble refusal of it because he feels she is still obligated to one of her own rank. Refused also by the Count of Roseneau, the Baroness Helena (like the Prince in *The Little Schoolmaster Mark*) joins Count Zinzendorf's Moravian community.

Again the plot line gives little indication of the weight of the story—it is probably the best of Shorthouse's smaller pieces—and if it is not very clear from the story what the "culture from intellect" is, the tale does, however, illustrate Shorthouse's ability to use the same lumber over and over again. The "culture which comes from intellect," if it is visible at all in the story, is revealed only through the unconsciously noble Richter's perceptiveness as an actor and the Baroness's education by a cultured but "progressive" father.

For an understanding of Shorthouse's habit of recycling materials it is necessary at this point to be reminded of the chronology of what may be called the Shorthouse canon. First, *John Inglesant* (1880), then "The Marquis Jeanne Hyacinthe de St. Palaye" and "The Baroness Helena von Saarfeld" (1882), then *The Little Schoolmaster Mark Part I* (1883), *Part II* (1884), then *Sir Percival* (1886) and "A Teacher of the Violin" as it was published in *Macmillan's Magazine* (November 1887). In the ambitious structure of *John Inglesant* it was possible for Shorthouse to balance the major themes which fascinated him: rank, culture, religion and art. In the later, slighter works a pronounced imbalance is evident but the original themes remain constant. "The Marquis Jeanne Hyacinthe de St. Palaye," for example, concentrates altogether on the necessity and obligations of rank; "The Baroness Helena von Saarfeld" repeats some of the arguments and extends them slightly to include the possibility of "nobility" in those not nobly born but condemning by implication any attempt to ignore the boundaries of rank. In *The Little Schoolmaster Mark* Shorthouse is again playing with the relationship of culture, religion, and the arts of theater and music. In *Sir Percival* he is back again to the culture inherent in rank and its connection with religion. In "A Teacher of the Violin" he concentrates on a particular art, music. In all the stories the important characters belong to the nobility, and are not easily distinguished from each other. At the end of *The Little Schoolmaster Mark* the Duke (and at the end of "The Baroness Helena von Saarfeld," also the Baroness) disappears into Count Zinzendorf's Moravian community. The "incompleat" gentlemen of *John Inglesant* reappear as the rebellious Chevalier in "The Marquis Jeanne Hyacinthe de St. Palaye" and the Count von Roseneau in "The Baroness Helena von Saarfeld," two figures betraying the established order, the first by placing desire above the conventions of his class, the second by his willingness to cross class boundaries to have his love. In *John Inglesant* amid the carnage of the Civil War there is noble action. At the end of "The Baroness Helena von Saarfeld" Helena makes her final proposal to the dying Roseneau on the battlefield. At the end of "A Teacher of the Violin" the former Princess Cynthia can show what stuff the nobility are made of as the French plunder the capital city.

"Ellie: A Story of a Boy and Girl" was printed for private circulation by W. Rickman King, printer for Cornish Brothers, Birmingham, 1883. Only five hundred copies were printed in small booklet form. It says something about the story and about Shorthouse that the copies were easily disposed of at church bazaars. The slight story stresses rather artfully that the guileless and pure in heart need no other justification for their actions than their innocence. One question is asked three times about the mystery of life, "Why did we travel down together, Ellie?" but it is suggested to the reader that only eternity will have the answer.

Lord Frederick Staines Calvert, "a good specimen of an English lad," at seventeen falls in love with orphaned Ellie, fifteen, a sort of poor relation given refuge by his family. They spend the summer alone on the ancestral estate while his family is touring the Continent. They travel unchaperoned on the train when Ellie is sent to finishing school in the South. While Lord Frederick is at Cambridge Ellie is stricken with the plague. He arrives at her sickbed too late.

Though the story is shorter and less well-muscled than either "The Marquis" or "Baroness Helena," it contains a generous quantity of Shorthouse's normal subject matter—the naturally noble noble; the calm, stately manorial life; the studied pictures of a handsome aristocrat against a background of armorial device; the antiquarian interest in feudal relationships; the instinctive love of religion. The story is lightweight, but it is soundly Shorthouse.

"An Apologue," an even shorter story, was first published in the

Nineteenth Century (July 1882) in the same month as "The Marquis" appeared in *Macmillan's*. Once again Shorthouse uses some of the ideas from *John Inglesant* rather neatly. (Slight as it is, "An Apologue" comes as something of a relief after the parade of "compleat" gentlemen.) In the twenty-third chapter, during a wide ranging conversation with Inglesant, the Cardinal, quoting Terence, says: "Life is like a game of cards, but of such as turn up you must make the most. . . . We did not make the world, and are not responsible for its state; but we can make life a fine art, and, taking things as we find them, like wise men, mould them as may best serve our own ends."

"An Apologue," worked out on the framework of a game of bezique, is a metaphorical form of the Cardinal's argument. The King of Clubs, "a stupid king" (evidently related to the King in "A Teacher of the Violin"), and the King of Diamonds, lying side by side during a pause in the game, discuss the relation of chance to destiny. The King of Clubs brashly avers, "It is all chance." The King of Diamonds, "very clever," "with his perfect culture" argues that there exists a presiding intelligence by which chance is "systematized and controlled." The trump Ace of Spades descending on the table terminates the game and the discussion.

The Cardinal in *John Inglesant* had said that even if chance dealt a person a bad hand in life it was still incumbent upon him to play the cards to the best of his ability, as a "fine art." But in this moral fable the King of Diamonds' argument suggests that what seems to be chance may actually be part of a pattern devised by an ordering mind. This would seem, then, to refute the Cardinal's viewpoint. But Shorthouse further muddies the waters by means of the setting in which the game (cards or life) is played. The Professor holds, by chance, a winning hand with which he defeats his adversary, the Herr Councillor, a friend from boyhood who (by chance) has grown "rich and great" while (by chance) the Professor, though he has acquired no wealth, has enjoyed the contentment of a life of thought, and feels that he has been given "everything, even a little girl." After the departure of the Councillor, the Professor's daughter tries to arrange the "royal cards" into a "pretty picture" but the picture is imperfect, for the "wise King of Diamonds had fallen by misadventure into the large pocket of the rich Councillor's embroidered coat and was gone." Is Shorthouse, then, saying that the Cardinal is both right and wrong, or that only expert bezique players can get the proper meaning from his fable?

IV   The Countess Eve
(1888)

The origin of *The Countess Eve* is obscured in the mist and silence. Nothing in Shorthouse's correspondence with his publisher indicates that he is working on another story until suddenly he writes to Maurice Macmillan (24 April 1888): "I think I shall have my book ready by the end of May: Should you advise its publication then or would it be better to wait till October? I hope that it will be longer than both parts of *Little Mark* but I fear not quite so long as 'Sir Percival.' I will make it as long as I can. I consider it powerful myself but of course public opinion may not coincide with mine." [47] Though apparently he agreed on October as a better publication time, nevertheless on 31 May he wrote again to Maurice Macmillan: "I sent you today the MS now because I understood you wished to have it as soon as finished." [48] After a spot of correspondence about the appropriateness of the French in the novel, *The Countess Eve* was published by Macmillan in October 1888 with an issue of three thousand copies, and a quick re-issue in December with another three thousand. It was quickly pirated in New York as a paperback by Lovell (Lovell's Library, No. 1305) and G. G. Munro (Seaside Library, No. 1148). Harper and Brothers arranged with Macmillan for a reprint and issued the novel in their Franklin Square Series (No. 633). *The Countess Eve* was issued only once more by Macmillan (July 1892) with two thousand copies.

Set in an unnamed (ancient) Burgundian city, in 1785, *The Countess Eve* is the temptation story of Eve, the beautiful, young Countess du Pic-Adam, unhappily married to a middle-aged diplomat strangely isolated from her by a silent brooding over memories of youthful indiscretion, his seduction of an innocent girl who subsequently killed herself. Unable to communicate with her husband, Eve is irresistibly drawn to Felix la Valliere, a mercurial actor, whose confusion of the realities of life and art have squeezed out any conscience he may once have had (as contrasted with the almost hypersensitive conscience of his musician friend, Claude de Brie, a paragon of moral purity). Eve and la Valliere, tempted, lured on and encouraged by the suggestion of the evil, ghostly figure of a French abbé and anxious to taste the sweet fruit of life, prepare to leave Paradise (the Count's private garden) for the "real" world and almost inevitable social ruin. An accidental delay in their flight makes possible, through the efforts of de Brie, the reunion of Eve and her husband, who has meanwhile discovered that his youthful crime has been imaginary, that the girl had not committed suicide but had entered a convent. The Tempter (the ghostly abbé) then disappears, foiled.

The "analysis and character of sin," Shorthouse claimed in the preface to *John Inglesant*, was one of his aims in writing the novel, but in *John Inglesant* there was fortunately too much else for him to do. He neither analyzed nor explained the nature of sin, except in passing, and then only obliquely. For instance, Richard Inglesant at the beginning of the novel cannot enjoy his reward for his part in the suppression of the monasteries (so one of the consequences of sin is unhappiness). In *The Countess Eve* Shorthouse takes a closer, though not necessarily a better, look at sin by focusing on the Countess Eve and her temptation in a modern, somewhat arbitrary, rewriting of Genesis 2, 3. The epigraph—one might call it his text—he takes from the litany in *The Book of Common Prayer*: "That it may please Thee to strengthen such as do stand, and to comfort and help the weak-hearted, and to raise up them that fall, and finally to beat down Satan under our feet." In one respect the epigraph may be considered a summary of the novel, for, when the hurlyburly's done, de Brie, who has been the most stable character, has been "strengthened"; the Duke, who has been "weak-hearted," is "comforted"; Eve, who had almost fallen, is "raised up"; and the Tempter, the ghostly abbé, has been "beaten down."

The parallel with Genesis is irritatingly obvious, and so badly bent that it is hardly useful. "Paradise" is a place, the Comte du Pic-Adam's private garden (though the Count is, if he is Adam at all, a rather gloomy one who is not even offered the apple; if he is God he is an ineffectual administrator). Paradise also, it is hinted, is a state of mind, even a state of grace. Like her counterpart in Genesis the Countess Eve is tempted to taste the forbidden fruit, life outside the garden and hence outside her social class. The Serpent is treacherous indeed, a *doppelgänger* embodied in la Valliere with the ghostly abbé at his good ear. The Abbess makes a strange Archangel, holding not the flaming sword but a crucifix, not expelling the sinners but inviting them back to Paradise.

In the opening paragraphs of *The Countess Eve* Shorthouse posits that just as in music there are overtones which enrich the sound so in life there are "unseen presences," "a crowd of unseen forms— Principalities and Powers and Possibilities" which are "unseen, but not unfelt." These presences may by nature be either good or evil.

Their effect may be either good or evil. They have always been; they always will be, everywhere. The "spirit world" is parallel and equal to the mundane and interactionary with it. This is, of course, not new ground for Shorthouse. He had played with the idea in many of the essays he wrote for the Friends' Essay Society, and from *John Inglesant* one easily remembers Strafford's ghost, the astrologer in Lambeth Marsh, and Inglesant's almost constant consciousness of the pressure of unseen forces.

The "unseen, but not unfelt" "Principalities and Powers and Possibilities" assumed, evil, then, is a ubiquitous malefic (he loved the word) presence, prompting, luring, sometimes clearly recognized, sometimes imperfectly perceived, sometimes only felt. Evil, in *The Countess Eve*, is embodied, if one can speak of him in that way, in the abbé (a clerical Mephistopheles), a mysterious figure who flits in and out, sometimes visible, at other times only a voice, but always an invisible force. Though both la Valliere and the Countess are tempted, la Valliere, as the more sophisticated of the two, sees the abbé when the Countess does not. De Brie, the "pure" character, sees him only once—and faints.

Negatively, Sin with a capital letter is a failure to resist temptation, and positively, Sin is the result of evil "unseen, but not unfelt" which is the cause of temptation. The only defence against temptation seems to be a "pure spirit." So la Valliere is tempted to dream selfishly of possessing the Countess. The Countess, though she puts up no resistance herself, is saved from falling (in the nick of time) by the efforts of the "pure" de Brie and the "purified" Abbess.

But it is really not so simple as that. "Yield not to temptation, for yielding is sin" are the opening words of a Sunday School hymn by Shorthouse's American contemporary, Horatio Richmond Palmer (1834–1907). But Shorthouse, probably without the hymn in mind, goes beyond the simple concept that "yielding is sin." Yielding to temptation is sin, he argues, but it is also the origin of Sin, a threatening, divisive force. Thus, what is really at the bottom of the misery in *The Countess Eve* is the Comte du Pic-Adam's early indiscretion, his seduction of his mother's maid. The consequences of his youthful enthusiasm are suffering and remorse which make him silent, undemonstrative, and morose, thereby erecting a barrier between himself and his wife—further sin. Neglected and hurt by his brooding, she is therefore tempted to look outside Paradise for excitement and affection. Shorthouse solves the whole matter of cyclic sin very easily if not very adeptly. At the last minute, just as Eve is about to leave Paradise for the alluring world beyond, sin is frustrated and the Count and Countess are happily reunited through the intervention of de Brie (Guardian Angel that he is). But though the Countess has been saved from inevitable social ruin she has still in her hair and eyes "an appalling mystic light—the singe and the glow of the flame of the pit!" (239). La Valliere (the real tempter) is merely thwarted; but Sin has been defeated and the abbé (visible again)—Evil—"so deadly in hate, so vindictive in disappointment and hate," creeps away.

If there has been an "analysis of sin" in *The Countess Eve* it has been rather left-handed. Shorthouse does not say what sin is; he manages only to convey that sin begets sin—"Wherever there is sin committed, then Sin is born into the world—is born but does not die" (151). He hints at sins without suggesting a distinguishing principle. The Count and his mother's maid, carried away by what on both sides is honest passion "in one moment of wild delirium," commit the act, presumably, whose consequences (sin, as Shorthouse meant it) are different for each. By committing the act each brings suffering on himself and directly or indirectly on others also. The Count is torn by remorse not for the act of passion but (needlessly, as it turns out) for the girl's presumed suicide. The girl is remorseful, not so much for the "wild delight" as for the betrayal of her mistress's trust. When, after long years, they meet—the girl, while the Count has been brooding over her death, has become an abbess—she says simply (and inscrutably): "Auguste, I am here. I have never seen you since that night, but I am here. God in his unspeakable pity has had mercy upon us, and has utterly abolished the whole *body* of sin" (178). What seems to give significance to their sin is the iniquity of crossing class lines—the Count for unconsciously lowering himself, she for presuming to forget her place. "When the devil entered into la Valliere as surely as he entered into Judas Iscariot" (189), in a "desperate insurrection against fate," he presumes to love a countess in order "to bring her down to his own level, nay, beneath it" (191). One is reminded here that in "The Baroness Helena von Saarfeld" the Baroness is saved from the consequence of such sin by Richter the actor's nobly refusing her offer of marriage because the union he himself desired would inevitably demean her.

If one of the weaknesses of *John Inglesant* is that Shorthouse attempted too much, in *The Countess Eve*, despite his narrowing of theme, he achieved too little. Though he considered the novel "powerful," he admitted that "public opinion may not coincide with mine." [49] But *The Countess Eve* exerts no great power over the ordinary reader who can tolerate a certain degree of nebulousness, light-struck mist, as it were, until he is lost in a fog of words, paragraphs of euphonious sound in "a tale of little meaning though the words are strong." The carefully descriptive paragraphs—an unobtrusive suspense device for delaying action—of room after great room of the chateaux, of the consecutive sights of mountain journeys (standard equipment in the novels) remind one of nothing so much as the wandering camera-eye and the excessive film footage of a movie chase.

But if one can overlook its faults and respond to its virtues *The Countess Eve* can provide a quiet retreat from the noise of the world, much as "Lansdowne," Shorthouse's Edgbaston home did in the days before steel and concrete and the roar of the throughway surrounded it. The scenes devoted in *The Countess Eve* to the gossipy, sybaritic, little Viscomte are more soundly true than anything similar in any of his novels. If de Brie's "purity" is too sensitive a conscience for la Valliere's taste, the cynicism of the Viscomte opens his eyes. And in de Brie Shorthouse no doubt unconsciously described himself without affectation or vanity:

There is no doubt that he was a happy man. His disposition was singularly sweet and placid, and he escaped by an intuitive recoil, everything that was coarse, cruel, or unpleasant. His religion consisted in following the good and the beautiful, and he avoided intuitively the disquieting aspects of both life and thought. The existence of beauty was to him a safeguard and an asylum from all the attacks of Satan and of doubt. It led him to a Father in Heaven. To him the range of white summits were indeed the heavenly Beulah. Every lovely chord, or sunset, or mountain rill, or rocky valley assured him of a higher life; and safe in this fairyland, he could defy the distracting sights of evil or the insinuating whispers of doubt. (153–54).

That, one gathers from what his wife and cousins record of him, is the kind of man Shorthouse was.

V   Blanche, Lady Falaise
(1891)

"I have finished the first draft of my tale," says Shorthouse, writing to George Macmillan (17 February 1891), "and am fairly satisfied with it so that I suppose there is no doubt that I shall finish

it now. . . . I call it *Blanche, Lady Falaise*, and am particularly
anxious to secure the title as it would spoil the story if I could not
use it." [50] Writing again (6 May 1891), he remarks on his progress:
"I have nearly finished my story for the second time so it will no
doubt be ready for publication in November. It is longer than Sir
Percival—I think." [51] By 16 June, then, he could say, "I am sending
off the MS in four parcels by book post registered to you today
which I hope will arrive safely as I have not a complete copy." [52]
Blanche, Lady Falaise was published by Macmillan September 1891
with an issue of three thousand copies, another two thousand in
November, and three thousand the following March. It was
Shorthouse's last novel, and, like *Sir Percival*, set for the greater
part in nineteenth-century England.

   Though setting and characters have been changed, the repetition
of theme in *Blanche, Lady Falaise* makes *The Countess Eve* and
Blanche, Lady Falaise close relatives. In *The Countess Eve* the
husband broods over his past transgressions; in *Blanche, Lady
Falaise* the wife broods over hers. Daughter of a former Oxford don,
rector of Clyston St. Fay, Devonshire, Blanche Boteraux declines
the proposal of her father's pupil, George Falaise, aristocratic scion
of an old Norman family. Blanche, "perpetually waiting for the
injunction of the Prophet to do some great thing" ' (41), longing to
"become a Sister devoted to work in the most terrible of the London
slums" (72), is charmed by a visiting preacher, Paul Damerle, a
"great 'missioner' among the poor in London" (74), and accepts his
proposal. However, when Damerle discovers from her father that
she is almost penniless, he breaks his engagement to Blanche and
marries the wealthy Lady Elizabeth Poer, hoping for her financial
support of his work among the London poor. But he rapidly goes
through her money, takes to drink and gambling, and is eventually
imprisoned for fraud. Shortly after Damerle's marriage, when
George Falaise again offers himself to Blanche, she drearily accepts
him, bears him two sons, but, indifferent to husband, children, and
family affairs, she suffers from an inexplicable, excruciating guilt
over the fate of Damerle. At length, on an expiatory trip to a Calvary
in the Austrian Alps, she is killed by lightning at precisely the
moment when Damerle in England emerges from prison, a worn
but presumably better man. In her will she settles on Damerle the
fifty thousand pounds she has unexpectedly inherited so that he may
continue his redemptive mission work.

   With *Sir Percival* and *The Countess Eve* behind him the reader cannot fail to recognize in *Blanche, Lady Falaise* some familiar materials: the usual thin narrative line which suspends an assortment of ideas; the fattening of the narrative with generous quotations, sermons, and letters; the recurrent themes; the descriptions of manors, churches, and landscapes; characters changed but little in name and situation; lack of action and pace; and an atmosphere of troubled calm which just escapes somnolence. Thus, in *Blanche, Lady Falaise* one is treated not only to the religious ideas which are the important matter of the book, but to incidental comments on art, music (especially church music), education, church restoration, preaching, the Salvation Army, Catholicism, and literary criticism. The motifs (religion, culture, gentility) reappear intermittently in much their usual costume. Large lumps from the Swiss mystic Henri-Frédéric Amiel's *Journal* (translated by Mrs. Humphry Ward, 1885) [53] added to other lumps from Count Zinzendorf, Walker of Truro, Wesley, and Tennyson give bulk to a slight structure, but they also have a small share in the characterization. Three short sermons on Shorthouse's favorite texts, and three long confessional letters also add to the bulk, but they are aptly used to reveal information about their speakers (and about Shorthouse's own interests). The description of Devonshire landscape (he was holidaying near Exeter when he was finishing the novel) is not only more affectionate and concrete but less stereotypical than the travel-book description of the Austrian Alps which he had never seen. [54] The churches, as usual, are described both inside and out. The furnishings of every manorial room are detailed in proper order. The characters seem to be first or second cousins of Inglesant, Percival, or Constance. And underneath a world that seems to be suspended in time, as in *Sir Percival*, lurks a timeless, brooding evil, as in *The Countess Eve*.

In *The Countess Eve*, in his "analysis of sin" Shorthouse had indirectly argued that sin created a chain of misery, or further sin. It is her husband's sin, his brooding over his "actual" sin, which alienates husband and wife and therefore makes Eve vulnerable to temptation, her sin. But in *Blanche, Lady Falaise* Shorthouse pushes the reader to the precipice and expects him to jump. In *The Countess Eve* the Count had something to brood about. He had seduced his mother's maid. His regret about his action is understandable. His brooding over her supposed suicide is ironic but equally understandable. But in *Blanche, Lady Falaise*, Blanche is conscious of sin she has not committed and can only conceive of

by means of the most remarkable mental gymnastics of any
character in fiction. Anxious for a life of useful service she accepts
Damerle, hoping to help him with his slum mission. When he jilts
her to marry a wealthy aristocrat, Blanche, far from considering him
a cad and a bounder, feels that she has ruined a noble nature with
her spiritual pride, and makes some very deserving people
miserable as a result, just as the Comte du Pic-Adam had done in
The Countess Eve. "In her excited nature it was she who was to
blame—it was she who was the sinner" (187)—before anything has
happened. Before she has any intimation of the mess Damerle has
made of his life she exclaims, "He is ruined for life—body and
soul—he is ruined for life—he who was so great and good, and it is I
who have done it" (177). The twentieth-century reader may be
excused his impatience with her.

But to Shorthouse she is not vexatious. In the first place, it is
possible that he knew of a case like Blanche's (at least so his wife
claims).[55] Second, he is not interested in anything so transitory as
human character when he is dealing with matters eternal. It is clear
from the very beginning of the novel that neither plot nor "the
actors of the story" are of any consequence, but the theme is. "The
consequences of one act of sin can never be revoked," says Claire
Wand the narrator. "If there be any lesson taught us by my story, it
is the deceitfulness of sin, and the pitiless insistence with which it
exacts its payment to the full. Nevertheless Sin will be slain, for the
Divine nature has known suffering . . . and thus won for itself this
supreme prerogative that it has achieved the revocation of an
irrevocable and appalling Past. God himself who is also the Son of
man, has become the divine and eternal redemption and rectifica-
tion of all wrong . . ." (3). There, in brief form, is a statement of
the only dogma Shorthouse seems to have consistently subscribed
to—usually in more nebulous terms (as at the end of *The Countess
Eve*). Claire Wand, patiently arguing with a frenetic Blanche, says,
"You are trying to take this man's Sin, this man's punishment upon
yourself. There is only One who can do that" (225). After Blanche
has been killed by lightning at the foot of the mountain-Calvary,
Shorthouse by some dark logic converts her into a Christ, "the One
who can do that." The pathetic victim of Damerle's inadequacy,
Lady Elizabeth Poer, has a dream in which she hears a voice
addressing not her but Blanche: "Thou hast tried to offer a sacrifice
which is not for thee to offer, and to bear a punishment which was
not thine to suffer or to bear. Nevertheless, the sacrifice which thou

hadst to offer is accepted, and the punishment which was thine thou hast fully borne. Thy prayer is heard. His [Damerle's] sins which are many, are forgiven him. He is turned, and shall be saved" (286–87). Blanche, of course, is only dead, and at this point, miracle of miracles, Damerle, with the odors of jail still upon him, enters the room, redeemed. The twentieth-century sceptic without a theological bent is understandably puzzled by Shorthouse's attempt to "justify the ways of God to men." "It [*Blanche*] is my favorite of my books," Shorthouse wrote to Macmillan (15 July 1894) [55] but few readers will share his enthusiasm.

CHAPTER 5

Refractions: Nonfiction

SHORTHOUSE'S nonfiction prose pieces, though separately slight and much less important than *John Inglesant* and his other novels—less well-known, too—nonetheless aid in an understanding of his novels, and, even more, of his distinctive "churchmanship."

I *Letters (1852–1903)* [1]

Shorthouse is not what someone somewhere has called "an epistolary artist." Though his letters cannot be considered great prose—even after editorial scrubbing—they are useful for illumination of a few matters which could find no room in Mrs. Shorthouse's *Life*. The letters disclose, in a way that Sotheby's catalogue for the sale of his library (published after the death of his wife, 1909) could not, that he owned a considerable number and variety of rare sixteenth- and seventeenth-century editions of historical and philosophical works—not to mention what was available to him in the rather good Birmingham Free Library—and, what is more important, that he had read them. It is no surprise, then, to come upon tell-tale tracks of his reading in his novels. In the letters can be traced, after a fashion, his response to what he was reading at a particular time—varied lightweight and heavyweight—and anyone alert to Shorthouse's normal method of composition learns early to suspect that what Shorthouse is reading while he is at work on a novel will find its way either directly or in some converted form into that novel before its completion—sometimes in the very phrases he uses in his letters. [2]

His contributions to the controversy in *Notes and Queries* (1863)—he was under thirty then—on the authenticity of the *Eikon Basilike* [3] show an early saturation in the seventeenth-century materials (and some of his biases) which later provide the historical base for *John Inglesant*. The correspondence with the Macmillans (*Macmillan Archive*, British Library), much of it involved with humdrum business, it is true, nevertheless authenticates an unusually warm—and agreeable, it should be noted—personal relationship between an author and a publisher. It shows his wrestling with misprints of the French and Italian in his novels which the reviewers so eagerly pounced upon to deprecate his imperfect education and provincialism. Though he was not writing novels for a living, nor, for that matter, even as a compulsive artist, his letters to Macmillan betray a sleepless business sense in the repeated, jovially discreet, postscript inquiries about his royalties "in these hard times." And one can enjoy the surprise of a protruding claw in Shorthouse's velvet writing paw in a letter otherwise benign in which he states that "the remark about an 'aristocracy' [in the preface of *John Inglesant*] is a hit at Professor Seeley, who is going about the country with a lot of nonsense in an 'inaugural address.'"

The publication of *John Inglesant* initiated a number of lasting, and most of them warm, friendships (and correspondence) with people, authors themselves, who might disagree with him on particulars but were in general agreement with him on matters he considered important: Canon Alfred Ainger, Master of the Temple, preacher, lecturer, author of a biography of Charles Lamb; W. Boyd Carpenter, Canon of Windsor, chaplain to Queen Victoria, later Bishop of Ripon; Dr. E. S. Talbot, first Warden of Keble, then Bishop of Rochester, who had an academic interest in Quietism; Lady Victoria Welby; Lady [Mrs. Leonard] Lyell; William Angus Knight, Professor of Moral Philosophy at St. Andrews; and Edmund Gosse. Each touched him on a different, welcoming spot. Lady Lyell was a descendent of the Ferrars and had authorially to her credit "Little Gidding in Huntingdonshire." Lady Welby (*Links and Clues*, 1882) had a "mystic" affinity with him (or he thought she had). Professor Knight was of course attractive as the editor of Wordsworth and a lover of Spinoza. Shorthouse's respect for erudition, culture, and rank made the cultured Anglicanism of the churchmen intellectually stimulating to him. Edmund Gosse's position near the throne in the realm of letters as poet, scholar, critic made his friendship particularly desirable to an unassuming but anxious author; but it is regrettable that the letters to Gosse [Brotherton Library] suggest an ingenuous eagerness for Gosse's good opinion from Shorthouse's side and also—for all his affability—

a distressing olympian condescension and reserve on Gosse's.

To his prelatical and aristocratic correspondents Shorthouse's letters are pleasantly formal, a bit studied, at times overly polite, and one turns almost with relief to the playfulness of his holiday letters to Rawdon Levett (with whom he lunched every Monday) to find the Shorthouse of those who knew him most intimately—the wit, the incurable anecdotist (despite a stammer), the genial host almost untouched by the "slings and arrows" of clever tongues in which "no kindness is." After some early diffidence, in the letters after the success of *John Inglesant* there is perceptible an increasing self-assurance amounting at times to boldness, which sometimes regrettably takes him beyond his wading depth in literary criticism. Even if one charitably assumes that revelation from the letters is piecemeal and incomplete, one cannot escape the conclusion that while Shorthouse may have been an independent thinker, he was not a systematic, nor sometimes even a clear, one. Though generous in his toleration of contrary opinion, he himself moves on a "scanty plot of ground." Wide in his Anglican views, he is almost narrow in his views of anything non-Anglican—Catholicism, for example, and Dissent. And if his novels do not already show this, his letters do.

II   *"On the Platonism of Wordsworth"* (1881)

"To my mind the greatest poet of the world," says Shorthouse, aged fifty-nine, speaking to Macmillan about Wordsworth who had been dead over forty years. Though he did not begin the serious study of Wordsworth until maturity, Shorthouse would have been hard pressed to remember a time when he was not conscious of Wordsworth's poetry. Rebecca Shorthouse had, as a child, saved her pennies to buy the *Lyrical Ballads*. It is unlikely that her grandchildren would have been unacquainted with the poetry of Wordsworth by the time they graduated to carving lines of poetry into the roof at Moseley. His cousins could not recall his participation, if any, in the discussion of Wordsworth they had on their Cumberland vacation; but they remembered well his sitting in Wordsworthian reverie while the others clambered about among the fells. Somehow he arrived at the opinion that Wordsworth was "the poet of middle age," and that he would begin serious study of his poetry at the age of forty. "I chanced one day," says his wife, "to read to my husband the 'Kitten and the Falling Leaves,' and it so caught his fancy that he entered on the study of Wordsworth sooner than he intended. Wordsworth became to him a constant companion, consoler, and friend. . . . He read and reread *The Excursion* often twice over in the same holiday. He took pains to collect other and rarer editions from time to time." [4] Eventually this enthusiasm for *The Excursion* prompted him to propose to Macmillan in 1893 "ideas for an edition of the 'Excursion' with a very large proportion of the other poems interleaved, as it were, with the poems." [5] He volunteered to undertake the editing (with pay) if Macmillan thought there was a chance of sales-success. Macmillan must have made some counterproposal, though it is not clear what it was, and apparently Shorthouse's editorial project was tabled.

He had been a reader of Plato since adolescence. He joined the Wordsworth Society when it was formed at Grasmere, 24 September 1880. Then a meeting with Professor William Angus Knight of St. Andrews ignited loose thoughts into an idea. Knight describes the meeting and its consequence:

In 1880 I happened to be lecturing on Spinoza, to the Birmingham and Midland Institute, and met Mr. Shorthouse at the residence of my host. Our talk was mainly on Plato, Spinoza, and Wordsworth; and a good deal of our subsequent correspondence referred to these three great writers. He had joined our Wordsworth Society at its formation, and I suggested to him the preparation of a paper on "The Platonism of Wordsworth" especially apropos of the two books of *The Excursion*—'Despondency' and 'Despondency Corrected'—and the great Ode, *Intimations of Immortality*. He liked the idea, and gradually worked it out. As he could not read it to the Society, it was published in Birmingham, first privately in quarto form, and afterwards in octavo for the public. It was subsequently included in our *Transactions*.[6]

Shorthouse's side is revealed by the correspondence which developed. In a letter to Knight shortly after their meeting, he says, with a mixture of caution and self-confidence, "If I can at any future time get any ideas upon paper concerning Wordsworth's Platonism I will do so, *but it is no child's play*. It will be necessary to concentrate the essence of Wordsworth's teaching (in the whole of his works) as regards the effects of material Law (Nature) upon intellectual Existence, by which it appears he conceived of absolute Being, but which as a system he has, I *think*, left somewhat vague; and on the other hand, it will be necessary to formulate Platonism which has never yet been satisfactorily done." [7] So much for his intention about the essay he eventually wrote. On 7 December 1880 he writes hesitantly: "Your suggestion with regard to an Essay on Wordsworth's Platonism is a very tempting one, but I cannot think myself equal to such an undertaking. I will see what I can do; and if I find myself getting on at all, I shall let you know." [8] He did get on. By 8 February 1881 he could say to Knight: "I send by this post a paper upon Wordsworth's Platonism for you to look at. I do not know whether it is anything like what you think the subject requires. . . . It would be easy, of course, to say much more on Platonism, but this does not seem to me what is wanted. If more could be said upon the subject as seen by Wordsworth, it would be much more desirable." [9] On 1 June (according to Knight) Short-house wrote: "You are perfectly at liberty to make any use of the paper you like, to read it at the meeting or to take any other course you think most likely to promote what alone we all have at heart, viz. the study and appreciation of the greatest poet-philosopher of any age or literature." [10] On 5 June (according to Shorthouse) Knight replied: "I have read your paper with increasing interest. . . . I should not be surprised if some of those present, whose opinion is of most worth, think it the most interesting of all the papers read at our meeting." [11] The paper was read by the Secretary [Knight] at the meeting of the Wordsworth Society at Grasmere, 19 July 1881. Because he was unable to deliver the paper himself (owing to his stammer) Shorthouse provided printed copies for members. Three weeks later he was restless and wrote to Knight (5 August 1881): "I have been thinking a good deal about the subject of my paper, as I have commenced my annual study of *The Excursion*, and I am more and more impressed with the possibilities which a perfect analysis of the poem would open in the direction of Platonic Thought. I *sincerely* think little of my paper, which in fact consists mostly of quotation, but the least thing may set people thinking upon a subject, and I should be very pleased to elicit the opinion of competent thinkers on the lines laid down in the paper on the synthesis of *matter* and *thought* as each was suggested to Words-worth's mind. The suggestion of the subject in your own book [*Studies in Philosophy and Literature*, 1879] makes it more fit that you should take it up." [12] Armed with Knight's recommendation (according to Shorthouse) that "it would be very interesting to have it published in a magazine," on 14 August he forwarded the essay which "might be much longer" to *Macmillan's Magazine*, and on 27 August bowed to editorial verdict that "as Mr. Grove cannot find room for the Wordsworth paper, as indeed I hardly expected he would, I think I shall print a few copies here, in antique pamphlet form." [13] Rickman King, Birmingham, printed the essay (for private circulation) in an eighteen-page, soft-cover booklet form (1882). There is no record of the quantity printed. It was reprinted in *Transactions of the Wordsworth Society*, No. 6 (1884–85). Knight must have considered it important enough to reprint as the opening essay in *Wordsworthiana* (1889), a selection of papers presented in the Wordsworth Society meetings between 1881 and 1886, and then it slumbered uninterrupted until Folcroft Press reprinted the essay in 1969.

In the essay, after an audience softening introduction, Shorthouse argues: "It is not asserted that Wordsworth consciously Platonized"; he possibly had "never read the Dialogues," but may have "talked to [Coleridge] on the matter." "Plato's Dialogues, just as much as Wordsworth's poems, form a volume of Philosophical Romance." (One remembers his label for *John Inglesant*.) Juxtaposing a selection of some fourteen lines from "Tintern Abbey"—the passage about the "gift of aspect more sublime"—and an extract from Plato's *Symposium*, he continues: "The meaning of the English poet and the Greek philosopher seems to be this: 'The forces of life, which we call intellectual may be actually of similar worth with the physical but phenomenally they stand out in clear distinction.' Nothing but the pure idea of the perfect object will exist in the intellect . . . in the pure intellect, in which alone all things exist (all things, that is, in their perfect form), and which is God," and "this pure intellect . . . some portion of which we have each of us received is none other than the all-perfect, all-containing intellect, the mind of God." Quoting from "Michael," lines 28–32, and "The Wanderer," lines 125–33, he adds: "They [these lines] . . . contain the key not only to Wordsworth's Platonism, but to that peculiar conception of his that an entrance into the world of abstract thought may be won by the help of material objects."

There was Baconian caution in Shorthouse's original title "On the Platonism of Wordsworth." Though he actually thought highly of the essay, as the correspondence shows, he considered it neither the first word nor the last on the subject. He wrote with a genuine love of Wordsworth and Plato. There was wisdom also in allowing Wordsworth to speak for himself by means of abundant quotation. Within his lights, it was an honest attempt to present a matter which interested him. But, for all that, it was a genial exercise which did little for the Wordsworth Society.

Reviewing the paper by J. V. Shorthouse [sic] for the Spectator, the writer (Was it R. H. Hutton who had heard the paper the previous July?) put the kiss of death on it: "The author of John Inglesant seems . . . to take a somewhat peculiar view of Platonism. . . . Mr. Shorthouse misunderstands Wordsworth, when he ascribes to him, in any strictly systematic sense, a philosophy; but he more than misunderstands, we think he perverts him." [14] Thus, like the "man without a wedding garment," the paper, if it was given entrance at all, was consigned to the "lower room" of Wordsworth bibliography.

III *"The Agnostic at Church"*
(Nineteenth Century *April 1882*)

It is easy to understand, in light of what has already been said, the position Shorthouse took when in the January issue of the *Nineteenth Century* (1882) appeared what A. W. Benn has denominated "a rather silly article by one Louis Greg, called 'The Agnostic at Church,' " [15] an article in which Greg argued that it is the duty of the agnostic to attend Divine service, but that he should not repeat the Creeds nor partake of the Eucharist. Shorthouse replied in the April issue with an article of the same title, agreeing in the main with Greg but taking exception to Greg's suggestion that the agnostic be barred from the Sacrament. Starting from the position that "there is a power *within ourselves* which makes for righteousness, and which may be cultivated," Shorthouse argues that participation cannot harm the agnostic and may do him good, for there "is one principle which underlies all church worship with which he cannot fail to sympathize, with which he cannot fail to be in harmony—the sacramental principle . . . the great underlying principle of life by which the commonest and dullest incidents, the most unattractive sights . . . become instinct with a delicate purity . . . become the 'outward and visible sign of an inward and spiritual grace.' Everything may be a sacrament to the pure in heart. . . . This principle, which underlies all things is concentrated in the supreme act of church worship." "Kneeling in company with his fellows," Shorthouse goes on, "it is impossible but that some effect of sympathy . . . should mollify and refresh his heart. . . . Strengthened, chastened, purified by this communion he will find his loins girded to run the daily race that is set before him." With a little assistance from Henry More's *Divine Dialogues*

Shorthouse can lyrically conclude, echoing John Inglesant's remark about "the supernatural to all who choose to come": "Looking into the future, I sometimes think I see a glorious Church, which without faltering in the announcement of what she conceives to be truth, gives her blessing with a kingly munificence, asking for nothing in return and leaving the result to the decision of the final assize, bestows her sacraments and benedictions like the Divine gift of sunshine, upon all mankind alike." Though rhetoric conceals what some would consider the speciousness of his argument, in the essay he had demonstrated how "Broad" and how "Sacramental" he was, and could therefore confidently express to Dr. Talbot (31 October 1882)—with whom he had had disagreement on the matter—"I do not think that it is a wild idea that the sacrament may yet be a basis of reconcilement between the Agnostic and ourselves." [16] How the agnostic was to circumvent the creeds and, as the "Exhortation" in the liturgy proclaims, "the danger great, if we receive the same unworthily" he does not say. And is it even faintly possible that his agnostic will ever experience "the stillness and peace unspeakable" of Inglesant at Little Gidding? It is difficult to avoid concluding that the essay is a sincere but rhetorical flourish.

IV *Preface to George Herbert's* The Temple *(1882)*

It was noted earlier that in creating the character of John Inglesant Shorthouse began with George Herbert (and a little of himself), for George Herbert, aristocrat, scholar, poet and priest represented what Shorthouse most admired and intended to incorporate in Inglesant, the gentleman-saint not removed from the world but moving daily in it, his saintliness undiminished by sweat, or squalor, or vice. In 1876 Fisher Unwin had issued a facsimile reprint of the first edition [1633] of Herbert's *The Temple*. The applause which followed the publication of *John Inglesant* encouraged Unwin to re-issue *The Temple* (1882) with an introductory essay by Shorthouse. When as a calculated risk the sixth edition was issued in 1903, just after Shorthouse's death, it contained a prefatory note:

So much interest was aroused by Mr. Shorthouse's Introduction that the Reprint, which had previously attracted but little attention, passed through several editions before it finally went out of print. . . . The publishers feel that, now the author of 'John Inglesant' has passed away, there must be many readers who will welcome a reprint of the volume, with its introduction so exquisitely delicate in style, and so peculiarly interesting as revealing Mr. Shorthouse's position in relation to the Church of England. [17]

If Shorthouse's position with regard to the Church of England had been rather indirectly conveyed by *John Inglesant* and his position in it obscured by his "The Agnostic at Church," the "Introductory Essay" to *The Temple* made it more plain. Jessie Montgomery, daughter of the poet James Montgomery and an admirer of *John Inglesant*, has an illuminating anecdote of a luncheon visit with Shorthouse and his wife which expresses more vividly than exposition can the satisfaction Shorthouse had in this expression of his belief. After the luncheon, as he was leaving, he remarked, "I want to send you something of mine, and am wondering what to choose. I think it shall be my Preface to George Herbert's *Poems*. It will give you a better idea of my churchmanship." When she protested that she had already learned this from *John Inglesant* he delightedly replied, "You could not have said anything to give me greater pleasure. I have been called Romanist, Agnostic—anything you please, but few have deduced English churchmanship from my book." [18]

In language at times half-lyrical and polished to brightness yet without the bluntness of the anti-Roman and anti-Dissent aspersions in his letters, he parades again the ideas implied if not always explicit in *John Inglesant*. With the beauty of the creation outside and the beauties of the communion service inside the church— "with no gaudy images, but with the 'fair white linen cloth' upon the wooden table with fresh flowers above"—the worshipper is uplifted in the Sacrament. "In these sacred places," Shorthouse continues, "sacred to the beauty of earth and of heaven alike, comes over us a blessed mood, in which all the fair scenes of life, the sunsets and the 'all-golden afternoons' come back upon the mind. The loved and lovely appear again. . . . They speak to us of that exquisite refinement which is the peculiar gift and office of the Church—a refinement so perfect that it requires an initiation to comprehend it." George Herbert, then, is "a type of this note of the Church: the ascetic priest who was also a fine gentleman," who, "eschewing alike the gaudiness of one ritual and the excitement and noise of other appeals to the uncultivated," "still holds forth this gospel of refinement and sacred culture." But at this point Shorthouse's contempt (also in the letters) for the "intelligent mechanics" puts a new ring, almost a clang, into his voice:

It is well that, in these days, amid the blatant idols of the market and the forum, culture and refinement, usually so silent, should for once be heard, and, the gage of battle being thrown down, this should be confidently asserted, that this constantly said service, this monotonous repetition, this simple ritual, has produced an effect which no undisciplined effort, no individual enthusiasm has ever wrought;—that this despised Church of England has produced a culture unequalled in the world beside; that it has produced families—generation after generation—which no other country, and no other class in this country, ever saw.

The Reformation, he continues, had overthrown "faith in a Church" to replace it with "faith in a Book." Donne, Wotton, Wither, Quarles, Vaughan, "all of them gentlemen and men of fashion," joined with George Herbert and Nicholas Ferrar to rescue the Church from disrepute. Thus, "these men were the true founders of the Church of *England*." Brushing aside the "insinuation" against Herbert that the "activity and sweetness that marked his pastoral life at Bemerton" were the result of disappointed political hopes, Shorthouse finds his defence of Herbert in "the spiritual instinct of a human life consecrated to God amid the pleasures, the temptations, the pains of this world's courts and cities." Herbert, one might say, is another John Inglesant, and even an extension of Shorthouse himself.

Herbert's poetry, he says, like his life, shows "the same sober, reasonable religion" of "a devoted Protestant 'Church of England man,' " of "an enthusiastic follower of his Lord." He does not say much more about the poetry except to comment on its "strength of expression and reality of feeling," a "strength of purpose and reality of insight, combined with quaintness and carelessness of expression." What really interests him is "the lesson and legacy that [Herbert] left behind him": "What seems to have been the peculiar mission of Herbert and of his fellows, is that they showed the English people what a fine gentleman who was also a Christian and a Churchman might be. They set the tone of the Church of England, and they revealed . . . to the uncultured and unlearned the true refinement of worship. They united the delicacy of taste in the choice of ornament and of music with culture of expression and of reserve, and they showed that this was not incompatible with devoted work and life."

And with all that Shorthouse, businessman, book-lover, People's Warden for nine years, could identify. His novels breathe—if they do not proclaim—a sacramental sense that finds fulfilment in the beauties and the discipline of the "Liturgy" as prescribed in *The Book of Common Prayer* of the Church of England by law established, with no Ritualist excrescences, and no Low Church excisions. He had more than a tourist interest in churches, for he was an unfailing attendant of his own church; he attended the businessmen's noonday service at St. Philip's; wherever he went on holiday he found a service to attend. He and his wife would "run over," as others would on a basket picnic, to attend the afternoon service at Worcester Cathedral. Every Sunday and Feast-Day he read aloud to his wife the appropriate passage from Keble's *The Christian Year*. Though he ranks Keble's poetry higher than Herbert's, Shorthouse finds Herbert's attitudes his own. If tolerance to dogma put him into the Broad Church, taste gave him a leaning for the High, but only so High as was laid down in *The Book of Common Prayer*.

V *"The Humorous in Literature"* (Macmillan's Magazine, March 1883)

In "Ars Vitae," which was possibly the last essay he wrote for the Friends' Essay Society (1870?), Shorthouse had touched on the subject of "Humour." Modestly asserting that "nothing beyond an attempt to direct attention to the subject is intended," he proceeded somewhat deviously toward a definition of "the faculty, or the art, which at present, for want of a better word, we call humour." By the Romans, he said, meaning of the word "was confined entirely to certain phenomena of the body"; "the old physicians taught that there were four 'humours' in a man," hence later "a humorist was understood to mean 'a man full of humours or conceits.' " Eventually a humorist "was understood to mean a man whose bias or habit, itself a humour, took the form of studying the humours of others," and "it became evident that the study of human life was nothing but the study of the humours of individual men." "It also became touchingly apparent that, well considered, nothing in a fellow human being is so truly pathetic as the ludicrous." "There is superadded to [the] sense of the ridiculous another of immortality: a conjunction producing mental sensation of which the man has hitherto been utterly unconscious," and "it becomes evident that the study of humours is as wide as that of human life itself." Therefore "the word most appropriate to the follower of this study [i.e. humor, life] is 'Humanist.' " And then with remarkable agility Shorthouse arrives at his conclusion that "Christ himself was, in the highest sense to which we have attached the word, a more perfect 'Humanist' than any who have hitherto spoken in His Holy Name."

Curious, idiosyncratic, the essay is representative of those essays he wrote for the Society in which from a suggestive title he drifts to a religious conclusion. But what strikes the reader is that the title "Ars Vitae" has a left-handed relevance to the actual (not ostensible) subject matter of the essay, and the relevance of the epigraph ("Who sees through tears the *masquer's* leap"), if it is concealed somewhere in the essay, is buried too deep for discovery. However, that mystery would be less dim twelve years later when this sentence drops into another essay from Shorthouse's pen: "For it would seem that beneath the masque of the comic actor lie the issues of great controversies, and in the jester's laugh can be recognized the truest test of what lies at the root of human existence."

Sometime in 1882 Shorthouse either offered to editor Sir George Grove, or Grove asked for, an article in *Macmillan's Magazine*. In either event, Shorthouse produced "The Humorous in Literature," which was published in *Macmillan's Magazine* (March 1883). Internal evidence indicates that if the essay was begun before mid-November 1882 it was not completed before that time. Shorthouse submitted it to Grove (30 January 1883) with a defensive note: "You will probably notice that I have not mentioned two names, Jane Austen and the late Mrs. Cross. I should like to have done both but it would have been absurd to drag either in in a paragraph or two." [19] (Jane Austen's *Persuasion* was possibly, next to Wordsworth's *The Excursion* and Keble's *The Christian Year*, Shorthouse's favorite reading. George Eliot's "Janet's Repentance" was close behind.)

The essay is perhaps less interesting for weight of content than for the manner in which Shorthouse has reworked an old sermon into a new one. Covering the same ground as in "Ars Vitae," he changes the approach by a series of swift, unanswered questions. The neglected epigraph of "Ars Vitae" becomes, with a new face, central to his argument in "The Humorous in Literature." Some of the old illustrations are replaced by more useful ones, swelling "Ars Vitae" to five times its former size. The line of argument is much the same,

but the manner is different. Thus he can argue "that the condition of
true humorous thought is individuality," that the source of humor is
"individuality of character." Don Quixote, Sir Roger de Coverley,
and Uncle Toby "all correspond to this highest mark of humorous
character—perfection in itself—the ridiculous and pathetic blended
into one." He finds "Addison's humour . . . permeated with
intention and purpose, and with insight into the whole of life."
Fielding (because of *Tom Jones*) is given short shrift because he can
"only see, and can therefore only describe part of life." Pope and
Swift are wits, not humorists. Thackeray, despite *Vanity Fair*, "one
of the masterpieces of humour," "lacks the ideal." Jean Paul Richter
is "the greatest and most perfect humorist, if we except the author
of *Don Quixote*, that the world has yet seen." And Jean Paul brings
him to the neglected epigraph of "Ars Vitae": "With its laughter and
its tears, this surely must be perfect humour, if such can be found."
"Can it be possible, then," he asks, "that the emotion which
displays itself sometimes in laughter and sometimes in tears is, in
fact, one and the same?" With a little help from Addison—"if
humour is nature, then—if the laughter in it is only a preliminary
step to the seriousness which is the highest joy"—he leaps nimbly to
the "humour in the Gospels." In "Ars Vitae" Jesus had been
nominated the great "Humanist." This time he argues the same
point by using the story of the Prodigal Son to arrive at his
conclusion that "Nature and humour cannot be far apart. The source
and spring of humour is human life. Its charm consists not merely in
laughter, or even in joy, but in the stirring of those sympathies and
associations which exist invariably in the race, for we inherit a
world-life and a religion, the earth-springs of whose realities lie,
perchance too deep for laughter, but not, Heaven be thanked, too
deep for tears." The bones of "Ars Vitae" are there, but not so
heavily fleshed that they are undetectable.

   In what must have been an unusually careless moment Gosse
seems to have commented to Shorthouse that the essay was "the last
word." Shorthouse's characteristic courtesy and modesty prompted
him to admit that "the subject was barely touched upon yet by
anyone." But Richard Holt Hutton spoke for most readers when he,
a Dickens-lover, deplored the omission of Dickens from Shorthouse's examples, objected to his assumption that "humour" was
"coextensive with individuality," and asserted that Shorthouse's
attempted definition would apply to "one species only." [20] It is
small wonder that Shorthouse's essay is in total eclipse.

VI *Preface to* Golden Thoughts from "The Spiritual Guide"
(1883)

· "There is a brilliant, but very fanciful, account of Molinos and his doctrines in J. H. Shorthouse's romance, *John Inglesant*," comments Viscount St. Cyr at the end of his article on Molinos in the eleventh edition of the *Encyclopaedia Britannica*. In one of the more effective sections of *John Inglesant* Shorthouse, drawing generously from Gilbert Burnet's *Three Letters Concerning the Present State of Italy* (1688), used a real historical figure, Miguel de Molinos (1628–96), Spanish-born mystic, to embody one of the seventeenth-century religious forces, Quietism, to which, after the death of his wife and child, Inglesant is drawn. On his arrival in Rome (1663) Molinos by his personality and mystical teachings attracted a large and influential following. The contemplative life, Molinos taught, leads to a state of internal repose through, first, a renunciation of all self-will, then through meditation, and finally through contemplation when the soul, indifferent to (and indeed beyond) all earthly ordinances, passively receives the celestial light. In other words, the way to God may be achieved through the intermediary of priest, ordinance, or Church, but these could be only means and not ends. In 1675 he published *Il Guida Spirituale*, which in six years went through twenty editions in French, Spanish, and Latin; an English translation appeared in 1688 (in the nineteenth century re-edited by Mrs. Arthur Lyttleton, one of Shorthouse's Cambridge friends). The popularity of "The Spiritual Guide" alarmed the Jesuits who felt that it threatened the authority of the Church. Molinos was arrested in 1685, tried, and after retraction condemned to penitential imprisonment in 1687. At a crisis in Inglesant's life Shorthouse thrusts him into a crisis in the Church. In defending Molinos Inglesant collides with the Jesuit order which had trained him, and, until then constantly drawn to the Church of Rome, he steps off the road to Rome to travel henceforth the *Via Media*.

The influence of *John Inglesant* is evident in another curious way, again indirectly through Fisher Unwin. In 1882, John Bigelow (1817–1911), an American editor, author, and diplomatist with Swedenborgian leanings, sent Shorthouse a copy of his latest book, *Molinos, the Quietist*, published by Scribners. At about the same time, when the popularity of *John Inglesant* was at its height,

Shorthouse was asked by a Glasgow publisher to write a preface to a selection from Molinos's "Spiritual Guide." Accordingly *Golden Thoughts from the Spiritual Guide of Miguel Molinos, the Quietist*, with a preface by J. Henry Shorthouse was published simultaneously by D. Bryce and Son in Glasgow, and by Fisher Unwin in London. Shorthouse's second postscript in a letter to Macmillan (11 June 1883) exhibits evidence of the leavening influence of *John Inglesant*: "I have written a few lines of introduction to a little volume of extracts from Molinos's *Spiritual Guide* a Mr. David Bryce of Glasgow wrote to me about. . . . He said he had been asked to publish it by readers of 'John Inglesant' and had got a Dr. Lindsay to make the extract. I read the ms. and think it will be a very interesting little book." [21]

The preface, sandwiched between the "Life" and the "Golden Thoughts" of Molinos, fills six pages of a purse-sized booklet. Brief as it is, it reveals a confidence in the validity of the "Mystic Way": "This message from a foreign country and a bygone age is not without a singular appropriateness at the present time, when the inquiring intellect is so much in the ascendant, and the soundings have become strange, and the old landmarks dim in the ever seething mist." The reader of *John Inglesant*, diverted by the sparks from Inglesant's collision with church authority in his defence of Molinos, is likely to miss the very point which makes Inglesant's (and Shorthouse's) sacramentalism perceptible if not plain. In this essay, speaking of Molinos's method, Shorthouse explains that

this method of the soul's training in mystical worship, is, in fact, conceived in the purest spirit of that Sacramentalism, which has nothing to do with priestcraft, and is the basis of that idea of the Church, which all its abuses in all ages, so far from creating, have only impeded and obscured. The "prayer of silence," the "spiritual martyrdom," the "mystical peace," the "entrance into eternal recollection through the most Holy Humanity of our Lord Jesus Christ," are all the offspring of the Sacramental principle which finds an utterance in outward fact, in formal and ceremonious usage, and not in human intellect and speech, is nowhere so clearly seen as in the worship of the Church Catholic in its purest form, and could nowhere, so Molinos insisted, more surely be expected than in the Communion of the constituent parts of that Holy Humanity, the Precious Body and Blood. [22]

For Shorthouse, then, as for Inglesant, the individual mystic communion with the divine is possible in the "Church Catholic in its purest form" (i.e., Anglican) in the celebration of the Eucharist.

But before Shorthouse closes he adds what was peculiarly important to him—the mystic's individual freedom within an historically authoritative structure, the "Liturgy": "The form is there, but form hallowed and mystical, without choice or alternative, without growth and without decay, and before the adoring individual sense, thus chastened and annihilated, is presented the God-given Humanity as God Himself restored it, and offered it before the universe as a sacrifice again."

"Brilliant and suggestive," the *St. James's Gazette* (29 October 1883) applauded. Dr. Talbot, Warden of Keble, was stimulated to compose an article "What is the Charm of Quietism?" for the *Pall Mall Gazette* (18 December 1883) in which, remarking on the "Golden Thoughts," he compliments Shorthouse on opening "a further and direct glimpse into one of the most remarkable of those phases of spiritual life to which 'John Inglesant' gave such fresh interest." When in the *Academy* (12 January 1884) Wentworth Webster reviewed a new translation of Juan de Valdes's "Considerations"—it will be remembered that Valdes first sent Inglesant to Little Gidding—and "Golden Thoughts of Molinos," Shorthouse seized an opportunity the following week in the same column to show that he knew more about Molinos than he had revealed in *John Inglesant*, and to openly express his admiration for Molinos: "Through the whole course of history few figures seem to me more calm, more gracious, and beneficent than this Spanish priest. His temperament was wrought to such fine issues that it appealed instinctively to the lofty and the pure. . . . So always is it with the finest natures." [23] This is an oblique comment on his intentions in *John Inglesant*, on the character of Inglesant, and on Shorthouse himself.

John Bigelow in his *Molinos, the Quietist* had remarked (101–02): "Molinos, doubtless, for the first time, figures as a part of the machinery of fiction . . . and one of [*John Inglesant's*] purposes seems to be to keep alive in the world a healthy distrust of the paganizing influence of the Latin Church. . . . Of Molinos and his martyrdom the author [Shorthouse] takes substantially the same view that is presented in these pages." It remained only for Henry A. Brann in *Catholic World* (July 1882) to rap what he considered the presumptuous knuckles of both: "Mystical theology is not a matter for pamphleteers like Mr. Bigelow and novelists like Shorthouse to meddle with safely." But Shorthouse having made his point could remain undismayed.

VII *"Frederick Denison Maurice"*
(Nineteenth Century, *May 1884*)

There is no evidence to indicate when Shorthouse's interest in
Frederick Denison Maurice (1805–72) began, but it is likely that at
seventeen he was well on his way to near-discipleship of that
controversial figure whom many considered the leader of the Broad
Church (though Maurice consistently denied the charge). Great
readers of weighty literature all, Shorthouse and his Southall
cousins in their teens constantly discussed their reading. During
this period Anna Mary Southall, says her sister Margaret, "read the
works of liberal churchmen, as we all did." [24] Of her sister Ellen she
says, "Kingsley [who called Maurice 'Master'] rose in her soul like a
new day, the dawn of a wider faith." [25] She comments on her
father's "reading Maurice's lectures on St. John with great
interest." [26] They read, they re-read, and discussed Dr. Arnold's
sermons which their father had given them. Later in life, in a letter
to Margaret (2 August 1899), Shorthouse remembers: "I never read
Dr. Arnold much; Maurice always absorbed me so much that I had
no time for other Divines at that time." [27]

Shorthouse's enthusiasm for Maurice is not hard to explain. His
early essays for the Friends' Essay Society already reveal a Quaker
yearning for the beauties of the Anglican liturgy. Maurice's "Letters
to a Quaker" (i.e., to his friend Samuel Clark, then a Quaker, later a
clergyman), collected later into *The Kingdom of Christ* (1842)—with
Evangelical, Catholic, rationalist tones in unpredictable succession—were to suggest the nature of John Inglesant's (and Shorthouse's) Anglicanism. Maurice, while enthusiastic about the Quaker
doctrine of the Inner Light, nonetheless emphasized the necessity
of "forms" through which the spirit works. Shorthouse, a Quaker
(without sacraments), drifting toward sacramental "form," felt an
affinity with (and saw an example in) Maurice, who, after having cast
off his father's Unitarianism, was baptized in the Church of England
(29 March 1831), thirty years before Shorthouse himself formally
joined the Church of England by baptism, and was ordained in holy
orders the year Shorthouse was born. In a defensive undated letter
(possibly 1861) to an unknown correspondent apparently re-
monstrating with him for his defection from the Society of Friends,
Shorthouse indicates his familiarity with the writings of Maurice:
"As Maurice has so clearly shown, it [*The Book of Common Prayer*]
has preserved over and over again the most vital truths which were

overlooked by those who profess to believe it and to use it. I have seen Maurice's late book, *What is Revelation?* [1859] in answer to Mr. Mansell's [Bampton] lectures. I should like thee to read it. It is, I think, more beautiful than any of his books, and very clear and plain—different from some of his writings." [28]

After the publication of *John Inglesant* he was drawn into warm friendships with admirers of his book, admirers differing in opinion but men themselves influenced by Maurice—Brooke Foss Westcott, F. J. A. Hort, R. H. Hutton (himself drawn into the Church of England by Maurice), W. Boyd Carpenter, Alfred Ainger. At the beginning of May 1882 Shorthouse and his wife, guests of Macmillan, in one swift swoop on London, experienced the lionizing of an author at the afternoon meeting of the Wordsworth Society (Ainger and Hutton among those present), and at an evening reception followed by the Prime Minister's reception (mostly princes present) where Shorthouse met Gladstone. This was followed the next morning by a breakfast party at 10 Downing Street (Hutton again present), and that evening by a publisher's reception at which Major Frederic Maurice, engaged on a memoir of his father, asked Shorthouse to write a review of the book after its publication. Shorthouse complied; his review was published in the *Nineteenth Century* (May 1884); publisher and author were apparently pleased because the review was elevated to an introduction in later editions of the *Life of Frederick Denison Maurice*, edited by his son, published by Macmillan.

Shorthouse wrote to Maurice Macmillan (6 February 1884) that he felt "the responsibility of the undertaking very much," that he had "made a beginning," and had "got on very well," adding in an admiring postscript that "no greater honor could be paid to any living man than to ask him to write upon Mr. Maurice." [29] A month later, in a letter to Boyd Carpenter (7 March 1884), again in a postscript, he announced both his enthusiasm and his hesitation: "At Colonel Maurice's request I have written an article on his father for the *Nineteenth Century*. It is a wonderful subject, and a great honor, but rather terrible." [30]

Considering Shorthouse's early enthusiasm for Maurice, and the "honor" already referred to, one is impressed in his review by the restraint, the lack of self-indulgence in the language, his attempt at a balanced and honest fairness by the subordination of his own biases and condescensions. Julia Wedgwood (*British Quarterly Review*, April 1884)—Shorthouse's essay having already been

written—pounced on Maurice's lack of "reverence for fact,"
something Richard Holt Hutton (having personal acquaintance with
Maurice) was to take issue with in *Good Words* (1882). In his own
review Shorthouse commented on the "uniqueness" of Maurice
among theological thinkers of his time. (Hutton, regarding Maurice
more personally, expressed the same conclusion in an epithet—
"Knight-errant fighting in the wars of the Lord.") Shorthouse
considered that this uniqueness which "caused [Maurice] to be
suspected of casuistry and rejected as obscure and unintelligible"
was evident in an "exquisite balance of mind and thought."
However, he admitted that, despite all his admiration for this
balance, "it has often appeared to me so subtle that I failed for some
time altogether to grasp it." [31]

To Talbot he wrote (25 February 1884): "Lady Welby tells me
that you are writing on Maurice. I am rather ashamed as I have been
persuaded to write an article for the *Nineteenth Century*. I have
kept out of controversy as much as possible." [32] Though he tried to
keep out of controversy, he could not refrain from dilating on the
disagreement of Maurice and Pusey on Baptism, naturally on
Maurice's side. Maurice and Shorthouse viewed the Sacrament of
such importance that they had both been baptized as adults in the
Church of England. With unwonted acidity he supports Maurice in
his dispute with Mansell (Bampton Lectures, 1858). He applauds
Maurice for breaking the control of the Evangelical party as he notes
"that a wonderful change has passed over the religious world of
England since Mr. Maurice took orders fifty years ago." But on
Maurice's "Christian Socialism," which other reviewers were to
linger on, Shorthouse finds restraint easy. One need only remember Virginia Clare in *Sir Percival* to understand why. However, on
the connection he sees between Maurice and Wordsworth he is
more expansive. Rather deftly, with the recollection of the "God
always, everywhere" of his childhood and a sprinkling of ideas from
his essay "On the Platonism of Wordsworth" he cements the
connection between the poet and the theologian who "believed that
he was very deficient in a love of Nature." And having done that, he
is prepared to close with some pulpit oratory which is among
Shorthouse's most dramatic and melifluous best.

VIII   *"Of Restraining Self-Denial in Art"*
(Century Guild Hobby Horse *1888*)

In 1888—possibly on suggestion from his friend Arthur Galton—
Shorthouse published in the *Century Guild Hobby Horse* (in 1892

reduced to *Hobby Horse*) an essay "Of Restraining Self-Denial in Art," which exhibits his strength and almost conceals his weaknesses. Using his own phraseology as much as possible, one can summarize thus: The Dorians taught Greece (and the world) "to seek after an advanced culture in the security of a patient reserve," and demonstrated that "there is no Art but the Art of Life," "the life of measured and ideal Art." Their "wise concession" to innovation resulted in "the most perfect music that the world [before the discovery of the violin] was to know and hear." But "as a people who saw life as a whole" they "allowed no one art to absorb or deteriorate the rest of life." By inference, then, it is the "insistence on the necessity of restraint in art" which is important, for "that art which boasts itself untrammelled and free" damages everything that is "noble and great in human existence." The "Art of Life," therefore, "the pursuit of the good and the beautiful," "the perfection of manhood" is moral, attained only "through restraint and sacrifice." Paradoxically, "self-denial that restrains is its own reward." By concentrating his "force and vigor" "within more confined limits" the artist achieves the work of art which he could not achieve by "fruitless wanderings in the walks of unrestrained fancy and frivolous self-pleasing." From a contrast between the worship of the Dorian deity ("Averter" and "Defender") and the worship of Christ by which "the whole of modern life has been transformed" one concludes that Christian (i.e. modern) art should be at least equal in quality to art of the past at its best. In literature and painting, then, "modestly, and with a restraining denial of self, following in the footsteps of the great masters" the artist creates, gradually "working into the fabric" his "own insight." Hence, "had the Pre-Raphaelites exercised more restraint," had their successors "been chastened by an unselfish, modest submission to the past, the world would have been spared many abortions of crude coloring, unreal grouping . . . and, latterly, of still worse sins against taste in morals. The result would have been different"—not so much art but better.

If in the essay Shorthouse preaches nothing new to the reader of *John Inglesant*, he preaches well. Moreover, he practices the self-denial which he recommends. He suggests rather than states; he limits his illustrations to a useful number; his language is temperate; his sincerity unquestionable. But most interesting, possibly, is what the art conceals, for the essay is a polished public performance and the meaning is narrower than at first it seems. In a letter to Gosse, two years after the essay was written, he remarks, "I have always contended, as I tried to say in my paper in the *Century*

Guild, that it is the duty of every artist to assimilate everything that
is true, and therefore permanent in every new development, from
whatever direction it may come." [33] It is true that by indirection he
has made the point in the essay without actually stating it. But when
he illustrates his point with examples from painting he suggests that
it is the innovation that is objectionable because it is not "true and
therefore permanent." The concessions he might have been
prepared to make to the great Romantics and their successors the
pre-Raphaelites are pushed underground by an insistence on their
weaknesses. Therefore the essay on the surface only partially
reveals what amounts to a prejudice against modern art (literature,
painting, music) because it is modern. He loved music but passed
up most of Birmingham's many offerings except for repeated
attendance at Handel's *Messiah* and *Elijah* (which he knew by
heart), the occasional opera, and of course cathedral music. When in
their teens his cousins were rhapsodizing over the great collection of
pre-Raphaelite paintings in the Birmingham galleries he kept a
thoughtful independence, but the significance of what he says about
the pre-Raphaelites in this essay becomes later more plain from his
dissuasion of his wife from viewing Burne-Jones's "Mermaid"
because he considered it "lascivious." (One would like to know what
he thought even later of Burne-Jones's "The Merciful Knight"
which might have been the painted form of that central scene in
John Inglesant where Inglesant forgives Malvolti.) And one notes
that the art he prefers is the art hanging in his own home and in the
mansions he furnishes in his novels, as he enjoyed it in "the old
masters of English [and Dutch] landscape." His two Piranesi
etchings and his collection of Dutch prints somehow find their way
into his novels.

If one can read between the lines of his correspondence with
Gosse, one gathers that Gosse, with one foot among the ancients
and one among the moderns, protested against Shorthouse's
wholesale condemnation of the moderns. Though it is clear from his
earliest essays where Shorthouse's homage lies—Cervantes, Dante,
LeSage, Jane Austen, Wordsworth—in his correspondence there is
a curious mixture of sense and whimsical nonsense, and statement
close to dogmatism, which, even if one makes proper allowance for
casualness, is impressionistic, even wayward. He says to Gosse (9
July 1890): "I loathe it [the modern school which 'reports instead of
creates'], beyond the power of expression; more than that, I believe
it to be a passing imposition, adopted because it is *easy*, and in fact

the only possible school for vulgar and stupid men, who have not the smallest particle of genius." [34] Speaking of Henry James's *Reverberator* he admits that "it is tempting at times for *even* a man of *some genius* to fall back upon the *easy* and the lascivious." [35] Despite his admiration for Jane Austen he could drop her into the same basket as Mrs. Sherwood. He "never could read Balzac." Though he was actually grateful to Mrs. Humphry Ward for introducing his *John Inglesant* to Macmillan, he nevertheless was reluctant to read her *Robert Elsmere* because he had "no sympathy for what [he] understand[s] to be its tendency. To say that God exists wherever a good action is performed seems to [him] to be *simply bosh.*" With his contemporaries in mind he says to Gosse (23 July 1890), "It is easier to *photograph* than to *create*. It is easier to grovel than to climb, it is easier to drivel and to maunder page after page (*especially if one is paid by the page*) than to create something of perfect beauty." [36] There is no doubt that he aimed at this beauty in his own novels, but when reviewers were unkind he could console himself with *Sir Percival's* "too good art," and resign himself to await a just verdict on *The Little Schoolmaster Mark* "when people wake up." To retain one's respect for Shorthouse's critical perception one needs to stay with his essay "Of Restraining Self-Denial in Art" and stay away from his letters.

IX *Preface to* The Message and Position of
the Church of England (*1899*)

In 1899 Shorthouse wrote a brief preface on the Royal Supremacy to Arthur Howard Galton's *The Message and Position of the Church of England*, the last public word from Shorthouse's pen. It is unfortunate that there is so little information on how this came about, for the relationship of Shorthouse and Galton reveals something about Shorthouse which is not perceptible in his relations with others. In the preface Shorthouse says only, "My friend and distant cousin . . . has asked me to write something in the fore-front of this volume," and expresses his admiration for Galton's competence. Galton concludes a letter to Gosse (14 December 1902)—he was collecting material for a memoir of Lionel Johnson—with "I think you know my dear friend and cousin J. H. Shorthouse. I send you a little sketch of his work, which Cornish asked me to do for their Christmas book list; but what can you do in a few sentences." [37] So far, then, only a recognition of distant kinship and mutual approval is evident. Though Shorthouse's published correspondence with Galton begins only at the end of 1898, there are indications that they had corresponded earlier.

Their kinship must have been distant indeed, and may have come about through the marriage into the Galtons of the daughter of one of Shorthouse's Southall cousins. Whatever the kinship, whatever the circumstances which drew them together, it is clear that they were attracted to each other by common interests. For six generations Quakers, the [Birmingham] Galtons had gradually dispersed into other faiths—Roman Catholic, Anglican, Plymouth Brethren, Unitarian—and Arthur Galton was born (1852) into the Church of England. Seeing no prospect of becoming a squire, but with an aversion to the army, at ease with his Roman Catholic relatives, with only a "blind literary instinct or taste" and "a passion for history," [38] he went to Cambridge, intending to enter holy orders in the Church of England. With (as he viewed it later) an insufficient grounding in Anglican belief, he became a Roman Catholic in 1875, and in 1880 was ordained priest. But his "passion for history" gradually eroded any confidence he had in Roman Catholic doctrine or practice. His appointment as curate at Windermere—he made a friend of Matthew Arnold there—proved "quite intolerable," and he asked his bishop to relieve him of his vows. He went "not back to Cambridge" but to Oxford—where Lionel Johnson was his intimate friend—concentrated on classics (instead of history), and it "was through Greek, finally, that the work of reconstruction came." After leaving Oxford (1890) he became a contributor to the *Century Guild Hobby Horse*, and wrote historical reviews for the *Academy*. After five years in Australia (1893–98) as private secretary to the governor of New South Wales, he returned to England, was readmitted into the Church of England, and again appointed curate (Anglican this time) at Windermere. He had published essays on Arnold in the *Hobby Horse* and he had dedicated his *Thomas Cromwell* to Arnold. His disappointment with Roman Catholicism and his championing of the Church of England were to be publicized later in a series of books and articles of which *The Message and Position of the Church of England*, with a preface by J. H. Shorthouse, was the first.

The friendships Shorthouse made with prelates and scholars such as Ainger, Carpenter, and Talbot were genuine enough, but these touched him on his Anglican side, and, on his part, though he was not too timid to disagree, he is often deferential and over-polite. His friendship with Gosse, also genuine enough, strikes one as a mastiff-terrier relationship. It is only with Rawdon Levett that there is a lowering of the guard which came from long acquaintanceship, similar interests, and mutual respect. But there is a meeting of minds in the relationship with Galton which reveals something about Shorthouse which is not evident in his relations with his other friends. The Galtons were an old, manorial, Birmingham family, part of Staffordshire history, distinguished by their civic service. His Quaker background some distance behind, Arthur Galton had been in and out of the Church of Rome. Almost a generation younger than Shorthouse, a promising young scholar (and Anglican clergyman) Galton was interested in precisely those aspects of the seventeenth century which interested Shorthouse. And, then, as a writer Galton could not fail to charm Shorthouse and arouse his paternal interest—particularly when they agreed on most matters. He found Galton "a magnificent correspondent, the best and most interesting I ever had." [39]

It is interesting, therefore, that from this relationship emerges Shorthouse's last public pronouncement, which makes clear what was rather less than clear in *John Inglesant*. In very small space he swiftly emphasizes the continuity of a *national* (here English) Church, and dismisses the charge of Erastianism (subordination of the ecclesiastical to the secular power): "His Sacred Majesty, the anointed of God, the Lords temporal and spiritual, the entire State is the Church." He attacks sacerdotalism ("priestcraft"). The King is head of the Church, and "this unbroken system produced in England a race of clergy such as no other system and no other country has ever produced; men who did not cease to be Laymen when ordained to the Sacrament of the Ministry." But he defends the Church of England with unwonted warmth by an attack on the Church of Rome with which he concludes the essay:

That proud boast of Rome 'everywhere and by all people and through all time' would seem to be more truly expressed by 'believed nowhere, is believed by none, never was believed'! Springing from the worst traditions of Pagan Rome, the Papal system never was a Church. It never was anything but a propagandist machine for extracting forced obedience and alms from an ignorant, a deceived, and a terrified world. The Papal Curia is founded on falsehood, and falsehood enters, consciously or unconsciously, willingly or unwillingly, into the soul of every human creature that comes under its influence. It has poisoned the wells of religious life. Its story is one of horror, and of crime, and of cruelty. . . . It has always been, and is now, the enemy of the Human Race.

Now it is clear how serious he was when he wrote to his cousin Margaret a month after the publication of *John Inglesant*: "Pure evil . . . only when it allies itself with what is supremely good (as in the Romanist Church) . . . becomes really dangerous to the child of God." [40] When he speaks (November 1880) to Dr. Abbott of "that fairyland (I will not say fools' paradise) in which modern Catholics live," he is in earnest.[41] He postscripts a letter to Professor Knight (7 December 1880) with "I flatter myself that [in *John Inglesant*] I have not unduly intruded the moral as few readers have perceived it without my pointing it out." [42] He writes to his cousin Isabel (7 April 1882): "I am expecting the great Roman attack [against *John Inglesant*] in the *Dublin Review* [by William Barry] every day. I am quite prepared to meet it. I have been too lenient if I have erred at all." [43] To an unknown correspondent he remarks (25 June 1882), "*John Inglesant* is *understated* all through." [44] After reading his preface to Galton's book, one is prepared to believe him.

X *Fragmentia*

Shorthouse left unpublished at his death three tales, "A Midsummer Night's Dream," "The Child in the Grave," and "The Fordhams of Severnstoke," and two undistinguished poems which had been written for the Friends' Essay Society. "A Midsummer Night's Dream" had apparently been prepared for publication, and one may conjecture that he had intended it for inclusion in the *Teacher of the Violin* volume.

It is a rather pleasantly instructive fantasy, a grownup children's story, a little longer and better than some of the musings he had contributed to the Essay Society. It is a pity that it was not allowed a public parade before it was immolated in the *Literary Remains*, for the earnestness which drove humor out of his normal writing is cushioned in this tale with quiet wit and a Lambian whimsicality that might have made him acceptable to those readers who find too much earnestness oppressive. It is a mystery that Shorthouse, known to his friends as a wit and an inveterate and sparkling narrator of humorous anecdote, should have had so little aptitude for humor in his writing. In the few instances when he attempts to insert humor, it is so heavy that one is embarrassed for him. But "A

Midsummer Night's Dream" indicates the kind of writer he might have been had he allowed his geniality to enter his art. He might have had to follow Charles Lamb at a great distance, but he might as an essayist have reached a larger approving audience—and a more permanent one—than he did with his later novels.

Into the changing fabric of little Julia's midsummer night's dream he weaves some old threads in new colors. The dream, which was such a useful device in the novels, provides the structure for this tale and enables Shorthouse to blur the boundaries of reality and unreality. The familiar gallery of the novels, lined with portraits breathing culture and lineage, in this tale is suddenly filled with life as the figures step from their frames and the centuries mingle. They are joined by "all the personages of fairy tale and legend," and by a spirit-host of forgotten thoughts and emotions. Nothing dies. The subject, as one might expect, is art, particularly music.

It has already been noted that Shorthouse looked forward to discovering the great musical romance, the great art novel. It has also been suggested that in "A Teacher of the Violin" he was trying his hand at this kind of art in a modest way. He had frequently expressed the desire to explore in an artistic way the effect of great music on the mind and emotions of the listener. He made little forays in *John Inglesant*; he tried again in "A Teacher of the Violin." "A Midsummer Night's Dream" is another example of his turning over and over again an idea which fascinated him.

In capsule form, his argument is that music has a wider appeal than any of the other arts and therefore has "no inconsiderable influence on mankind." One of the spirit forms separates from the brilliant, heterogeneous assembly and addresses Julia in her dream: "We are the people who live in sound. . . . We live in sound, but we are not born of sound. We are born of the union of art and human thought, wedded in the aisles of the glorious cathedral-church of sound." Julia in her dream asks a question which is really an explanation: "Then you are what everybody has thought after they have been listening to beautiful music?" The spirit-figure (a magician) continues: "Thought, when it is once conceived, has an existence of its own . . . [and therefore] affections and events which the actors themselves, perchance, forgot on the morrow . . . live on . . . as parts of the life of sound." Then he (the magician) narrows his meaning: "We continue our existence only in harmonious sound . . . nor can we breathe freely in sound which . . . is not under the influence of mind, or if you prefer the word, soul. . . . There is an art so perfect by long training and instruction, by something higher than itself, that it supplies the place of soul. In sound evoked by this art-soul we exist freely." But Julia's dream fades into sound sleep before the lecture is concluded, while the magician makes other distinctions among the pleasures derived from the arts. In this rather charming tale Shorthouse added something to the "musical passages" of *John Inglesant* and "A Teacher of the Violin," but whether he moved nearer to a solution of the "musical problem" is doubtful.

"The Child in the Grave" was bound into the middle of the 1865-70 volume of the essays of the Friends' Essay Society [since 1959 in the Birmingham Reference Library]. It would, then, have been written around 1867 when Shorthouse was beginning *John Inglesant*. "The Fordhams of Severnstoke" was a story which might have been intended for publication. These two tales require little critical consideration except the mention that through their content and manner they remind the reader of the possible extent of Hawthorne's influence on Shorthouse. Margaret Southall comments: "Nathaniel Hawthorne had a perennial charm—his influence on our cousin was permanent—and we turned from all other books to Hawthorne with fresh delight. There is in existence a well-worn copy of the *Twice-told Tales* that was seldom out of our hands." [45] Writing to her from "The Hole," his father's office (16 August 1853)—he would be nineteen then—Shorthouse expresses his admiration for Hawthorne: "If I ever write anything, I intend to make my *debut* as one of his disciples. I am sorry you have not got the *House of Seven Gables*, though the more we read the *Scarlet Letter* the more we like it. I think the "Haunted Mind" in *Twice-told Tales* one of the most perfect things ever written." [46] Shorthouse's "The Ringing of the Bells" (*LR*, 35) and "Sundays at the Seaside" (*LR*, 87) surely have more than a casual relationship with "Sunday at Home" in *Twice-told Tales*. Some indebtedness to Hawthorne in *John Inglesant* has already been commented on. Forsaking reality for "Reality," both Shorthouse and Hawthorne adopted the romance form to get at the dark truths of "the nightmare of the soul."

"The Child in the Grave" is the story of a dead child's influence on its mother; the mother's refusal to accept the fact of death adversely influences everyone about her. It is another form of the probing for sin in *The Countess Eve* and *Blanche, Lady Falaise*. "The Fordhams of Severnstoke," a well-drawn-out story, uses the supernatural—the ghost of a man who has just died—to sober up the gathered Christmas-eve company with the lesson that there is a spiritual world co-existent with a physical one, and that one of the facts of life is death.

"A Sunday Afternoon" was published in the *English Illustrated Magazine* (June 1895). Mrs. Shorthouse writing to Macmillan (2 February 1905), when she was compiling the *Literary Remains*, explains: "The story was almost the picture of a scene which my husband saw one Sunday afternoon at Llanfairfechan [near Conway where they were on holiday in September 1894], though the characters are of course fictitious." [47] The writer reviewing the *Life, Letters, and Literary Remains* for the *Edinburgh Review* (July 1905) comments that "A Sunday Afternoon" shows "the artist in Shorthouse triumphing over the controversialist." Shorthouse's pleasure in the scene at Llanfairfechan is unmistakable, and for once he views the Salvation Army and Dissenters with benevolence.

For comment on Shorthouse's poetry one needs only a short breath. "A Shadow of George Herbert," the best of his surviving poems, was written for the Friends' Essay Society when he was twenty-three. It is a modest tribute to Herbert by attempted imitation of Herbert's matter and manner. "The Little Graveyard" was written for the Essay Society later that year (1857). During their first year of marriage Shorthouse and his wife, then still technically Quakers, were visiting relatives near Shrewsbury. Mrs. Shorthouse remarks: "Their [Friends'] meetinghouse stood on the crest of a steep hilly road. My husband was fascinated with it." [48] In thirteen stumbling, five-line stanzas the poem is Shorthouse's equivalent of "Elegy Written in a Country Churchyard." "My Wife's Valentine", an undistinctive poem, ("recording the facts of my own boyhood") was, though written earlier, published in the *English Illustrated Magazine* (May 1884).

CHAPTER 6

Epilogue

I N the latter half of the nineteenth century many voices (not all of them new) were in the wind—admonitory, polemical, prophetic voices sounding an ever-changing discord which made the "Victorian Agony" variously audible. Because they reached a numerically greater, generally less critical and more diversified public than other writers, the novelists were particularly audible. "Fiction," says Margaret Maison, "became the pulpit, the confessional and the battlefield for countless Victorians, and the novel was used by them more than any form of art to portray the religious movements of their time, to be a vehicle for all manner of theological and ecclesiastical propaganda, to conduct debates and controversies, and to tell the world of their doubts and conflicts, their spiritual travels and phases of faith." [1] Through the characters of their novels or by authorial attitudes, the novelists pressed on the Victorian consciousness a variety of religious beliefs and some substitutes for or alternatives to orthodoxies which had ceased to be convincing.

The impact of biblical criticism on religious thought, of science on philosophical thought, and a resultant change in the concept of history forced on the Victorian a number of alternatives to orthodox belief. He could perversely ignore the new and valiantly cling to the old; he could discard the old and follow the new; he could try to reconcile the new with the old or work out an acceptable compromise. If he was resolute enough to adopt the first course, he could maintain his faith but endure possible ridicule (illustrated by the Huxley-Wilberforce debate), or, like Philip Gosse, dissipate his energy in an attempt to disprove the fossil "testimony of the rocks." If he took the second course and chose to discard the old and follow the new, he ended with either openminded indifference, agnosticism, atheism, or the new religion of science. And if he attempted to reconcile the old with the new, to work out a comfortable compromise, he was headed for a quicksand of "isms" and cults

152

distinguished from each other by the nature of the compromise, or by their novelty. Choices were further complicated by individual differences of temperament, personal needs, and social pressures which not only determined the choice but often gave it direction.

Because of the increasing scientific information which he felt he could not refute, the thinking Victorian was plagued with uncertainty about what to believe. He was wracked sometimes with agonizing doubt about the validity of any Christian dogma. It is therefore to be expected that many novels of the time, whatever their religious stripe, should be concerned with the problem of doubt. In resolving his doubt into a positive belief the Victorian in many instances tailored Christian dogma to his own personal requirements. Or, if he found the resolution impossible, he denied Christianity altogether and substituted for it a new belief in man, in progress, in morality, or in the occult.

In the welter of belief, disbelief and unbelief during the 1880s, when the popularity of *John Inglesant* was highest, the many novels of doubt suggest the variety of choice in matters of faith open to the uncertain Victorian, and reveal the pressures of thought, temperament, and circumstance which could determine the choice. In 1880 alone, besides *John Inglesant* which spoke out for Anglicanism, Edward Dering's *Freville Chase* spoke for Roman Catholicism; Gissing's first novel *Workers in the Dawn* halfheartedly preached Comtean Positivism; Olive Schreiner's tale of agonizing, unresolved doubt, *The Story of an African Farm*, had already been written, though it was not published until 1883. And as the 1880s progressed other dissonant voices joined the chorus.

For the purposes of this study an arbitrary selection has been made from novelists contemporary with Shorthouse, whose novels in the 1880s suggest the religious ferment of the time and indicate some of the pressures on the Victorians: George Gissing (1857-1903), Samuel Butler (1835-1902), Mrs. Humphry Ward (1851-1920), Walter Pater (1839-94) and William Hale White (1831-1913). Gissing's *Workers in the Dawn* was published two months before *John Inglesant* and through the protagonist Arthur Golding explores the possibility of a faith in art, philosophy, or political action. Butler's *The Way of All Flesh* (though published posthumously in 1903) was written between 1873 and 1885 and can be considered contemporary with *John Inglesant*. In 1880 Butler published a philosophic-scientific essay *Unconscious Memory* which is the base of the "Creative Evolution" offered in *The Way of All Flesh* as an alternative to an untenable Anglicanism. *Marius the Epicurean* (1885), closest to *John Inglesant*, shows a tailoring of Christianity to meet Pater's personal requirements. Mrs. Ward's *Robert Elsmere* (1888) sets up the defence of an undogmatic Christianity which is manifested in social service. In *The Autobiography of Mark Rutherford* (1881) and *Mark Rutherford's Deliverance* (1885) William Hale White evolves a working faith in doubt which is independent of dogma for those who, like himself, must believe something.

I

Shorthouse and Gissing had little in common. As one might suspect, they approach the problems of faith and doubt quite differently in *John Inglesant* and *Workers in the Dawn*. Shorthouse through Inglesant never denies Christianity. He merely makes a choice from among a number of orthodoxies; in fact, the choice is essentially between two systems, the Church of England and the Church of Rome. It was to be clear in Shorthouse's later writing that his Broad Church sacramentalism was an adaptation of Anglicanism to his own requirements. Half-mystic by nature, Shorthouse began with a religious base, "God always, God everywhere," and a residue of Quakerism on which he superimposed a distinctive Anglicanism which amounted to religion as an art. Religion, his religion, was a solution to the questions of his time, and, for that matter, of any time. *John Inglesant* is a record of indecision, not of doubt. Inglesant is a puzzled and vacillating seeker, not a sceptic, but his voice at the end of the novel when he has made up his mind is confident and sure.

Gissing began without religious convictions of any kind. By studying German philosophers (like Helen Norman in *Workers in the Dawn*)—Goethe, Haeckel, Schopenhauer—and by reading Auguste Comte in the British Museum reading room he fought his way to a purely intellectual conclusion. His solution to the problems of his time takes place not in religion (as Shorthouse conceived of it) but in Comtean Positivism. Writing to his brother shortly after the publication of *Workers in the Dawn* Gissing remarked:

The book in the first place is . . . a very strong . . . attack upon certain features of our present religious and social life. . . . First and foremost, I attack the criminal negligence of governments which spend their time over matters of relatively no importance, to the neglect of terrible social evils which should have been long since sternly grappled with. . . . As regards religious matters, I plainly seek to show the nobility of a faith dispensing with all we are accustomed to call religion, and having for its only creed belief in the responsibility of intellectual and moral progress. Hence it follows that I attack (somewhat savagely) the modern developments of Ritualism, which, of course, is the absolute antithesis of my faith.[2]

In *Workers in the Dawn* Gissing's emphasis is on the problems of slum poverty and the ineffectuality of orthodox religion in dealing with them. Arthur Golding at the age of eight is charitably rescued from the slums by Edward Norman, the Anglican incumbent of Bloomford near London. With only a smattering of religious instruction Golding escapes to the slums and after considerable misery is befriended by Samuel Tolladay, a printer. Impatient with all theologies, Tolladay has come to possess a faith in a "Religion of Humanity." He arouses in Golding a passionate desire to alleviate the miserable condition of the poor. Golding joins a workingmen's club with a political program for the "New Dawn," but eventually leaves it, disillusioned. He entertains for a time a humanitarian dream of improving the world through his art. But that vision fades. Frustrated, he takes his life. So, by indirection Gissing is saying that political, social and philosophical "isms" are ineffectual in solving the problems of human misery; and orthodox religion is equally ineffectual.

By his rough handling of the Anglican clergy in *Workers in the Dawn* Gissing suggests also that organized Christianity is no alternative to the religion of "Humanity." Of all the characters in the novel, scholarly Edward Norman comes closest to what Shorthouse believed an Anglican clergyman would be or should be. But when Norman's daughter asks, "What *is* God?" he replies that it is *something* "which gives you the power of distinguishing between a good and a bad action" or "bids you choose the good and beautiful rather than the bad or ugly." In a moment of despondency he remarks to Gresham, his cynical artist-friend: "I should walk down to the church next Sunday morning, mount the pulpit as I am, devoid of ecclesiastical mummery, and proclaim aloud to the congregation, 'Behold! Here am I, Edward Norman, who have been your pastor for so-and-so many years, preaching the gospel to you day after day without in reality believing a word of what I preached.' " Norman's Ritualist curate is caricatured by Gissing as silly beyond redemption; his son is portrayed as a hypocritical profligate, a divinity student who has any characteristic but godliness. Frankly confessing her Positivist views Helen Norman offers her service to the Anglican clergy working in the slums. She receives no reply from one clergyman, and from the other only a pompous, indignant reprimand and a request for a donation. But despite her "unchristianity" she is accepted by Heatherley, who, with untainted faith, continues his futile plodding in the slums mission, a genuine Christian, but (unfortunately, Shorthouse would think) a Dissenter. In Shorthouse's politically conservative mind—and not in his only—Dissent was associated with the Reform Bills, as it well might be, and he was apprehensive of advancing democracy which he felt could lead only to socialism (Gissing's "Dawn"?) and the triumph of vulgarity. Nothing in Gissing's picture would have allayed his fears.

But in *Workers in the Dawn* Gissing's voice, though insistent, quavers with uncertainty as Shorthouse's in *John Inglesant* does not. Samuel Tolladay, opposed to all organized religion, despite his religion of Humanity and his discreet philanthropy, dies in poverty, ineffectual; Helen Norman, having abandoned the mild Anglicanism of her childhood for Positivism, uses up her body and her money in a humanitarian effort with little perceptible effect; Arthur Golding, after testing all, and finding the "isms" of his time unworkable or futile, takes his life. So Gissing's answer to doubt is really no answer, or at best a wistful hope. Shorthouse could, of course, sound the more cheerful note, for though there were slums in Birmingham, they did not extend to patrician Edgbaston. He could have had only a tourist's view of the London cesspool as he rode in Macmillan's carriage between Euston Station and Tooting. Though never rich, he had always been comfortable. But Gissing had actually endured some of Arthur Golding's misery in London and could justifiably be cynical about well-meant attempts to lift the human animal out of its mire. By temperament and experience different, Shorthouse could not sing the same tune as Gissing no matter where the truth lay.

II

Nothing in *John Inglesant* or in his other writing indicates Shorthouse's attitude toward the mushrooming scientific information which caused so many of his contemporaries to question the religious belief of their fathers. Lyell's *Principles of Geology* was published shortly before Shorthouse was born a Quaker; Darwin's

The Origin of Species was published two years before Shorthouse was baptized in the Church of England. One can only assume (or speculate) that, though necessarily conscious of science, he somehow absorbed the new scientific information as supporting rather than in contradiction of religious belief. If there was religious indecision, there seems to have been no period of scepticism during his passage from the Society of Friends to the Church of England. The new faith in science seems for him never to have been an alternative to either Quakerism or Anglicanism.

In this respect he differs from those who, like Samuel Butler, chipped a faith of some sort out of the new science. Butler's *The Way of All Flesh* suggests, if it does not expound, a faith in biological principle as an alternative to the Anglicanism in which he had been reared and which at nineteen he had abandoned. Behind and under *The Way of All Flesh* (begun in 1873; completed in 1885) lies some of Butler's philosophical-scientific writing, particularly *Life and Habit* (1877) and *Unconscious Memory* (1880). A religious sceptic even before 1862 when as a young sheep-farmer in New Zealand he read *The Origin of Species*, he was unlikely to join the throng which by invective or ridicule was trying to protect the "Holy City of Orthodoxy" against the infidel. On the other hand, for all the warmth of his original response to *The Origin of Species* he gradually developed his own view of evolutionary progress. Darwin, as Butler claimed to read him, had banished "Mind" from the universe by suggesting that modifications in the species were the result of fortuitous circumstances, thus ruling out design in evolution. Butler maintained that design was implied by the organism's will to live. Accepting Lamarck's theory that species are modified by transmission of characteristics acquired through adaptation to environment, he argued that through a sense of need the individual organism, by repeated volition, struggles to adapt itself to change. Variation, then, is due not to "luck" (chance) but to "cunning" (conscious striving) of the individual in adapting to environmental circumstances, and is passed on to following generations by inheritance of an "unconscious memory" of acts incessantly repeated. Professor Robert Lee Wolff in a recent discussion of Butler comments pertinently on the significance of Butler's thinking on this matter:

In the "continued personality" passing not only from parent to child, but also from each entire generation of mankind to the next, Butler found the substitute for the personal Deity of which Darwinism had originally robbed him. Since men live in their descendents, they obtain a form of immortality. The mere wish to live, to know, to do, is in itself an act of faith. Thus is "the vital principle." And the presence of unconscious memory provides the best possible life, and the inverse is equally true.[3]

Thus in *The Way of All Flesh* Ernest Pontifex, a maladjusted "animal" in an uncongenial environment, discards the religious beliefs he has always meekly accepted but never understood and begins to struggle for survival, for independence ("volition"). Conscious of his own stultifying religious education, he places his children into the care of a bargeman's family at Gravesend that they may grow up healthy and normal, trained in useful work, learning what they want or need to know. In effect, this is a cyclical return to the healthy condition of his great-grandfather, John Pontifex, but with an infusion of Ernest's own "volition," "striving," "cunning" which will be transmitted by "unconscious memory." Butler's alternative to orthodoxy, then, is a "faith" in "Creative Evolution," in biology. There is no evidence that Shorthouse ever considered this alternative to the orthodoxy which Butler was flagellating in *The Way of All Flesh*. But his wide tolerance of belief different from his own made no great choice of alternatives necessary. He could cheerfully assert: "I believe that every dogma of Christianity is based on scientific truth . . . and I believe that if ever agnostics would adopt my position, they would be drawn on to believe as we believe." [4] He seems never to have indicated what he meant by "scientific truth." One can only surmise that by "scientific" he meant either "demonstrable" or "experienced."

III

The only real, influential rival to *John Inglesant* in the 1880s was Mrs. Humphry Ward's *Robert Elsmere* (1888). For those doubters of dogma who needed assurance of the validity of Christianity the novel provided an answer—Christianity revealed in action, humanitarian service. The popularity of *Robert Elsmere* suggests that the Victorians had other concerns than the cleavage between the Church of Rome and the Church of England. Shorthouse's passage from the Society of Friends to the Church of England seems placid when one considers Mrs. Ward's attempts to find a satisfactory religion. Her background (unlike Shorthouse's) was a motley of religious belief. She was the granddaughter of the great Dr. Thomas Arnold of Rugby, the niece of Matthew Arnold, the niece (by marriage) of W. E. Forster [Education Bill 1870] who lost his membership in the Society of Friends by his marriage to an Anglican; she was the daughter of a fiercely Protestant mother of Huguenot descent married to Dr. Arnold's second son Thomas who shuttled between the Church of England and the Church of Rome. Her brothers were brought up as Catholics, her sisters as Protestants. When in 1867 she joined her family in Oxford, she, as an eager and charmed adolescent, moved socially and intellectually in the charged atmosphere created by Benjamin Jowett, Mark Pattison, Thomas Hill Green, Lewis Nettleship, Henry Sidgwick. Thus she was fanned during her most impressionable years among the "patient scholars and thinkers of the Liberal host" with what she called "the spiritual winds of an agitated day." [5] Mrs. Ward recalls her "shock of indignation" excited by John Wordsworth's first Bampton lecture (on the subject "Doubt as Sin") which, she says, "led directly—though through seven intervening years—to 'Robert Elsmere.' " [6] "How," she asks, "would one show England what was going on in her midst?" Her first response to the question was to write a pamphlet "Unbelief and Sin" which, against the advice of friends, she posted in a bookseller's window. She completed *Robert Elsmere* in March 1887. "Elsmere," she says, "was to be an exponent of a free faith. I wanted to show how a man of sensitive and noble character, born for religion, comes to throw off the orthodoxies of the day and moment, and to go out into the wilderness where all is experiment, and spiritual life begins. And with him I wished to contrast a type of the traditional and guided mind—and to imagine the clash of two such tendencies of thought, as it might affect the practical life, and especially the life of two people who lived together." [7]

Elsmere is a young clergyman, by family influence and character happy in the "stateliness and comely beauty of the Church order as it was revealed to him at Oxford." The sacraments and the ceremonies of the Church mean less to him than its social gospel, but still he believes that the Church of England by law established is the only institution capable of making a social gospel effective. But various influences, particularly those of the freethinking Squire Wendover, raise doubts in Elsmere's mind about the validity of his untested beliefs and eventually destroy his faith. When he concludes that he can no longer hypocritically continue in his pulpit, he leaves the Church to practise the social gospel in the slums, and finally dies of overwork. In *Workers in the Dawn,*

Gresham, Edward Norman's sophisticated artist friend, has a pragmatic solution to Elsmere's problem. Gresham advises Norman to remain in the Church in spite of his doubts because no one will know the difference. Helen Norman is defeated by the magnitude of her humanitarian service, but Heatherley labors on. Shorthouse in *Blanche, Lady Falaise* was later to give a bilious cast to the social gospel by making Damerle a sincere but weak instrument. Mrs. Ward was also eventually to revise her opinion about the necessity of doubters leaving the Church in *The Case of Richard Meynell* (1911), but in 1888 in *Robert Elsmere* she is saying that there is such a thing as respectable scepticism and that doubt is not a sin as John Wordsworth had asserted in his Bampton lecture. A social gospel unattached to dogma is her answer to doubt about dogma. She is singing as confidently as Shorthouse but not quite in tune with him. And Gissing, though he would like to believe in the social gospel unattached to dogma, sings too uncertainly to support her.

IV

Shorthouse had so little in common with Gissing, Butler, or Mrs. Ward that one could expect him to be unaffected by their alternatives to orthodoxy. But with Walter Pater he had a surface affinity which almost conceals the difference between the two men. Edmund Gosse defines Shorthouse as a Birmingham Pater. Certainly, a similarity between the "Birmingham Pater" and the Oxford-London Pater is discernible in their interest in Platonism, their aesthetic enjoyment of liturgical ritual, their affection for the past, their careful writing. On the other hand, Shorthouse was a part-time, eager but unsystematic, vagrant scholar; Pater was an Oxford don, a professional scholar with no daytime duties at the "Warehouse." By temperament Shorthouse was cheerfully half-mystic; Pater was intellectual and philosophic rather than religious.

As was suggested earlier, *John Inglesant* may be considered Shorthouse's *apologia*, his defence of the Anglican position he had arrived at on withdrawal from the Society of Friends, a satisfactory alternative to Quakerism. In a slightly different manner *Marius the Epicurean* is Pater's *apologia*. The "Conclusion" to Pater's *Studies in the History of the Renaissance* (1873) had excited considerable discussion about his "hedonism." Pater, alarmed by what he considered a misinterpretation of his meaning, omitted the "Conclusion" from the second edition. W. H. Mallock in *Mallock in The*

New Republic (1877) mercilessly satirized Pater in the decadent "Mr. Rose." In 1881 Pater began *Marius*, which was published in 1885. The offending "Conclusion," slightly altered,was reinstated in the third edition of *The Renaissance* (1888) with Pater's explanatory note: "This brief 'Conclusion' was omitted in the second edition, as I conceived it might possibly mislead some of those young men into whose hand it might fall. On the whole I have thought it best to reprint it here, with some slight changes which bring it closer to my original meaning. I have dealt more fully in *Marius the Epicurean* with the thoughts suggested by it." In July 1883 he had written to Vernon Lee [Violet Paget]: "I have hopes of completing one half of my present chief work—an Imaginary Portrait of a peculiar type of mind in the time of Marcus Aurelius, by the end of this vacation. . . . I regard this present matter as a sort of duty. For you know I think that there is a . . . sort of religious phase possible for the modern mind, the conditions of which it is the main object of my design to convey." [8]

"The sort of religious phase possible for the modern mind," for such a mind as his own, Pater had already suggested in "The Child in the House" (*Macmillan's Magazine* August 1878). There he records (about himself, presumably): "[Florian] began to love, for their own sakes, church lights, holy days, all that belonged to the comely order of the sanctuary, the secrets of its white linen, and holy vessels, and fonts of pure water, and its hieratic simplicity became the type of something he desired always to have about him in actual life." [9]

What is germane to discussion here is Pater's reference to the "comely order," the sensuous, aesthetic enjoyment of the forms, the symbols, the externals of religion. This sensuous love of the "comely order" Shorthouse shares with Pater. Passage after passage, not only in *John Inglesant* but in Shorthouse's other novels and essays, lingers on the sensuous, uplifting beauties of the church service. In *John Inglesant* (Ch. 4) when Inglesant takes communion with the Ferrars, he feels that he can never "lose the sense of that touching scene, of that gracious figure over the altar, of the bowed and kneeling figures, of the misty autumn sunlight, and the sweeping autumn wind." But a difference of attitude (or belief) between Shorthouse and Pater is perceptible from their handling of similar "scenes." In Chapter 31 of *John Inglesant* Inglesant participates in mass at the Church of the Lateran. In Chapter 23 of *Marius the Epicurean* ("Divine Service") Marius, on the brink of Christianity, observes "for the first time the spectacle . . . of those who believe." The respective episodes are handled by Shorthouse and Pater in similar manner to bring out the beauties and drama of the service. But one can be pardoned for feeling that Shorthouse, like Inglesant, is a participant, and Pater, like Marius, is a spectator of worship. In the act of worship, the aesthetic experience for Shorthouse is inextricably combined with the religious experience; it intensifies and heightens the religious experience. For Pater the act of worship *is* the experience. One can suspect that Pater in *Marius the Epicurean* is arguing that an acceptance of Christianity is necessary for the dispelling of doubt, but one can infer also that Marius's "Christianity" is a series of "sensations," a focusing of "impressions," rather than a statement of belief. Pater implies that a Christianity without codified dogma is a workable hypothesis by means of which doubt can be resolved and some sort of faith attained. Shorthouse, as much aware as Pater of the "comely order," the "becoming attitude," is already sure of his faith in a particular form of Christianity, a national, English church.

V

William Hale White is representative of those Victorians who, without altogether discarding inherited dogma for an alternative, selected, rethought, restated that dogma in terms acceptable to them. In the *Autobiography of Mark Rutherford* (1881) and *Mark Rutherford's Deliverance* (1885) White traces the intellectual and emotional journey of Mark Rutherford from the untested belief of his childhood, through the doubt of his early manhood, to resolution into a form of faith. Hale White is a "modern" Puritan. Sceptical of the Calvinist dogma which disturbed his youth (as it did Rutherford's) he turns his scepticism to use as an instrument in validifying Christianity for this modern mind. In the *Autobiography* (Ch. 9) he points out that "what we believe is not of so much importance as the path by which we travel to it." It is only through doubt that one can achieve a firm belief. Without any consciousness of heresy, Rutherford realizes fairly early in his sceptical period (Ch. 2) that "nearly every doctrine in the college creed had once had a natural origin in the necessities of human nature [validity], and might therefore be so interpreted [restated] as to become a necessity again." Because of the complexity of the universe the finite mind can understand but little of it and of God and therefore can find little certainty. There will always, then, be a margin of doubt. But some sort of faith one must have. Because doubt is normal, the struggle for a supporting faith will be unending. Because the intellect cannot grasp everything (and much must needs remain a mystery), one can but hope that from a chaos of ideas, principles, motives, actions, one can by an intelligent selection of those which are wholesome and ennobling give proper direction to one's life. In extremities one must rely on "insight," on what Miss Arbour in the *Autobiography* (Ch. 5) calls the "voice of God" (and Rutherford calls the "inner oracle"). It comes to the earnest seeker only in the silence, in repose, and it must be obeyed.

What strikes one here is the similarity of Rutherford's "inner oracle" to Inglesant's "Divine Light." Commenting on Peter T. Forsyth's *Religion in Recent Art* (1889) Shorthouse remarked: "He [Forsyth] is naturally, somewhat in a fog, *being a Dissenter*, but what he says seems very reasonable." [10] Shorthouse had greater affinity to Hale White, this dissenter from Dissent, than he might have surmised. By temperament Hale White and Shorthouse were "religious" in a sense that Butler, Mrs. Ward, Pater, and certainly Gissing, were not. If Shorthouse is the more mystically inclined, Hale White is not without a trace of mysticism, though he (like Rutherford) is more steadily conscious of "fact" than Shorthouse (like Inglesant) is. Both in the formulations of their belief owed a debt to Wordsworth and Spinoza. Though they interpret differently, both emphasize the "idea of Christ" as central to their belief. Shorthouse justified that "idea" by means of Platonic philosophy. Hale White took the simpler route by considering the example of Christ as a pattern for human conduct. Both were sin-conscious. Sin is a fact, and expiation of and atonement for sin a necessity. Shorthouse, though never very clear on the point, conceived of an ever-present evil lurking in the universe. Sin, as Hale White reveals it through Rutherford, constitutes thinking of *self* alone, as if the self were not part of a whole; atonement is a fact of life, for the innocent always suffer because of the guilty; salvation comes through love by an abandonment of Self for the Universal.

But the most important difference between the two men can best be discerned in their attitude toward institutionalized religion. Though Shorthouse's Anglicanism was so "Broad" and so "High" as to be in fact a personal made-to-order religion, he nevertheless required an institutionalized form—a well-appointed church edifice, an unchanging ritual, a creed—through which his religion could be realized. Hale White, having dismissed systematized religion for a creedless one, retains one of the fundamental concepts of Puritanism, that the state of a man's soul is an internal, private matter between man and God, and cannot be judged, as conduct can, by measurement against a creed, or practice, or a "system." Therefore, churchgoing is of no great importance. Though the picture of Christ in Gethsemane hung over his bed at Groombridge and Hale White read his Bible every morning, he seldom entered a church. "What would I learn there? he remarked. Shorthouse's greatest regret during his last illness was that he was deprived of "the beautiful service" of his Church. Like many others, Hale White, lapsed Calvinist independent, an "expert in pain," remains to the end a Puritan who admits no outside interference or distraction in the communion of man with God. Like many others, Shorthouse sensuously stimulated by the drama of ritual and the beauties of organ music and stained glass windows is elevated to a communion of man with God.

Shorthouse and Hale White differ in one other important respect. Shorthouse places his hope for an improvement of the human condition in what he considers the elevating power of aristocratic ideals from times past, culture—Inglesant's experience. Hale White places his in the salutary, present experience of the "mystery of the commonplace," in the lessons to be learned from one's own suffering and that of countless ordinary people. Salvation comes only through love of one's neighbor, which is an emanation of the Divine Love—Rutherford's experience.

VI

It is a truism that every age is an age of change. What distinguishes, then, one century from another is the rate of change and the nature of the change. Almost a century has passed since these Victorian voices of faith, hope, doubt, and despair were raised in the ever-changing discord along the highway (always under construction) from the Industrial Revolution to the Atomic Age. For the Victorians the economic, political, social (inevitably including philosophical and religious) changes which were the direct and indirect results of the Industrial Revolution did not automatically create a new heaven nor suddenly dismantle an old hell. And in the twentieth century the ever-accelerating rate of change in institutions, modes of thought, and attitudes has not managed to dispel the uncertainty which afflicted Shorthouse's contemporaries. Though some matters which perturbed the Victorians are no longer in doubt, an important question remains: "What shall, or must, or can a man believe?" The condition of the underprivileged which was grieved over in *Workers in the Dawn* has been modified but not eliminated. The social gospel of *Robert Elsmere* was adapted and expanded—even during Mrs. Ward's lifetime—into all sorts of philanthropical enterprises, but the well of misery still is deep. *The Way of All Flesh*, which has still some small pertinence in the battle of the biologists, has become curiously more pertinent as a blunt instrument for sociological and psychological demolition than as a guide to belief. Denominational boundaries have been blurred, if not erased, by ecumenical overtures and the redefinition of old creeds. But there remain still the normal shades of belief, disbelief, unbelief. The survival in the twentieth century of some of the cults on the fringes of Victorian religion—and the rise and fall of new cults—is evidence of man's almost frenetic desire, amid falling temples and "th' encircling gloom," to believe *something* which can give consolatory joy, or hope, or certainty.

Workers in the Dawn is no assuring guide to belief. Arthur Golding, eventually with no faith in anything, despairingly takes his life, and hope, faint to a glimmer, shines only in Heatherley who does believe something which enables him to bear defeat and to wrest a modicum of joy from meager success. In *Robert Elsmere*, Elsmere, though he discards a particular orthodox belief, nevertheless believes in the nondenominational humanitarian cause which eventually kills him. Ernest Pontifex in *The Way of All Flesh*, too late bereft of religious dogma, believes in the future of his children with a Butlerian hope in the improvement of the species. Pater's Marius, his ancestral religion abandoned, after a vacillation between epicureanism and stoicism, hovers on the brink of a belief that seems to promise joy and hope—a Christianity as yet undogmatic and unformalized. In the *Autobiography* and the *Deliverance* Mark Rutherford works out a faith for those who must believe—a creedless, unorganized belief that will work at any time. Though it can promise only accidental joy, only occasional hope, and no real certainty, it enables the believer to endure what endure he must. And to those who still require, among contemporary confusions and dissolving institutions, the authority of a form to channel and enhance their belief, *John Inglesant* can convey Shorthouse's sense of joy and hope and certainty. Amy Cruse comments: "Into a troubled and restless world it [*John Inglesant*] came like a quiet voice reminding men that there remained for those who would seek it an inner center of peace untouched by the controversies that raged without." [11] Shorthouse was perhaps not a great novelist; he was not a great, nor even a consistent, thinker, but even if he is only one voice in the Victorian discord, he carries his tune with the confidence of one who has to his own satisfaction solved the problem of belief. In the twentieth century, his pertinence lies in the slender possibility that for "those who [like Mark Rutherford and John Inglesant] seek it" there can be "an inner center of peace" which will make it a matter of indifference whether the world ends with a bang or with a whimper.

Notes and References

Chapter One

1. *Memorials of the Families of Shorthouse and Robinson and Others Connected with Them, Printed in Commemoration of the One Hundredth Birthday of Sarah Southall,* 12 September, 1901. Printed for private circulation (Birmingham, 1902), pp. 94–97. Cited hereafter as *SR.*

2. Grove House School in Tottenham ("the Birmingham of London") was founded in 1828 and continued until 1878 on the site now occupied by the Tottenham Polytechnic. A former country mansion situated on six acres of land and surrounded by gentlemen's residences with fine gardens, the school normally gave instruction to between thirty and forty students. A carefully chosen staff on high salaries accounts for the high tuition fee of one hundred pounds per annum. A wide curriculum offered English grammar and literature, Latin and Greek (normally considered "pagan" subjects by Quakers) German, French, mathematics, drawing (but not painting), natural and experimental philosophy, Principles of Religious Liberty, the British Constitution, natural history, geography, history, and the Practice and History of the Society of Friends. Thus Grove House was one of the progressive, expensive Quaker schools which tried to combine religious tenets with the study of science and modern languages. Shorthouse and his brother John were listed among the students in 1850; his brother Edmund was listed for 1852.

3. The phrase is used by a number of reviewers. It would be difficult to determine whose property it is.

4. This is Robert Barclay's epithet in the title of his exposition of Quaker doctrine *An Apology for the True Christian Divinity as the Same is Held Forth and Preached by the People, in Scorn, Called Quakers* (1687). The phrase and its variants became a cliché in Quaker literature. A broadside petition (1661) listing "sufferings" of the Quakers is made by "The People of God called Quakers."

5. Shorthouse's grandfather William Shorthouse in 1830, and his uncle William Nutter in 1843, had been victims of distraint. Some Quakers got around the difficulty of the church-rate in a number of ways; for example, one practice was to "leave" the rate-money where the proper official could "find" it. In this way they were technically obeying the Society of Friends by making no direct contribution to the support of "Steeplehouses," and the law of the land by having paid the church-rate.

167

6. Moses Morris's oldest daughter, Mary Knowles (1733–1801), the painter, was a friend of Dr. Johnson. She is one of the few Quaker painters—Benjamin West (1738–1820) and Samuel Lucas (1805–70) are two others—in the early nineteenth century, for the Quakers' "age-old fear of color" discouraged the use of pigment in art, as well as color in clothing. Shorthouse and his cousins had lessons in sketching and drawing but not in painting.

7. *SR*, p. 4.

8. *Life, Letters, and Literary Remains of J. H. Shorthouse*, 2 vols., edited by his wife (London, 1905), Vol. I, p. 22. Hereafter *Volume I (Life, Letters)* will be cited as *LL* and *Volume II (Literary Remains)* as *LR*.

9. *LL*, p. 6.

10. George Bainton, *The Art of Authorship* (London: Jas. Clark & Co., 1890), p. 146.

11. *SR*, p. 19. Shorthouse was called Henry by his parents, cousins and friends, but Harry by his brothers. His normal signature is J. Henry Shorthouse. It is pleasantly ironical that after the publication of *John Inglesant* Shorthouse's name appears frequently as *John* Henry in reviews, obituaries, and critical notices. Shorthouse smarted patiently until in a letter to Macmillan (8 October 1886) he complains: "When my name is advertised at full length I should be glad for it to be correctly stated; my name is *Joseph* Henry, not *John*. I have a brother named John." *The Bromley Express* (4 March 1903) gets the prize for taking Shorthouse's name in vain. In their notice of Shorthouse's death they refer to him as John Harry Shorthouse. Even the famous Sandys portrait of Shorthouse in the Macmillan Authors Collection is inconspicuously labelled "J. H. Sorthouse."

12. Ibid., p. 47.

13. Ibid., p. 53.

14. *LL*, p. 32.

15. *SR*, p. 79.

16. Ibid., p. 70.

17. Ibid., p. 71.

18. Ibid., p. 74.

19. *LL*, p. 17.

20. In John W. Shorthouse's diary for 1853 a number of entries allude to repeated visits by a Monsieur Duval who was apparently trying to cure his brother's stammer. It appears to have been a last attempt at therapy. Mildred F. Berry and Jon Eisenson in *Speech Disorders; Principles and Practices of Therapy* (New York: Appleton-Century-Crofts, 1956) suggest that parents "anxious about the speech of the child" may hasten the child into trying "to master adult speech too soon," and therefore cause a nervous child to stammer. They also make a connection between nervous disorders, like epilepsy, and stammering.

21. In a tribute to Shorthouse after his death, in the *Pall Mall Gazette* (5

March 1903), "By One Who Knew Him," the writer says: "It was a cruel impediment of speech which reduced Mr. Shorthouse's social enjoyments within . . . narrow limits. Once, when a guest at a classical play which has been kept up at the Oratory School as a tradition of Cardinal Newman, Mr. Shorthouse rose to speak on behalf of his fellow-visitors, but his usual nervousness overcame him, and his gratitude remained for ever unexpressed."

22. *LL*, p. 9.

23. Ibid., p. 10.

24. *Yorkshire Post* (7 March 1903).

25. A. G. Gardiner, *Life of George Cadbury* (London: Cassell, 1923), p. 18.

26. *T. P.'s Weekly* (13 March 1903), p. 554.

27. Ibid., (29 January 1904), p. 146.

28. James Bain, *A Bookseller Looks Back* (London: Macmillan & Co., 1940), p. 140.

29. Henry Scott Holland, *A Bundle of Memories* (London: Wells, Gardner & Co., 1914), pp. 137–38.

30. *Macmillan Archive* MS 543934, pp. 178–79 (letter d. 22 May 1905).

31. Gosse's review was later included in his *Portraits and Sketches* (London: Heinemann, 1924). Gosse dedicated his *Questions at Issue* (London: Heinemann, 1893) to Shorthouse.

32. William Boyd Carpenter, *Further Pages of My Life* (London: Williams & Norgate, 1916), p. 216.

33. Arthur Sidgwick and Eleanor Mildred Sidgwick, *Henry Sidgwick: A Memoir* (London: Macmillan & Co., 1906), p. 459.

34. *LL*, p. 379.

35. Ibid., p. 12.

36. Ibid., p. 30.

37. Ibid., p. 29.

38. Ibid., p. 33.

39. E. Edwards, *Personal Recollections* (Birmingham: Midland Education Trading Co., 1877), p. 4.

40. *SR*, p. 71.

41. *LL*, p. 13.

42. Ibid., p. 37.

43. Ibid., p. 39.

44. *Life of George Cadbury*, p. 15.

45. *SR*, p. 79.

46. *Friends' Quarterly Examiner*, LVI (1922), 51.

47. *Mary Howitt an Autobiography*, ed. by her daughter Margaret Howitt (London: W. Isbister, 1889), I, 219.

48. *Friends' Quarterly Examiner* (July 1822).

49. *SR*, p. 83.

50. Ibid., p. 83.

51. Ibid., p. 83.
52. *LL*, p. 64.
53. Ibid., pp. 66–67.
54. Ibid., p. 64.

Chapter Two

1. J. D. Hunter, "The Early Years of the Birmingham Friends' Reading Society," *Journal of West Midland Regional Studies*, 2 (1968), 44.
2. *Essays of the Friends' Essay Society*, Vol. 16 [n. d.], p. 4.
3. Letters from Mrs. Shorthouse to Macmillan (dating from 25 March 1903 to 28 November 1907) are in the *Macmillan Archive* (British Library), MS 543934.
4. Elfriede Rieger, *Joseph Henry Shorthouse und sein "John Inglesant,"* Ein Beitrag zur Geschichte des englischen Romans im 19. Jahrhundert Diss. Georg-August 1927 (Göttingen: Göttingen Tageblat, 1927), p. 29.
5. *LR*, p. 6.
6. Ibid., pp. 41–43.
7. Ibid., p. 207.

Chapter Three

1. The letter referred to is in the Berg Collection, New York City Public Library.
2. *LL*, p. 76.
3. Part of a letter to Charles R. Aston was published in the *Church Times* (9 April 1903).
4. *LL*, p. 329.
5. Ibid., pp. 130–31.
6. It is difficult to determine what Shorthouse really had in mind. Probably he meant only that he would be unwilling to undertake a major reorganization of the book which might make it more like "the novels of the day" he disapproved of. Shorthouse saw the 1880 edition through the press himself, and it is therefore not surprising that the text of *John Inglesant* shows the same faults as his essays and letters before they were edited: whimsical punctuation, erratic capitalization, faulty syntax, misspelling (particularly of Italian proper names) which cannot be blamed on imperfect proofreading. Careful refinement by Macmillan's editors considerably improved the text, and made it syntactically more sound. Some sentences were omitted; others were altered; some were added. For some reason Shorthouse changed a few dates in Inglesant's life. Dr. Henry More in the 1880 edition is consistently called Dr. Mole, but reassumes his own name in the Macmillan edition (1881).

7. *Macmillan Archive, MS* 55935, IV, 45.

8. This is William Angus Knight's version of the much repeated story (*Retrospects, First Series,* [New York: Scribners, 1904] 296). There are only two common factors in the various versions—Gladstone and *John Inglesant*; other details of place, position, volume vary with the teller. I have failed to find a copy of the photograph.

9. Paul Elmer More, "J. Henry Shorthouse," *Shelburne Essays, Third Series* (New York, 1906), p. 236.

10. The phrase is Charles F. Keary's in "The Work of J. Henry Shorthouse," *Edinburgh Review,* XXII (July 1905), 125.

11. See Edmund Gosse, "The Author of 'John Inglesant,' " *Portraits and Sketches* (London: Heinemann, 1924), pp. 149-62.

12. *LL,* p. 137.

13. Ibid., p. 122.

14. Ibid., p. 123.

15. Ibid., p. 130.

16. Ibid., p. 124.

17. *Friends' Quarterly Examiner,* XXXIX (1905), 400.

18. *LL.* p. 132.

19. Shorthouse may never have been in the Beringtons' house but it is interesting that the house does contain a portrait such as he describes in the house at Lydiard. Herbert Bartleet in " 'John Inglesant,' Its Author, and Little Malvern," *Transactions of the Worcestershire Archeological Society* (1923–24), pp. 41–49, states in a footnote that the portrait at Little Malvern Court has inscribed on its back: "Joseph Williams, Priest of the English Carthusians in Nieuport, Flanders, son of Thomas Williams Esq., of Trellynian, Flintshire, A.D. 1779." Also he says, "In the Burial Register of Little Malvern Church is the following entry: 'Buried 8 January 1797, the Rev. Joseph Williams.' " Some years ago, after some persistence, I was allowed a glimpse of the portrait without a glimpse of the inscription on the back, and concluded then that the portrait was much as Shorthouse had described it without, presumably, his having seen it. While he was on holiday at Malvern, Shorthouse may, of course, have seen the church register, and heard about the picture in the house. In furnishing his stage Shorthouse may not even have needed Anthony à Wood to supply him with the name "Lydiard," for when the story proper opens its setting is several miles south of Malmesbury in Wiltshire. In the same area, in a large park stands a mansion, Lydiard House, and a private family church, noted by John Aubrey, one of Shorthouse's favorite sources. But the mind staggers under the burden of trying to make a firm connection between the Benedictine "tonsured head" of John Inglesant, of Flemish extraction, and the portrait in the Berington house of the Carthusian Williams, eighteenth-century Welsh priest in Flanders, and Lydiard Mansion with its private church in the park. Even the Flemish name "Inglesant" Shorthouse could

have met in the *Register of Freemen of York* and the *Yorkshire Poll Tax Returns* which mention a William, though not a John, Inglesant.

20. In the first edition of *John Inglesant* (1880) Inglesant is born in 1612. In the first Macmillan edition (1881) dates are moved up by ten years to fit Inglesant's birthdate 1622. Perhaps Shorthouse changed the dates to bring Inglesant's life into line with John Aubrey's (1626–97), or more likely with John Evelyn's (1620–1706). Certainly it is more than coincidence that Inglesant's tour of Italy follows the itinerary of Evelyn's continental tour in 1644.

21. Gardiner's criticism was made in *Fraser's Magazine*, NS., 25 (May 1882), 599–605. Lord Acton's detailed criticism of the historical background of *John Inglesant* can be found in *Letters of Lord Acton to Mary, Daughter of the Right Hon. W. E. Gladstone*, edited by Herbert Paul (London: Macmillan, 1904), pp. 126–23; 135–48; 150–51. Shorthouse apparently tried to answer Acton, but I have been unable to find the letter. Fleming's *Quarterly Review* article years later indicated that Shorthouse was sometimes right when the historians were wrong.

22. Shorthouse would have had available J. E. B. Mayor's first volume of *Cambridge in the Seventeenth Century* (1855) which contains Jebb and John Ferrar. Peckard he would have found in Christopher Wordsworth's *Ecclesiastical Biography* (1810).

23. So effective is the result that many readers with no suspicion of the assistance from Peckard expressed surprise that Shorthouse—who readily admitted he had never been to Little Gidding—had managed to wield the brush so well. Little Gidding became a tourist attraction for excited admirers of *John Inglesant*. One enthusiast brought some flowers from Little Gidding as a gift and tribute to the author, flowers which Shorthouse carefully preserved between the pages of his own copy of *John Inglesant*. At Shorthouse's funeral an anonymous admirer from King's College, Cambridge, left a large wreath as "a tribute of admiration and reverence from one who owes all that is best in him to 'John Inglesant.' "

24. See A. L. Maycock, *Nicholas Ferrar of Little Gidding* (London: Society for Promoting Christian knowledge, 1938), and W. K. Fleming, "Some Truths about 'John Inglesant,' " *Quarterly Review* CCXLV (July, 1925), 130–48.

25. *LL*, p. 365.

26. Anthony à Wood, *Athenae Oxonienses* (New York: Burt Franklin, 1976), vol. 3, col. 1221. Shorthouse owned the 1691–92 edition.

27. John Aubrey, *Brief Lives and Other Selected Writings*, ed. by Anthony Powell (London: Cresset Press, 1947), p. 121.

28. A good example is found near the end of Chapter 14: "A revolting coarseness marks every detail of the tragic story; the flower of England on either side was beneath the turf or beyond the sea, and the management of affairs was left in the hands of butchers and brewers. Ranting sermons, three in succession, before a brewer in Whitehall, are the medium to which

the religious utterance of England is reduced, and Ireton and Harrison in bed together, with Cromwell and others in the room, signed the warrant for the fatal act."

29. *LL*, p. 329.

30. Robert Lee Wolff, *Gains and Losses: Novels of Faith and Doubt in Victorian England* (New York and London, 1977), p. 172.

31. *N&Q*, 11th Series, XI (10 April 1915), 278.

32. Quotations from Aubrey are in *Aubrey's Brief Lives*, ed. by Oliver Lawson Dick (Ann Arbor: University of Michigan Press, 1962). See also the Anthony Powell edition of *Brief Lives and Other Selected Writings* (London: Cresset Press, 1949). There is no hard evidence that Shorthouse owned Aubrey's *Brief Lives* or the *Miscellanies* (1696) or *Letters Written by Eminent Persons in the Seventeenth and Eighteenth Centuries* (1813). However, included among his books sold after his wife's death, were Aubrey's *Wiltshire: The Topographical Collections, The Natural History of Wiltshire*, and John Britton's *Memoir of John Aubrey, F.R.S.* (1845).

33. There is a careless assumption in some comment on *John Inglesant* that the book given to Inglesant was Richard Crashaw's "The Flaming Heart." The book which meets the description in *John Inglesant* (Ch. 3) is an earlier edition of a book which Shorthouse owned: *The Flaming Hart or the Life of the Glorious S. Teresa, Foundresse of the Reformation, of the Order of the All-Immaculate Virgin-Mother, our B. Lady of Mount Carmel . . . written by the Saint herselfe, in Spanish; and newly, now, translated into English, in the yeare of our God, 1642* (Antwerp: Johannes Meussius, 1642). The book is dedicated to "the incomparable Soveraigne Princess, Henrietta-Maria of France, Queen of Great Brittaine, France, and Ireland." In fact, the books which Shorthouse's characters read are usually from his own library and bibliographically described.

34. *LL*, p. 329.

35. Ibid., pp. 122–23.

36. Shorthouse's letter to W. A. Wickham (5 October 1883) was published in the *Guardian* (18 March 1903): "In reply to your letter I am a devoted adherent of the Church of England *as by law established.* More particularly I should call myself a 'Broad Church Sacramentalist.' The assertion that I am an agnostic merely shows that the majority of persons who use the phrase are totally ignorant of the meaning. . . . The entire tone of 'John Inglesant' is that of *understatment*—it has been compared to what is known as Aristotelian irony or what might perhaps be called 'Christian Agnosticism.' "

37. *LL*, p. 124.

38. Edward, Earl of Clarendon, *The History of the Rebellion and Civil Wars in England*, ed. W. Dunn Macray (Oxford: Clarendon Press [1888], 1958), VII. 222.

39. *LL*, p. 122.

40. Ibid., p. 124.

41. Gilbert Burnet, *Three Letters Concerning the Present State of Italy, Written in the Year 1687* (London[?], 1688).

42. *Macmillan Archive*, MS. 55935, IV, 45.

43. *LL*, p. 174.

44. Ibid., p. 290.

45. Writing to his cousin Isabel, Shorthouse comments (*LL*, 147) that part of the passage "was composed during service in Wells Cathedral, and is, I think, more appropriate to that building than to the Santa Chiara at Naples. Do not make the fact public (in print, I mean); there is no necessity to assist critics to detect flaws."

46. Edith Batho and Bonamy Dobrée, *The Victorians and After* (London: Cresset Press, 1950), p. 295.

47. From a letter to Miss Beever quoted in the *Westminster Gazette* (11 March 1903).

48. Andrew Lang, "Theological Romances," *Contemporary Review* LIII (1888), 815.

49. Henry Festing Jones, *Samuel Butler a Memoir* (London: Macmillan & Co., 1919), I, 373.

50. Herbert Hensley Henson, *Retrospects of an Unimportant Life* (London: Oxford Press, 1946) I, 11.

Chapter Four

1. This letter and following letters cited were originally examined in the London office of Macmillan and Company, before the individual letters became part of the *Macmillan Archive*, British Library in 1965. Therefore only dates of letters are here noted. The letter to George Macmillan is dated 10 February 1883.

2. *Macmillan Archive*, letter to Alexander Macmillan, dated 21 April 1883.

3. Ibid., letter to Frederick Macmillan, dated 29 August 1883.

4. *Academy* XXIV (29 December 1883), 427.

5. *Westminster Review* CXXI: NS 65 (January 1884), 279.

6. *LL*, 223.

7. *Macmillan Archive*, letter to Alexander Macmillan, dated 21 December 1883.

8. *LL*, 202.

9. Ibid., 212.

10. Ibid., 211, 216.

11. *Macmillan Archive*, letter to Frederick Macmillan, dated 17 July 1884.

12. *Part II* was reprinted twice February 1885 and again in August 1891; the complete edition was reprinted 1891, 1894.

13. All page references are to the complete edition.

14. *LL*, p. 203.

15. *LL*, p. 205.

16. In the preface to *The Little Schoolmaster Mark*, Shorthouse acknowledges indebtedness to Stilling: "I have made use of some passages in the childhood of Heinrich Jung-Stilling to create the character of Little Mark. The experience of the Princess as to private religious societies was also that of Stilling." Shorthouse's access to Stilling more than likely would have been through Samuel Jackson's translation of Stilling's autobiography which was available from the 1840s on.

17. Shorthouse wrote to Alexander Macmillan (30 January 1883): "I have been much taken with 'Vernon Lee's' 'Studies of the 18th century in Italy'. . . . I am glad that I did not see it before I wrote *John Inglesant*. I might have got confused between the centuries." In the preface to *The Little Schoolmaster Mark*, which was not published until later that year, he admits that as "a matter of common honesty I should wish to express the pleasure I have had in reading another delightful book, *Studies of the Eighteenth Century in Italy*, by Vernon Lee," but he does not say that he has borrowed from the book.

18. Quoted in the entry for *Bordoni* in *Grove's Dictionary of Music and Musicians*, ed. Eric Blom (New York: St. Martin's Press, 1954), vol. I, 814.

19. *LL*, p. 228.

20. Ibid., p. 234.

21. Ibid., pp. 228–29.

22. Ibid., p. 231.

23. Ibid., p. 232.

24. Ibid., p. 234.

25. Ibid., p. 236.

26. *Westminster Review*, CXXVII: NS 71 (January 1887), 265.

27. *Saturday Review*, LXII (27 November 1886), 725–26.

28. *Academy*, (13 November 1886).

29. *Blackwood's Magazine*, CXV (December 1886), 793–97.

30. *Macmillan Archive*, letter to Maurice Macmillan, dated 17 November 1886.

31. *LL*, p. 237.

32. Ibid., p. 244.

33. Ibid., p. 230. Later in the letter he adds that "Sir Percival is written against a certain very definite school of thought in London, and especially against 'Vernon Lee.' "

34. In later printings of *Sir Percival* the name De Lys was changed to De Foi. On 20 February 1887 Shorthouse wrote to Macmillan: "I have been much annoyed as you may have seen in the Athenaeum by a misunderstanding which has arisen through my using the name of De Lys in 'Sir Percival' *together with the mention of a real Dr. De Lys in the preface*. When I chose the name I was under the impression that the family had long since returned to France but I find that the last remaining member, the widow Marquise de Lys is still living in Worcestershire and it has troubled

me very much that the use of her family name has given her pain. I wish to substitute another name. . . . I have thought of De Foi as having a similar number of letters to the word to be replaced." In a letter to George Macmillan (24 May 1891) he remarks: "I won't have the original preface *at any price*; it was a mistake altogether, and I am thankful to get rid of it. The allusion to Dr. De Lys was a great mistake and got me into that awful row with 'La Marquise de Lys.' *Now* it would be a mistake to put it in as I have altered the name to De Foi."

35. *TLS* (11 March 1903)

36. *LL*, p. 226.

37. Ibid., p. 234.

38. W. S. Peterson, "J. H. Shorthouse and Mrs. Humphry Ward: Two New Letters," *Notes and Queries*, (July 1971), p. 260.

39. *LL*, p. 284.

40. *Macmillan Archive*, letter to Maurice Macmillan, dated 27 July 1887.

41. Ibid., letter to Maurice Macmillan, dated 17 January 1888. Mrs. Shorthouse published only the last half of the letter in *LL*, p. 261.

42. Shorthouse must have been led to this unusual name through a paper "The Theism of Wordsworth" read to the Wordsworth Society by a Professor Veitch, 9 July 1886. "A Teacher of the Violin" was not completed until the following summer.

43. *Life of Jean Paul F. Richter*. Compiled from Various Sources. Together with his *Autobiography*. Translated from the German. 2 vols. (London: John Chapman, 1845), vol. I, 31.

44. *Characteristics of Goethe*. From the German of Falk, von Müller, etc., With notes, original and translated by Sarah Austin, 3 vols. (London: Effingham Wilson, 1833), vol. I, 77.

45. *LL*, p. 161.

46. Shorthouse writes to George Macmillan (13 October 1882): ". . . a young lady, an acquaintance of ours, an American by birth but brought up in France, has translated the first novelette 'The Marquis.' She is a very clever girl with a great talent for composition and has done it very well. Her professor says that the tale itself is remarkably true to French feeling, and that no French writer has described the finest type of old noblesse better. I should hope that she may get it printed in France to repay her for her trouble."

47. *Macmillan Archive*, letter to Maurice Macmillan, dated 24 April 1888.

48. Ibid., letter to Maurice Macmillan, dated 31 May 1888.

49. Ibid., letter to George Macmillan, dated 24 April 1888.

50. Ibid., letter to George Macmillan, dated 17 February 1891.

51. Ibid., letter to George Macmillan, dated 6 May 1891.

52. Ibid., letter to George Macmillan, dated 16 June 1891.

53. Mrs. Ward, negotiating about the publishing terms for her translation of Amiel's journal, wrote to Macmillan (5 February 1884): "I should

dislike nothing more than that the book should be a loss to you considering
how generously the firm has always treated me. There are good grounds for
hope however that this will not be so. The 'John Inglesant' public seems to
me just the public which Amiel ought to please."

54. Mrs. Shorthouse wrote to George Macmillan (23 January 1907):
"Only last night when I was alone for an hour or two I read some pages of
'Blanche, Lady Falaise,' and realized afresh the rare beauty of the style and
the depth and spirituality of its teaching. I seemed to live again in the lanes
and moors of North Devon when he was so often telling me of his progress
in the book and talking of the tints and wild hedgerow flowers." (*Macmillan
Archive* MS 543934, pp. 199–200).

55. "Some were inclined to dispute the possibility of a girl's finding it
possible to blame herself for the cruel usage and desertion of another, but,
curiously enough, long afterwards, when reading the *Life of Mrs. Booth*, I
found in this unlooked-for quarter the true story of a young Wesleyan lady
who had, like Blanche, given her heart with no reserve to a minister, and
was trying in every way to prepare herself for the life which lay before her,
when her faithless lover left her for a richer lady. This poor girl distressed
Mrs. Booth by persistently blaming herself instead of her unworthy suitor"
(*LL*, 250).

56. *Macmillan Archive*, letter to George Macmillan, dated 15 July 1894.

Chapter Five

1. Most of the letters referred to here were published in *Life, Letters,
and Literary Remains of J. H. Shorthouse*, edited by Mrs. Shorthouse.
Another one hundred and thirty unpublished letters of Shorthouse's
correspondence with Macmillan and Company are in the *Macmillan
Archive* (British Library). About thirty-five unpublished letters from
Shorthouse to Edmund Gosse are in the Brotherton Library, Leeds. Other
letters are scattered through the correspondence columns of newspapers
and periodicals.

2. For instance, Shorthouse in a letter to Edmund Gosse (10 August
1890) mentions that he is reading Comte De Vogue's *Histoires d'hiver*
(1885), a book he had received from Bain, the London bookseller, on the
recommendation of Gosse (*LL*, 286): *Blanche, Lady Falaise* must have been
well under way by that time, for Shorthouse finished the first draft in
February 1891, the second in May, dispatched the manuscript to
Macmillan in June, and the novel was published in September. Clair
Wand, the narrator, in the last chapter of *Blanche*, is reading *Histoires
d'hiver* and makes comments on the book very similar to those Shorthouse
makes in his letter to Gosse. After the publication of *Blanche* Shorthouse
writes to Gosse (24 November 1891): "You will see what good use I made of
your introduction to De Vogue. This is one of the benefactions I must thank
you for."

3. Discussion of the *Eikon* was carried on in *Notes & Queries* from IS:I: 137 to 5S:I: 199 when the discussion was closed by the editor. Shorthouse's contributions were 3S:III: 128 (14 February 1863); 3S:III: 220 (14 March 1863); 3S:VIII: 396–97 (11 November 1865); 3S:XII: 1–2 (6 July 1867).

4. *LL*, p. 79.

5. *LL*, p. 322.

6. *Retrospects: First Series* (New York: Scribners, 1904), p. 294.

7. *LL*, pp. 128–29.

8. Ibid., p. 129.

9. Ibid., p. 131.

10. *Retrospects: First Series*, p. 301.

11. *LL*, p. 137.

12. Ibid., p. 135.

13. *Macmillan Archive*, letter to Alexander Macmillan, dated 27 August 1881.

14. *The Spectator* (18 February 1882), p. 238.

15. A. W. Benn, *A History of English Rationalism in the Nineteenth Century* (London: Longman's, Green, 1906), p. 416.

16. *LL*, p. 173.

17. *The Temple. Sacred Poems and Private Ejaculations by Mr. George Herbert.* Sixth edition with introductory essay by Shorthouse, (London, 1903).

18. *LL*, p. 398.

19. *Macmillan Archive*, letter to Grove, dated 30 January 1883.

20. Richard Holt Hutton, *Brief Literary Criticisms* (London: Macmillan & Co., 1906), p. 74.

21. *Macmillan Archive*, letter to Alexander Macmillan, dated 11 June 1883.

22. *Golden Thoughts from the Spiritual Guide of Miguel Molinos, the Quietist.* With a preface by Shorthouse (Glasgow: David Bryce & Son, 1883).

23. *LL*, pp. 199–200.

24. *SR*, p. 76.

25. Ibid., p. 79.

26. Ibid., p. 55.

27. *LL*, p. 371.

28. *LL*, p. 67.

29. Ibid., p. 220.

30. Ibid., p. 221.

31. *LR*, p. 293.

32. *LL*, p. 220.

33. Ibid., p. 284.

34. Ibid., p. 282.

35. Ibid., p. 288.

36. Ibid., p. 286.

37. *Gosse Correspondence*, Brotherton Library.

38. This and following quotations are from Galton's essays in the *National Review* XXXV (1900), 481–91; 580–91; 850–65: "Why I Entered, and Why I left, the Roman Catholic Church;" "Some Final Impressions of the Roman Catholic Church."

39. *LL*, p. 372.

40. Ibid., p. 123.

41. Ibid., p. 125.

42. Ibid., p. 130.

43. Ibid., p. 148.

44. Ibid., p. 159.

45. Ibid., p. 28.

46. Ibid., p. 40.

47. *Macmillan Archive*, MS 543934, pp. 127–28.

48. *LL*, p. 63.

Chapter Six

1. Margaret Maison, *Search Your Soul, Eustace* (London and New York, 1961), p. 5.

2. *Letters of George Gissing to Members of his Family*, ed. Algernon and Ellen Gissing (London: Constable, 1927), p. 73.

3. Robert Lee Wolff, *Gains and Losses: Novels of Faith and Doubt in Victorian England* (New York, 1977), p. 447.

4. *LL*, p. 203.

5. Mrs. Humphry Ward, *A Writer's Recollections*, (London: Peter Smith, 1918), p. 168.

6. Ibid., p. 169.

7. Ibid., p. 196.

8. Quoted in A. C. Benson, *Walter Pater* (London: Macmillan & Co., 1906), pp. 89–90.

9. *Selected Writings of Walter Pater*, ed. Harold Bloom (New York: New American Library, Inc., 1974), p. 13.

10. *LL*, p. 272.

11. *After the Victorians* (London: Allen & Unwin, 1971), p. 27.

Selected Bibliography

PRIMARY SOURCES

John Inglesant, A Romance. The first edition, published by Cornish
  Brothers, Birmingham (July 1880), limited to one hundred copies, is
  practically unavailable, but the reprint by the Garland Publishing Inc.,
  in 1975, has again put this edition into circulation. Macmillan and
  Company published a two-volume edition (1881), a "Large Paper
  Edition," limited to two hundred and fifty copies, in two volumes
  (1882), a one-volume edition (1883), a one-volume "Six-Penny Edition"
  (1901), and an "Edition de Luxe," limited to five hundred and ten
  copies, in three volumes (1902). After Shorthouse's death Macmillan
  added *John Inglesant* to their *Illustrated Classics* series (1905) and
  later to their *Cottage Library* series (1933). It is these last two editions
  which are most likely to be available to the general reader.
The Little Schoolmaster Mark. A Spiritual Romance. London: Macmillan
  and Co., 1883–85. *Part I*, published by Macmillan, October 1883, and
  re-issued only once more in December 1883, is the most frequently
  available copy. *Part II* was published December 1884. Parts *I* and *II*
  were combined into one volume in 1885.
Sir Percival. A Story of the Past and of the Present. London and New York:
  Macmillan and Co., 1886.
A Teacher of the Violin and Other Tales. London and New York: Macmillan
  and Co., 1888.
The Countess Eve. A Novel. London and New York: Macmillan and Co.,
  1888.
Blanche, Lady Falaise. A Tale. London and New York: Macmillan and Co.,
  1891.
"On the Platonism of Wordsworth." Birmingham: Cornish Brothers, 1881.
  Privately printed.
"The Agnostic at Church." *Nineteenth Century*, XI (April 1882), 650–52.
HERBERT, GEORGE. *The Temple*. Facsimile rpt. with "Introductory Essay" by
  Shorthouse. London: Fisher Unwin, 1882.
"An Apologue." *Nineteenth Century*, XII (July 1882), 51–53.
"The Marquis Jeanne Hyacinthe de St. Palaye." *Macmillan's Magazine*,
  XLVI (July 1882), 177–91.
"The Baroness Helena von Saarfeld." *Macmillan's Magazine*, XLVI (August
  1882), 257–78.

"The Humorous in Literature." *Macmillan's Magazine*, XLVII (March 1883), 248–80.

Golden Thoughts from the Spiritual Guide of Miguel Molinos, the Quietist. With a "Preface" by Shorthouse. Glasgow: David Bryce and Son, 1883.

"Ellie: A Story of a Boy and Girl." Birmingham: W. R. King, 1883. Printed for private circulation only.

"Frederick Denison Maurice." *Nineteenth Century*, XV (May 1884), 849–66.

MORSE, FRANCIS. *Peace the Voice of the Church to Her Sick.* With a "Preface" by Shorthouse. London: Christian Knowledge Society, 1888.

"Of Restraining Self-Denial in Art." *Century Guild Hobby Horse*, III (1888), 3–7.

"A Sunday Afternoon." *English Illustrated Magazine*, XIII (June 1895), 257–65.

GALTON, ARTHUR. *The Message and Position of the Church of England.* With a "Preface on the Royal Supremacy" by Shorthouse. London: Kegan Paul, French, Trübner and Co., 1899.

SECONDARY SOURCES

1. Bibliography

WAGNER, FREDERICK J. "J. H. Shorthouse (1834–1903): A Bibliography." *Bulletin of Bibliography and Magazine Notes* 28 (1971), 84–87; 108; 141–44. Annotated and useful, but marred by typographical error; needs updating.

2. Biography

SHORTHOUSE, SARAH. *Life, Letters, and Literary Remains of J. H. Shorthouse.* 2 vols. London: Macmillan and Company, 1905. The official *Life* so far, domestic rather than public, and uncritical. *Volume I* contains a selection from Shorthouse's letters; *Volume II* includes a selection from essays written for the Friends' Essay Society, some of his more important published articles, and a few previously unpublished ones.

Memorials of the Families of Shorthouse and Robinson and Others Connected with Them. Printed in Commemoration of the One Hundredth Birthday of Sarah Southall, 12 September 1901. Birmingham: Morland and Henson, 1902. For private circulation. A compilation by members of the family about other members on matters not touched on in the *Life*.

3. Criticism

BAKER, JOSEPH ELLIS. "Joseph Henry Shorthouse: Quaker-Catholic," in *The Novel and the Oxford Movement*. Princeton: Princeton University Press, 1932. *John Inglesant* considered as "the greatest Anglo-Catholic novel of the Victorian Age."

BARRY, WILLIAM. "John Inglesant," *Dublin Review* 90 (1882), 395–426; rpt. in *Heralds of Revolt*. London: Hodder and Stoughton, 1909. A generally appreciative review which maintains that the Jesuits and the Roman Catholic Church are misrepresented in *John Inglesant*.

BISHOP, MORCHARD. "*John Inglesant* and its Author," *Essays by Divers Hands*, NS 29 (1958), 73–86. A very readable, sensible, nonpartisan defence of Shorthouse.

BRODRICK, JAMES PATRICK. "A Prince of Plagiarists," *The Month*, 146 (October 1925), 338–43. Renewal of Jesuit assault on Shorthouse with fresh ammunition from Fleming's *Quarterly Review* article.

CHAPMAN, RAYMOND. "The Zeal of a Convert," in *Faith and Revolt: Studies in the Literary Influence of the Oxford Movement*. London: Weidenfeld and Nicolson, 1970. Stresses Shorthouse's Quaker background in determining his Broad Church sacramentalism.

DRUMMOND, ANDREW L. *The Churches in English Fiction*. Leicester: Edward Backus, 1950. In a review of the nineteenth-century English religious novel, discussion of Shorthouse and Pater (pp. 86-98), Shorthouse and Catholicism (pp. 134–36), Shorthouse and the Broad Church (pp. 166–69).

FLEMING, WILLIAM KAYE. "Some Truths about 'John Inglesant,' " *Quarterly Review*, 245 (July 1925), 130–48. An important article with chapter and verse evidence of some of Shorthouse's borrowings from seventeenth-century writers.

FRAUCHIGER, HANNA. *Das "innere Licht" in "John Inglesant" von Joseph Henry Shorthouse*. Diss. Zürich 1928. Mulhouse: Alsatia, 1928. An examination of Shorthouse's mysticism and its connection with seventeenth-century neo-Platonism.

GARDINER, SAMUEL. "John Inglesant," *Fraser's Magazine*, NS 25 (May 1882), 599–605. Generally favorable review but critical of Shorthouse's misuse of historical fact.

GOSSE, EDMUND. "The Author of 'John Inglesant,' " in *Portraits and Sketches*. London: Heinemann, 1912. Gosse had a twenty-year acquaintance with Shorthouse. A rpt. of Gosse's review of Mrs. Shorthouse's *Life*, inaccurate on a few unimportant details; Shorthouse is viewed as an "epicurean quietist."

KEARY, CHARLES F. "The Work of J. Henry Shorthouse," *Edinburgh Review*, 22 (July 1905), 110–31. Stresses the "aristocratic ideal" and the "religious element" in Shorthouse's writing.

MAISON, MARGARET MARY. *Search Your Soul, Eustace: A Survey of the Religious Novel in the Victorian Age*. London and New York: Sheed and Ward, 1961. American title is *The Victorian Vision: Studies in the Religious Novel*. In a short chapter, "Towards Beauty," Shorthouse compared and contrasted with Pater.

MEREDITH, GERTRUDE E. "Sir Percival and Mr. Shorthouse," *Church Review*, 49 (June 1887), 608–19. One of the few favorable reviews of *Sir Percival*.

MORE, PAUL ELMER. "J. Henry Shorthouse," *Shelburne Essays, Third*

Series. New York: G. P. Putnam's Sons, 1905. Sees *John Inglesant* as "the one great religious novel of the English language," "the direct fruit" of the "Battle of the Churches," and stresses the union of Quaker mysticism and Platonism in Shorthouse. Most important of the early evaluations.

PAUL, HERBERT ed., *Letters of Lord Acton to Mary, Daughter of the Right Hon. W. E. Gladstone*. London: Macmillan and Company, 1904. Lord Acton's detailed complaints about historical inaccuracy in *John Inglesant*, pp. 126–28; 135–48; 150–51.

POLAK, MEIJER. *The Historical, Philosophical, and Religious Aspects of "John Inglesant."* Purmerend: J. Muusses, 1933; Oxford, 1934. The only full-length study of Shorthouse in English. Rather less important than the title suggests; capitalizes on Fleming's discoveries; scolding in tone.

RIEGER, ELFRIEDE. *Joseph Henry Shorthouse und sein "John Inglesant": Ein Beitrag zur Geschichte des englischen Romans im 19. Jahrhundert*. Diss. Georg-August-Universität, 1927. Göttingen Tageblatt, 1927. A fairly comprehensive study which shows that Shorthouse was "borrowing" materials for his minor novels as well as for *John Inglesant*.

WOLFF, ROBERT LEE. *Gains and Losses: Novels of Faith and Doubt in Victorian England*. New York and London: Garland Publishing, Inc. 1977. Indispensable for any study of the English religious novel in the nineteenth century. Shorthouse and Pater discussed, pp. 168–190.

Index